PAVILION PRESS

JEWISH GERMAN REVOLUTION

SAVING CIVILIZATION IN 400 CE

by LEE CRANE

PAVILION PRESS

Philadelphia

Books by Lee Crane

Jewish German Revolution

Survivor from an Unknown War

Treasury of Jane Austen Illustrations (ed.)

Horatio Alger Jr.: A Century of Covers and Illustrations (ed.)

Wolfowitz on Point (ed.)

Anti-Federalist Papers (ed.)

Fathers of the Constitution (ed.)

For a complete list of authors, titles, special offers, discounts and future products visit

www.pavilionpress.com

contact us at

webmaster@pavilionpress.com

Pavilion Press, Inc.
Philadelphia
Copyright ©2010 by Pavilion Press, Inc.

Jewish German Revolution
by Lee Crane

ISBN: .
Paperback: 1-4145-0716-X

Library of Congress
Cataloging-in-Publication Data

1. History 2. Jewish Studies
3. Medieval History 4. Spain 5.Visigoths

Thanks to Elli Fischer for help in translations.
Cover: *Genseric Sacking Rome* by Karl Briullov, *Roman Slave* by Gerome, Triumphal Arch in Rome, Romans killing infants in the Visitation Church mural, Jerusalem
Editors: Anika Abbate, Leah Goodwin, Naomi Long, Michael Whelan

A SAMPLE OF OTHER POPULAR BOOKS FROM PAVILION PRESS:

The authors and editors of Pavilion Press are generally available for speaking engagements. For specific information, contact us at webmaster@pavilionpress.com and refer to the web site for further information. www.pavilionpress.com.

MURDER THRILLER - *LETHAL RHYTHM* by Dr. Peter Kowey and Marion Fox.

Philip Sarkis was a good doctor—maybe a little too good. So when he is sued for malpractice after a young patient dies suddenly and unexpectedly, he sinks into an alcoholic depression, losing his family and his career. With the help of two remarkable women attorneys, Sarkis discovers some astonishing things about his patient, her husband and his diabolical mistress, and himself.

MIDDLE EAST - *ISRAEL 3000* - *by Jerome Verlin.*

Just how long have Jews continuously lived in Israel? Even since the battle of Jericho, and that is a long time, over 3000 years. In meticulous detail and using historical and archeological discoveries, the book documents the this habitation and asks the question, shouldn't Israel celebrate it's 3200 anniversary?

Jane Austen - a whole series.

From books that can not be found anywhere else, like *Jane Austen's Letters, Great Ilustrations*, and Her *Homes and Friends* to her wonderful novels, this is the place for Austen lovers.

ADVENTURE BIOGRAPHY - *SURVIVOR FROM AN UNKNOWN WAR* by Stephen Crane

You only really know about WWII, The Soviet Union, romance, and breathtaking danger after reading about the life of Jay Narzikul, a boy from Central Asia who avoided death traps of dictators and divulges secrets hidden by entire national governments or ignored by history.

FEDERALIST PAPERS AND ANTI-FEDERALISTS

Passionate debates about the nature of our government started at the time of drafting our *Constitution*. In these two books, leaders like Jay, Madison and Hamilton proposed a strong central power while critics like Patrick Henry worried about limits on taxation. Sound familiar? Read the beginning of national debate to understand today's discourse.

With Love, to Marci

TABLE OF CONTENTS

JEWISH GERMAN REVOLUTION
PROLOGUE

The ascent to the Throne of Imperial Rome by Constantine in 306 CE resulted in a spread of slavery and oppression not seen since Pharoah. This did not bode well for enlightenment. However, a mere century later, a corrupt Rome succumbed to an onslaught of Germanic tribes who promptly established suzerainty over most of Europe. The depiction of these peoples as barbarian could not be further from the truth. Steeped in Judeo-Christian culture, they implanted the foundation of law recognized today as modern civil society.

The Jewish German revolution shaped the Europe-to-come and America-to-come. American Revolutionaries acknowledged their debt to the Exodus and its new governance. That Exodus tradition survived because the Jewish German Revolution of 400 defeated the attempt of mighty Rome to extinquish it in favor of absolutism. German military victories allowed codification of modern civil society based on the culture of Moses in the soil of Europe and laid the groundwork for the eventual Renaissance and Enlightenment. This revolution of 400 and its successors in Europe triumphed despite the massive and oppressive force of imperial Rome. The ultimate failure of the Roman imperial model and the success of Mosaic law allowed humanity's instinct for respecting both self and neighbor to prosper.

Certain traits define a regime that represses its population, including establishment of special rules for the privileged, abrogation of contracts, permission of false witness and theft, forced religious observation, murder, deprivation of simple rights, and partial judges. For these reasons, Moses cried, "Let my people go!" His oppressed people instituted a new for of government with separation of powers and agreement of the governed. Centuries later, in the same vein, the United States Congress declared, "That to secure these (certain) rights, Governments are instituted among Men, deriving their just powers from the consent of the governed, — That whenever any Form of Government becomes destructive of these ends, it is the Right of the People to alter or to abolish it, and to institute new Government." The U.S. is definately a child of the Hebrew Exodus.

What happens after revolution? Hopefully not the chaos of the French Revolution or the repression of the Soviet and Maoist Revolutions. A successful revolution is different. Modern civil society in the United States and other democratic nations adopted a certain combination of responsibilities and rights. Included in that combination is the belief that murder, lies, stealing, and coveting are wrong; that the sins of the father do not extend to the sons; and that merit and work trump noble heredity or plunder. In Judeo-Christian culture, the basis of morality lies in doing unto others as you would have them do unto you; no person exalted or low is exempt from a moral code of laws; judges must be impartial; and science and religion are brothers. Also expressed in such a culture is the need to extend charity; to improve the world; and to disperse power. And finally we enjoy property rights, exegesis; the respect of minority opinion; women's rights; abolition of slavery; unbiased education; community health practices; and freedom of religion and thought. These above constitute Judeo-Christian ideals as first set out explicitly in the five books of Moses (the *Pentateuch*), as well as Prophets, Writings, Talmud, Midrash, Responsa, Zohar, and New Testament. Moses' passion extended beyond the legal realm into the arena of faith and culture. In addition, he introduced concepts only recently recognized in the wider world, such government's need to obtain the consent of the governed.

The brutal and violent imperial Rome attacked these ideals with a zeal not seen since the Pharaoh of Exodus. Herein we see how remarkable partnerships: Jews, together with Visigoths, Muslims, and Catholics stood up to a great military machine in order to preserve and then deliver the possibility of a modern civil society. And herein we also see the intense fear and loathing that any dictator or highly centralized government posses towards the laws of Moses. No murder? Rulers obey common law? Contract law rather than the whim of aristocrats? Women's rights? Consent of the governed? Impartial judges? and so on. No modern or ancient despot abides such things.

Modern civilization began with the ancient Hebrews, resided in Greece, moved to southern Europe (where it prospered despite the oppression of Rome), and then advanced worldwide. We should be clear that the Judeo-Christian culture as proposed by Moses and then elaborated upon goes beyond religion, rules of conduct, and law to include concepts such as the compatibility of religion and science, the necessity of community health, and the importance of education in understanding the tradition.

This present work sets forth the mechanisms of how political alliances between Jews, Arian Christians, Muslims, and Catholics stood up to the terrible onslaught of imperial Rome. It also touches on the philosophical lineage, but in-depth analysis of the manner in which modern civilization mirrors Hebrew culture has been admirably completed by others.

An interesting literature chronicles the influence of Hebrew culture on modern society, with recent books published and classics including authors as Joseph Jacobs, Leo Schwarz, and Gabriel Sivan.

This book, *Jewish German Revolution,* connects the dots as to who stood up for freedom, and gives personal credits to those who made possible the journey from Exodus to America's Declaration of Independence.

THE JEWISH GERMAN REVOLUTION OF 400 CAME ABOUT BECAUSE EMPEROR CONSTANTINE TURNED ROME INTO A VAST REGIME OF SLAVERY, TORTURE, CONFISCATION OF PROPERTY, AND PAMPERED ARISTOCRATS. EXILED FOR HIS RESISTANCE, THE THEOLOGIAN ARIUS TAUGHT JUDEO-CHRISTIANITY TO GERMAN TRIBES. GERMANS, TOGETHER WITH OPPRESSED SLAVES, CHRISTIANS, GREEKS, AFRICANS, AND JEWS REVOLTED AND WON.

Arius

Constantine

THE REBELS REPLACED ROMAN DEPRAVITY WITH THE LAWS AND CULTURE OF MOSES. THEREAFTER, FOR OVER 1000 YEARS, VARIOUS CHRISTIAN, MUSLIM AND JEWISH LEADERS MAINTAINED SUPPORT FOR JUDEO-CHRISTIAN CULTURE. FINALLY THE RENAISSANCE AND ENLIGHTEN-MENT TRIUMPHED.

Pedro III of Aragon in Spain continued Hebrew-based law

German Visigoth Architecture

MAKING MODERN CIVILIZATION
STEP 1 ANTIDOTE FOR TYRANNY

2000 BCE   Jewish prophets taught that emotional, material and intellectual existence are universal and granted by a Master incomprehensible to humanity. No line was drawn between "science" and "religion" except in the minds of certain backward thinkers. The idea of universalism as opposed to the fragmented nation-by-nation laws of nature, adds rationalism to our heritage.

1300 BCE   Before this time, tyranny and oppression ruled humanity, and in Egypt the worst of this system prevailed. Then the Hebrew people determined that the oppressed had the both right and the obligation to establish freedom. With the help of their Almighty, they revolted and escaped (the story of the Exodus). Having survived the tortures of slavery, they were determined to form a new civilization, what we call today modern civilization, where murder, stealing, and false witness are prohibited, where prince and pauper follow the same law with impartial judges, where rulers must seek consent of the governed, where scales must be true and craftsmanship trumps plunder. Morally, citizens should leave part of the harvest for the poor, love the neighbor as themselves, give women rights, obey contracts and be good samaritans. These and more we know as the *Laws of Moses* and they form the backbone of what we consider civil society. These laws go even further to promote public health, ensuring a weekly day of rest, and engendering family values.

These laws were commented on and expanded by various sources including the rest of the Old Testament (Tanakh), New Testament, and Talmud, causing despots to tremble because of their simple expression, clarity, and power.

Red Sea by Nicholas Poussin   Ten Commandments by Aron de Chavez

STEP 2 SPREAD THE WORD

1000 BCE The ideas of Moses spread throughout the world, especially during the reign of Israel's King Solomon, in activity that pointedly included Europe.

Peoples of the world always have conducted extensive trade, and their activities have transmitted ideas as well. Solomon oversaw trade in everything from horses to chariots, glass to spices, and metals to wood, from Spain to India. Ideas travelled with this trade. Jewish and Phoenician allies settled the Mediterranean, especially in the grand Spanish cities of Cadiz and Tartessus (Tarshish).

Solomon

Solomon-Era Ship

19th Century Carpet

Word of a new culture spread, one that preached a world of craftsmen and jobs rather than nobility and serfs. Songs, straightforward wisdom, laws and religion based on Mosaic morality, as well as trade, circled the world.

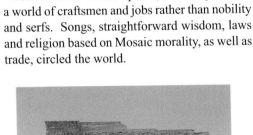

Jewish and Phoenician Sarcophagus & Ruins at Cadiz.

11

Deborah   *Gregory*

Having introduced a new concept of civilization, Greek, Jewish, and Christian leaders expanded its content with songs, proverbs, and crafts, thus adding more substance to civil society. The *Canticle of Deborah* started the tradition of chanting in Judeo-Christian religious services. (*Judges* 5). In the book of I Samuel, the Lord orders chanting (I Samuel 10:5). Singing was codified under David in services at the time of the second Temple. (500 BCE 1 *Chronicles)* and helped develop the tradition of Gregorian chant. These chants show the close partnership between the Christians and Jews.

Popular wisdom spread with sayings such as "land of milk and honey," "apple of your eye," "eat, drink and be merry," "answer a fool according to his folly," "the race is not to the swift," "deliver us from evil," "fear no evil," and words like *"Psalter," "Psalms,"* "hymn," "amen," and "Hallelujah."

The occupations of crafts were favored over plundering. During their Exodus journey, Jews wove linen and goat hair clothes of violet, purple and scarlet; mounted precious stones; engraved; worked wood; made tents; and shaped metal. Glass blowing was an early Hebrew craft.

The Torah talks about wine in a number of places as a trade. In Spain, the wine merchants were among the most influential, but other activities included mining shepherding, tanning, leather products, soapmaking, candlemaking, timber production, wool spinning, weaving, minters, and so on.

Symbols like the Lion of Judah identified the Hebrew presence.

In order for a Judaic, soon to be Judeo-Christian, culture to take root in Europe, Hebrews needed to settle there and spread the word.

Just about every Spanish, Portuguese, and French town and city has a Hebrew quarter in its oldest section

Caceres Juderia   *Hervas Juderia*   *Sagunto Juderia*

Toledo Juderia   *Barcelona Juderia*   *Besalu Juderia*

Cadiz Juderia   *Calahorra Juderia*   *Cervera Juderia*

Pamplona Juderia   *Plasencia Juderia*   *Lucena Juderia*

Ribadavia Juderia   *Seville Juderia*   *del Rey Catolico*
Juderia

Tarazona Juderia   *Segovia Juderia*   *Lleida Juderia*

14

Cordoba Juderia   Girona Juderia   Granada Juderia

Huesa Juderia   Leon Juderia   Malaga Juderia

Murcia Juderia   Murviedro Juderia   Palma Juderia

Alfama Lisbon Juderia   Valencia Juderia   Granada Juderia

Castelo Juderia   Coimba Juderia   Lisbon Juderia

Jaen Juderia   Faro Juderia   Belmonte Juderia

200 CE Even after Rome solidified control of the Mediterranean with military victories in Egypt and Israel, the region continued to flourish under light-handed rule. Alexandria continued as queen of the Mediterranean Renaissance. Multi-ethnic, philosophical, religious, and business interests succeeded in the Judeo-Christian-Greek society.

Lighthouse at Alexandria >>

Library at Alexandria

Hypatia >>>

Women contributed to many disciplines. Hypatia gained fame as a mathematician and philosopher.

Jewish women continued to enjoy rights and opportunities from the times of the prophetess Miriam and Abraham's wife Sarah. Beruriah contributed to the *Talmud*. Women weavers engaged in trade and banking with excess stock and profits. Jews and Christians translated the Old Testament into Greek.

17

All kinds of industry prevailed, and with the industry came trade. Jews excelled at glass-making and continued using their symbols such as the Lions of Judah. Ships of all sizes plied the waters of the Mediterranean.

300   A civilized society prospered, but a serious problem loomed: Alexandria welcomed Judeo-Christian values and hosted arts, trade, science, industry, tolerance, law, and invention. Rome, however, dominated in the area of military prowess and despotism.

Constantine promoted himself to Roman Emperor, instituted rule by nobility and dictatorship, subsumed the Church to his ends, and then proceeded to kill, intimidate, and expropriate the property of Greek intellectuals, Jews, Arians, Copts, and others. (Picture by Rubens)

STEP 3: JEWS AND GERMANS
300 - 600 CE

FROM THE ROMAN THEODOSIAN CODE

-- GUILT EXTENDS TO WHOLE FAMILY
-- DEATH FOR MARRYING A BARBARIAN
-- NON CATHOLICS DEEMED INSANE
-- NOBILITY EXEMPT FROM TORTURE
-- PURPLE RESERVED FOR NOBILITY
-- COMMONERS BARRED ADVANCEMENT
-- PRISONERS SUBJECTED TO TORTURE
-- FUGITIVE SERFS & SLAVES RETURNED
-- TRADESMEN & HEIRS MUST CONTINUE
   IN THEIR TRADE OR SUFFER
-- SECRET SERVICE HAS SPECIAL PRIVI-
   LEGES
-- PUNISHMENT EXTENDS TO WHOLE FAMILY
-- A SOLDIER SHALL NOT ADVANCE TO SENATOR
-- UNAPPROVED RELIGIONS MAY NOT CONGREGATE

Theodosius

Successors to Constantine formalized imperial suppression in the Theodosian Code (codified after his death), which they forced on the Catholic Church, in direct opposition to the Judeo-Christian traditions outlined in the Five Books of Moses (Torah), the Old and The New Testament, the Talmud, and other works. Theodosian Catholics opposed Judeo-Christian Catholics. Noble Romans incited mobs to murder opponents like the philosopher Hypatia.

Death of Hypatia

Roman arrogance and oppression seemed endless as Bishop (later Saint) Theophilus of Alexandria stirred up mobs to destroy Greek temples, pagan property, and opposition buildings. Property in these structures was seized for profit. The predilection of the imperial state to concentrate on oppression left the defense of the Empire compromised.

Theophilus

19

Both by law and by culture, the Romans enslaved large populations.

The plunder of peoples both external and internal to the Empire gave aristocrats wealth.

Dictators and absolutists murder innocents. This was a Roman mainstay. (One should not confuse modern Italians with ancient Romans, as many on that peninsula suffered.)

The decadent life of nobles, the special laws to favor them, and their struggle for power at any cost created much discontent.

Disobedience or free thought often resulted in mutilation or death by brutal torture.

MEDIEVAL AGES: NOBLE ROMAN THEO-DOSIAN SOCIETY DECLARED WAR AGAINST THE JUDEO-CHRISTIAN SOCIETY

This set a culture of nobility and serfs against one of craftsmen and jobs. Christians, especially Catholics, split between those controlled by the Theodosian rulers and those adhering to true Judeo-Christian values. The teachings of Moses, Akiba, and Christ were suppressed.

Moses - Bible

Akiba - Talmud

Christ - the First Judeo-Christian

21

Intimidated but allied were Greek thinkers, Jews, minority Christians, Judeo-Christian Catholics, and the mighty Arian Germans. Germans such as Visigoths practiced a form of Christianity that could be called the first Protestant tradition, a tradtition theologically between most other Protestants and Judaism. These people saved the concept of "civil society" from oblivion.

After his expulsion from Rome by Constantine in 320 for rejecting the notion of trinity and other opinions, the theologian Arius created a tolerant Judeo-Christian church. (The "Arian" church should not be confused with the 20th century Nazi Aryan movement.) His church (an example on right above) celebrated the Jewish holidays including Yom Kippur, Rosh Hashanah and Passover. In the multicultural Alexandria where Jews and Christians translated the Bible into Greek, Arius conversed with rabbis, as reported by the Jewish scholar Rashi (woodcut). Roman noble St. Athanasius (center) disparagingly refered to Arians as "modern Jews."

Imperial Rome, unable to corrupt or intimidate Arius, physically attacked him (See St. Nicholas above left punching him), and exiled him from its councils (center) to Germania. Arian Visigoths produced fine art (above right).

Constantine set about burning the books of those who disagreed with his views. A later law cannon from 825 CE boasts about burning the works of Arius, who faced passible burning himself had he remained in Roman territory.

Burning the Books of Arius

Greek Tiles in Cologne

Germans had already welcomed Greek and Hebrew communities into their midst and therefore had interacted with the basis of Judeo-christian-Greek culture, and compared it with Roman.

Constantine's Proclamation
Recognizing Colonge's Jews

In accepting the Arian Religion, Vandals, Goths, Burgundians, and others thoroughly placed themselves in the Judeo-Christian tradition, in opposition to the Roman autocracy. Arian altars reflected the designs of other Christians (Picture at right.

23

410: Rome was sacked, defeated by Germans, much to the relief of the slaves, minorities, Jews, Berbers, Copts, and others. Arian Christian Visigoths, Vandals, and Burgundians occupied France and Spain.

The most famous noble Roman writers of the era laced their books with descriptions of the Arian Visigoths. St. Gregory of Tours (left) described their tolerance in sneering terms. Sidonius (book in center) said their royal court was every bit as civilized and gracious as the Roman royal court (center). And so Germans like Visigoth King Euric (right) used precedents from the Talmud in order to create the Visigothic Code of Law, a Judeo-Christian force in opposition to the Romans and Theodosian law. This was one of the most important events of the Middle Ages and served to preserve Judeo-Christian values for the world. Aspects of the code included: -- WOMEN MAY INHERIT -- ROYALTY AND COMMONERS SUBJECT TO LAW -- ONE LAW ONLY -- NO FALSE WITNESS -- JUDGES MAY SUBPOENA -- FRAUDULENT JUDGES PAY FINE TO DEFENDANT -- IGNORANCE OF THE LAW IS NO EXCUSE -- PROPERTY DESTRUCTION = COMPENSATION -- CONTRACTS ARE ENFORCEABLE -- LAST WILLS ARE VALID -- THEFT IS PUNISHED & COMPENSATED -- A WIDOW MAY NOT DISINHERIT THE UNBORN

When the German Vandals sacked Rome, they showed remarkable restraint, sparing many and much. As noted in the painting above by Briullov, African Berbers and former slaves joined the Vandals. Recaptured for or by Jews was the treasure looted from Jerusalem by Titus and shown in the Arch of Titus (see p. 20.)

Visigoth art compared with the finest, as shown by the Arian chapel in Ravenna commissioned by Theodoric and showing the sacrifice of Isaac.

STEP 4: JEWS AND MUSLIMS

Just when Europe was organized for spectacular advances under Judeo-Christian values under the protective shield of Visigoth Arians, a Visigoth king, <u>King Recared,</u> in **587** converted to radical Theodosian Imperial Roman Catholicism and threw most of Europe into a century-long tailspin of revolution, counter-revolution, repression, and catastrophe.

Once again, for modern civilization and renaissance to advance, an ally had to defeat the forces of imperial Rome. Those liberating forces came from Africa.

Berbers and Arabs in **711** rapidly gained control of Spain, which they called Andalusia. Muslim Caliph Abd al Rahman with Jewish master diplomat Hasdai ibn Shaprut sponsored many of the world's most prolific thinkers, greatly expanding the scale of renaissance.

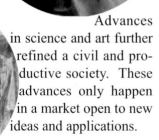

Advances in science and art further refined a civil and productive society. These advances only happen in a market open to new ideas and applications.

In such a civil society, the process of civilization building can proceed by expanding the knowledge of humanity. Judeo-Christians had long recognized the compatibility of science and religion as per the cycle of rain (Eccl 1:7; Job 26:8, 36:27, 37:11,16), wind has weight (Job 28:25), plant and animal reproduction by seed (Gen. 1:11-12), and the concept that geometry and astronomy are appetizers of wisdom Pirket Avot, 3:23. In Spain the cooperation of Muslims, Christians and Jews brought peace.

About **900 CE**, the Jewish Marshallah advanced astronomy with the spherical astrolabe. His comments on Earth's shape, astronomy, moonlight, daylight at the poles and equator, the global wind patterns, lunar tides, and the rain cycle elevated science. The famous Rabbi Chasdai imported his works into the Spanish Muslim area. The Works of Marshallah were

translated, engraved, used and published by countless voyagers and intellects. His *De Scientia Motus Orbis* is widely distributed.

The physician, philosopher, mathematician and astronomer Avicenna penned the Cannon of Medicine which described the circulation of blood, the nature of internal organs, and the skeleton. It was a standard text for 500 years. The *Aid to Health* by Avenzoar followed. Maimonides wrote of poisons and antidotes still with relevance today. *New England Journa.* 3/2009 found that male circumcision reduces risk of various diseases.

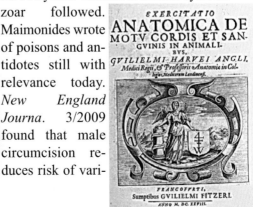

Rabbi Solomon ibn Gabirol was the first significant philosopher in Spain. He discussed the relationship between faith and reason, concluding that they are one and the same. His *Fons Vitae* is still studied today. He is quoted by name extensively by William of Auvergne, Alexander Hales, and Roger Bacon in his *Summa Universae Theologiae.*

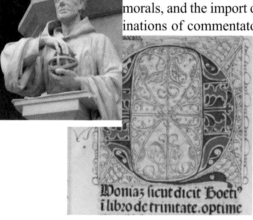

Later Maimonides (bottom center), one of the world's greatest thinkers, wrote, among many other titles, *A Guide to the Perplexed*, which explains philosophical controversies and, like Gabirol, concluded that science and religion are one and the same. Maimonides also disapproved of any sort of superstition,

Rabbi Gabirol's (right) revival of the ancient Jewish mystical Kabbalah expressed spirituality,

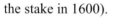

morals, and the import of the soul. It fired the imaginations of commentators across all schools of religion and philosophy. Included in this deluge were Roger Bacon (left) and, Duns Scotus (bottom left) and continuing through Dominicus Gundisallimus, William of Auvergne, Alexander of Hales, Bonaventura, William of Lamarre, and Giordano Bruno (burned at the stake in 1600).

Donias ficut dicit Boeti? i libro de trinitate. optime

28

STEP 5: JEWS AND CATHOLICS

Charlemagne

Charlemagne and His Father Pepin

Situated next to the Islamic Caliph in Andalusia, French King Charlemagne, as well as his entire dynasty, loved renaissance. As Catholic kings, they embraced Judeo-Christian values and rejected the extreme discrimination of the Roman Theodosian code. Jews and Catholics studied and worked together in France. Since Charlemagne needed alliances to counteract his Muslim enemies in Spain, his Jewish diplomat Isaac performed diplomatic missions to the Muslim Baghdad empire, which also considered Spain an enemy.

Christians and Jews fought together under Charlemagne. They formed the legions that accompanied Roland in Spain and were slaughtered on the way home. Rabbi Makhir Natronai Kalonymos or his son wrote the epic *Song of Roland* to commemorate the slain soldiers.

One of the most important parts of the Judeo-Christian heritage, namely education, received much attention, truly earning Judeo-Christians their "children of the book" appellation.

Jewish children were compelled to begin learning at a very young age.

At the yeshiva (university) level, subjects included Talmud, theology, philosophy, science, optics, logic, geometry, astronomy, music, mechanics, and metaphysics.

CHARITY Right from the Five Books of Moses, Judeo-Christian attention to charity is important.

The majority of Christians, Muslims and Jews have always been poor. From time of Moses, Judeo-Christians were instructed to help the poor by leaving a corner of the fields for them to harvest. Even slaves had rights.

<u>**TRADE**</u>   Jews routinely traveled from India and China to France, Spain, and everywhere in between carrying out trade in spices, silk, musk, and camphor.

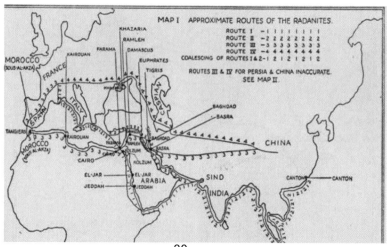

STEP 6: SYMBOLS

Jews and Christians both worship the same Almighty and share a scriptural heritage. Their cooperation is expressed beautifully in their shared symbols such as the lion of Judah described in *Genesis* and *Numbers*, often shown on its rear feet. Early kings, including Jeroboam used the lion, as did Jewish glassmakers and the Saltiel family, descended from the biblical David and settled in Zaragossa.

The Lion of Judah in the Seals of Jerusalem and Jeroboam; glass art; the seals of the Shealtiel family and their Zaragossa home; and also the flag of Christian/Jewish Leon.

As Christians and Jews read about the twelve tribes of Israel, they also adopted the symbol of Simeon, a fortress usually shown with three parapets.

Despite claims of Theodosian Romans, Judeo-Christian peoples including tolerant Catholics, Arians, minority Christians and Jews worked together famously. Medieval cities of Jews like Carcao in Portugal and Lucena in Andalusia displayed the same castle/fortress as the Jewish/Christian Kingdom of Castile with its capital of Toledo.

The Lion of Judah, together with the fortress of Simeon were on a flag of Castile - Leon, a Hebrew grammar book, and the front of the Halevi Synagogue in Toledo. And we see the bold shield with four prominent red stripes in Spain. Some early Jewish Counts of Urgell, Cerdanya, and Barcelona used these stripes which became the symbol of Barcelona, then Aragon, then Catalunya. The four stripes signify the people of Passover.

The Exodus holiday of Passover is the seminal holiday for Christians and Jews. These Haggadot, Jewish guides for the celebration of the Exodus, all have four bold stripes. The number four is mystical for Passover due to the presence in the liturgy of four cups of wine, four questions, four sons, and four promises of the Almighty.

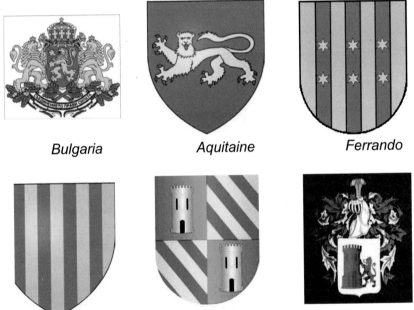

Bulgaria   Aquitaine   Ferrando

Aragon   Aristizabel   Abravanel

Christian and Jewish families and places frequently used the Hebrew symbols of Moses and Passover. It was only natural, as they employed the same value system initiated by the Ten Commandments.

33

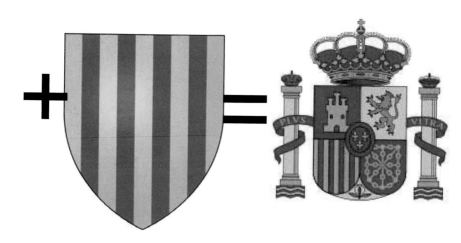

The Spanish flag, a masterful acknowledgement of Christian and Jewish brotherhood.

STEP 7: MORE
CHRISTIAN JEWISH HARMONY

1100 CE With the demise of the tolerant Muslim administrations in Andalusia, the remarkable partnership of Catholics and Jews continued in Northern Spain, including Castile-Leon, Aragon and Portugal along the traditions of the original Visigoth Arian and Jewish cooperation.

Christian *Eleanor of Aquitaine, wife of two kings, mother of kings and queens, writer of Judeo-Christian morals, descendant of Catholics and Jews.*
<<

The Tolerant Alfonso VI

Tomb of Ferdinand III with inscriptions in Hebrew, Latin, and Arabic

Alfonso X, son of Ferdinand, Court of Christians, Muslims, Jews, and Ally of Italian Judeo-Christian Ghibellines who opposed the Theodosian Guelphs (of Romeo & Juliet fame). A quote from his court: The Almighty is, "One who can pardon Christian and Jew and Moor." Catholics composed important Cantatas.

An וִסוֹת is a law

based on Judeo-Christian principles in the tradition of the original Visigoth code. The *Usatges* formed the basis of law in Barcelona and Aragon.

With laws in place following the lead of Moses, those in the Catholic kingdoms of northern Spain enjoyed a continuation of cultural renaissance.

Abraham Zacuto presented navigation maps to the explorer Vasco da Gama and Levi ben Gerson invented Jacob's staff, used by ship pilots for hundreds of years.

*Moses de Leon
Advanced Kabballah*

Friends of the Usatges paid a dear price for opposing Theodosian principles. The King of France burned the Templar Knights in order to seize their wealth.

A crusade against Albigensian Christians and the Catholic King Pedro of Aragon resulted in the king's death and the death of all types of people, including Viscount Trencavel.

Another crusade with the French against the grandson of Pedro was part of the bloody War of Sicilian Vespers.

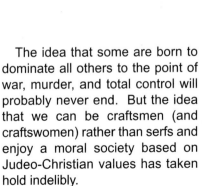

The idea that some are born to dominate all others to the point of war, murder, and total control will probably never end. But the idea that we can be craftsmen (and craftswomen) rather than serfs and enjoy a moral society based on Judeo-Christian values has taken hold indelibly.

STEP 8: BREAKTHROUGH TO MODERN CIVILIZATION

In a display of interfaith cooperation, Pico Mirandola, Henry More, Galileo, Dante, Fibonacci, Roger Bacon, and St. Thomas Aquinas all read Hebrew or had Hebrew assistants or used Hebrew texts. Many of these thinkers were excommunicated.

GERMANS RULE EUROPE AND NORTH AFRICA: 400-700 CE

Various German tribes lived East of the Rhine from the earliest times, trading with Greeks and Jews in places like Cologne. Many converted to a Judeo-Christian religion. Pressures from other agressive tribes further east and a corrupt Rome caused then to migrate westward. After skirmishes with Franks, the Vandals crossed the Rhine in 406 to invade Gaul (France), and proceeded all the way to Africa, there establishing a kingdom. Various Goths and Burgundians followed closely, conquering Italy, France, and Spain in the process. They swept out oppressive Roman imperial laws and embedded Judeo-Christian laws in Europe that became the basis of modern civil society. After 700, their territory decreased, but the shadow of their influence is today stronger than ever.

(Map below is simplified as boundaries were always changing.)

GERMANS RULE OF EUROPE

SAXONS
ANGLES
SAXONS
FRANKS
VISIGOTHS
THEN
FRANKS
GOTHS
BURGUNDIANS
OSTROGOTHS
VISIGOTHS
LOMBARDS
VANDALS

GERMANS AND JEWS
THE EARLY YEARS
IN SEARCH OF MOSAIC LAW

By 400, Imperial Rome had pretty much trashed the empire. The famous libraries of Alexandria stood in burnt ruins from the activities of Roman thugs; Greek schools were shuttered and their possessions confiscated by nobles; the new rulers forced the Catholic Church into a compromised position under supervision of Emperor Constantine's government and placed hacks or patronage bullies in key positions. Intimidation prevailed that included voiding municipal contracts such as transport of grain from Africa to Rome with long-standing Jewish vessels, oppressive laws cementing privilege for aristocrats, and placement of craftsmen, labor, and the general population into bondage or outright slavery.

Catholics had based their observance of law upon the Torah, the Old and New Testaments, and traditions from Judeo-Christian culture. The Romans forced the laws of the Roman Empire on Catholics, even though they contradicted traditional teaching. Many Catholics however remained true to their heritage and subverted imperial dictates. The civil war that placed Constantine on the Roman throne in 306 brought in a code of laws, later known as the Theodosian Code, that promulgated the type of brutal dictatorship familiar since the times of the pharaohs. These laws violated those of Moses and the Judeo-Christian tradition.

This set the stage for the revolution of 400. A practice session for the revolt took place in 378 when members of the German Visigoth tribe killed Emperor Valens and soundly defeated his imperial army. Roman hegemony stood exposed.

Long-standing victims of Roman aggression noticed the defeats, and the first to take advantage of the situation came from the vast German forests and the Hungarian plains. From there, Visigoths penetrated the Empire and sacked Rome in 410. A tribe called Vandals joined with another group called Alans and cut a swath through the Empire as they raided Roman treasures in Gaul (France) and pressed into Spain. The derogatory implication of the word "vandal," serves as an example of successful Roman propaganda, as that word should really mean "liberator." Hordes from the Roman underclass broke loose from their masters to march for liberation from Roman laws and magnates. They then crossed the Straits of Gibraltar from the rich Spanish area to the even wealthier North Africa.

429 CE

Suddenly these land-based tribal peoples had access to the fleet of Carthage, courtesy of those North African merchants discriminated against by Rome. With their new allies and new fleet, Vandals challenged Rome/Byzantium on the open seas, raiding their cargo ships and attacking coastal cities. This African invasion succeeded due to the disgust of oppressed Jews, dark-skinned Berbers, and other people desiring the over-throw of Roman Byzantium[1]

The invaders started to throw out Romans, causing loss of ground for the Empire. They ruled with tolerance, but did, however, engage in vengeance stemming from past suppression Vandals had suffered under Romans. The Vandal king signed legislation, using old Roman laws against minority Christians and other "heretics," but substituting the word "Catholic," thus continuing an unfortunate association of imperialism with Catholicism. Otherwise, Vandals ruled with intelligence, patronizing the arts and encouraging both secular and diverse religious education.

The Vandals conquered North Africa and suspended Roman-Byzantine hegemony; the control of the Roman bishops faltered, and religious tolerance regained respectability. Jews came down from the hills, and those who had converted to Catholicism under duress reversed themselves and again took up positions of freedom and prosperity. Trade in North Africa increased, as bishops could no longer preclude Jews and others from conducting business transactions. Danger increased for those in the comfortable manor houses of the Roman elite.[2]

The combination of Berbers, Jews, and Germans, all of whom had suffered immensely under the harsh rule of Rome, created an historic alliance. All dictatorships fear this type of interaction among the oppressed. Rome and its state religion worked hard to portray these peoples, Berbers, Jews, minority Christians and German tribes, as inferior in faith, prowess, and civilization, but the reality of Roman losses struck at the heart of the theory that G-d willed an imperial dictatorship.

Black Berbers continued their allegiance to the Vandals and contributed troops to the Vandal army. In 455, Vandals and Berbers embarked on a convoy of ships, disembarked from Carthage, and landed in Italy. Honoring pleas of the pope, the raiders spared residents of the Holy City from torture and slaughter, but plundered Rome itself According to some reports, they took into their possession large parts of the Jewish temple treasure that Titus had brought to Rome after his sacking of that city. The invaders returned to Africa with trophies that included senators and their wives as booty. Thereafter the Vandals established bases in Sardinia, Corsica the Balearic Islands, and Sicily. [3]

Catholic apologists heaped abuse on the Germans, more on Goths than the Vandals, as Bishop Isadore of Seville wrote, "The Goths are descended from Magog... from a good Roman Catholic background, the Vandal king instead of following Romans, converted to the Arian (Christian) falsehood.... He then ravaged Sicily, besieged Palermo, introduced the Arian pestilence through the whole of Africa, drove priests from their churches, caused many to be martyrs, and, as in Daniel's prophecy, after altering the mysteries of sacred worship, delivered the churches to the enemies of Christ."[4]

The German tribes, called "barbarians" by Roman apologists, followed laws and religious practices far more civilized than Rome. Vandals, Goths, Visigoths, Burgundians, and Lombards followed the Arian religion, not to be confused with the perverted 20th century Nazi Aryan practices.

The Germans followed the religious practices of Arius. Arius was a Christian presbyter from Alexandria, Egypt who engaged in the lively religious and philosophical community that existed prior to the imperial dictator Constantine. That community shared thoughts in an ecumenical manner, with Jewish rabbis, Greek thinkers, and Christians of many denominations. In that atmosphere the Hellenic Jewish philosopher Philo supervised the translation of the Bible from Hebrew to Greek.

Arius practiced the seven Jewish feasts (Passover, Unleavened Bread, First Fruits, Summer Harvest or Shavu'ot, Shofer or Ram's Horn as in Jericho and New Year, Atonement, and Tabernacles or Wilderness Shelter). He emphasized the Father's divinity over the Son, and he opposed trinitarian Christology. According to his contemporary Epiphanius of Salamis as interpreted by Warren Carroll, Arius was ""tall and lean, of distinguished appearance and polished address. Women doted on him, charmed by his beautiful manners, touched by his appearance of asceticism. Men were impressed by his aura of intellectual superiority." Unfortunately, Arius preached at the time of Emperor Constantine, who outlawed his teaching and burned his writings. Constantine exiled Arius to Germany where Arius and his successors converted tribes to the Arian religion, with tolerance, its closeness to Judaism and its roots in the Five Books of Moses.

German Visigoths, Vandals, Burgundians and others took to this teaching. It depicted a moral approach to life and stood in stark contrast to the immorality of Rome. Even though Arius could no longer enjoy the splendid surrounding of Alexandria, Germania possessed a great deal of culture that came about from trade and other exposure to the world at large. The Greek and Jewish communities in Cologne could provide some of the stimulation Arius had absorbed in Alexandria. Constantine, while curtailing many religions in the year 321, recognized the Jewish community in Cologne and Greek mosaics from the era survive today.

In possession of the Judeo-Christian tradition of human behavior and civilization building, Germania understood the makings of a civil society, unlike the Huns who only contemplated marauding, or the Romans, who only understood raw centralized power rather than anything associated with "freedom," be it free markets, rights, or religion.

In the fifth century, Arian Christians from Germany occupied large parts of the Empire stretching from Gaul to Spain to North Africa and even Italy. They had no need of the Roman laws that had discriminated against them. The religion of Arius stood, in Roman minds, as a dangerous heretical movement to be opposed and oppressed.

Officially, the Romans did not admit their need for any other peoples or ideas besides their own. Unofficially, the case differed. In his hometown of Hippo in North Africa Saint Augustine submitted disputes about the Bible to Jewish rabbis.[5] Augustine justified the Roman Empire and endowed it with heavenly grace, "In this book it is proved that the extent and long duration of the Roman Empire is to be ascribed... to one true God, the author of felicity, by whose power and judgment earthly kingdoms are founded and maintained.'"[7]

Roman apologists including Augustine, whose homeland in Africa was lost, wrote that the Empire deserved to rule. This idea had been developed in better days by Polybius, Saint Jerome and Rufinus. Augustine continued the thought in *The City of God*. *The City of God*, along with *Etymologies,* by Isadore of Spain and *Books Against Pagans* by Orosius stood in the libraries of influential Romans.[7]

Augustine wrote about the glories and virtues of the Roman Empire. He attempted to explain the reliance of the Church on dictators and military leaders such as Constantine to forcefully recruit Catholics. This, of course, stood in contrast to the methods of early missionaries who relied on verbal persuasion and example. Augustine wrote:

"Wherefore let us go on to consider the virtues of the Romans and why the true God, in whose power are also the kingdoms of the earth, condescended to help in order to raise the empire...

For the good God ... gave to the Emperor Constantine, who was not a worshipper of demons, but of the true God Himself, such fullness of earthly gifts as no one would even dare wish for. To him also He granted the honor of founding Constantinople, a companion to the Roman Empire, the daughter, as it were of Rome itself, but without any temple homage to the demons. He reigned for a long period as sole Emperor, while he held and defended the whole Roman world. Constantine introduced and continued war in a most victorious manner." [8]

Augustine supported the passage of laws against those he labeled pagans and heretics. He recommended the use of force in order to bring them into his City of God:

"What shall I say as to the infliction and remission of punishment in cases where we only desire to forward the spiritual welfare of those we are deciding whether or not to punish: What trembling we feel in these things, my brother.

For many have found advantage in being first compelled by fear or pain, so that teaching might afterwards influence them. Roman disasters came from tolerating paganism, heresy and immorality."

He supported passage of laws against pagans and heretics in instituting "correctio."[9] (law of correction)

After a century of desperate attempts, the emperor finally took back Northern Africa and recovered great treasure for the Roman Empire. Howefer, France and Spain, then used the names of the conquering tribes such as "Gothia," or "Burgundy," and remained largely German.

So in Clermont, France, Romans held onto control while close by, in Toulouse, Visigoths established a capital. One Roman noble, Sidonius attempted to maintain relations with his neighbors, whether they were Roman or not. And so Sidonius came to befriend a number of Jewish residents, a task easily done because Clermont served as a small Hebrew center. In spite of the official attempts to discredit non-Roman thinking, Sidonius admired education, the benefits of business, rational discussion, and traditional Judeo-Christian values. His Jewish neighbors provided all of those things. He admired their business practices above those of other communities.

"In the area of business the Jews are the most honest in negotiation," discovered Sidonius.

He spoke often with his friend Gozolas, a Jewish man who supplied an important link to the outside world for Sidonius. The outside world grew ever more dangerous as Visigoths to the west threatened to gain ever more land. Travel by a Roman noble outside his realm could bring danger and arrest. [10]

Sidonius lamented, "The armed bands of the tribes that surround us are terrifying our town, which they regard as a sort of barrier restricting their frontiers. So we are set in the midst of two rival peoples and are become the pitiable prey of both; suspected by the Burgundians, and next neighbors of the Visigoths, we are spared neither the fury of our invaders nor the malignity of our protectors." [11]

Jews were especially friendly with the Visigoths and could pass between the two sides more easily than many others. Gozolas performed

favors for Sidonius, as Sidonius wrote thanks for his delivery of letters outside the city walls.
Indeed, both the Burgundians and the Visigoths alternately fought each other and various Roman factions. But the Arian Christianity of Burgundians and Visigoths lent religious fervor to wars against Rome. While Visigoths fought Romans, Clermont came under siege for some years, trapping Sidonius inside the town on the side of the Roman nobility.
Arians harbored no resentment towards other faiths. including many of their Roman Catholic adversaries. Traditional Catholics, other Christians and Jews looked at the Goths as liberators from harsh Roman religious laws.[12]

470 CE

Sidonius advanced to the position of Prefect of Rome, and then Bishop of Clermont, holding the office of the Holy See for the third generation with no liturgical or ecclesiastical credentials. His political connections impressed the powerful. He added the title of "Count" to his legacy.
Now if one thing upsets a gentleman, it must be the freedom of his slaves. One the the friends of Sidonius fell on hard times, and so when this humbled friend faced the bleak prospect of life separated from his slaves, Sidonius felt compelled to help,
"Greetings to Riothamus (man of rank),
"Things are always happening about which it is obviously impossible for a man of my rank and cloth to speak without incurring unpleasantness or to be silent without incurring guilt... The bearer of this letter, who is humble and obscure, and so unassertive that he might even be taxed with harmless indolence, complains that his slaves have been enticed from him by underhand persuasions of certain Bretons..."[14].
Like his father-in-law, the late Emperor Avitus, Sidonius attempted relationships with those in the Visigoth leadership who favored rapprochement with Rome. Theodoric, King of the Visigoths lived close to Sidonius, in his capital of Toulouse where he maintained a court like a Roman emperor.
Much to his own surprise, Sidonius lived to see peoples (Germans) of low birth with no Roman blood living in a way that rivaled imperial culture. That realization flew in the face of Rome's claim to solely represent divine will due to the superiority of its aristocrats. Few Romans other than Sidonius ever admitted to equality with other peoples. Sidonius wrote to his dear brother-in-law Agricola, son of Emperor Avitus, and made comments regarding the Visigoth king:
"Greetings,
I have recently seen a report that commends to the world the graciousness of Theodoric, King of the Toulouse Goths.[15] You have often asked me to describe to you in writing the dimensions of his person and the character of his life. I am delighted to do so, subject to the limits of a letter, and I appreciate the honest spirit that prompts so nice a curiosity. Well, this is a man who deserves review even by those not in close relations with him. In his build the will of God and Nature's plan have joined together to endow him with a supreme perfection. His character is such that even the jealousy that hedges a sovereign has no power to rob it of its glories.
And now you may want to know all about his everyday life, which is open to the public gaze. Before dawn he goes with a very small retinue to

the service conducted by the priests of his Arian faith, and he worships with great earnestness, though one can see that this devotion is a matter of routine rather than of conviction. The administrative duties of his sovereignty claim the rest of the morning. Nobles in armor have places near his throne; a crowd of guards in their dress of skins is allowed in so as to be at hand, but excluded from the presence so as not to disturb. They keep up a hum of conversation by the door, outside the curtains but within the barriers. Meanwhile deputations from various peoples are introduced, and he listens to a great deal of talk, but replies shortly, postponing business which he intends to consider, speeding that which is to be promptly settled. The second hour comes: he rises from his throne, to pass an interval in inspecting his treasures or his stables....

When one joins him at dinner, there is no unpolished conglomeration of discolored old silver set by panting attendants on sagging tables. The weightiest thing on these occasions is the conversation, for there are either no stories or only serious ones. The couches, with their spreading draperies, show an array sometimes of scarlet cloth, sometimes of fine linen. The viands attract by their skilful cookery, not by their cost; the platters by their brightness, not by their weight. Replenishment of the goblets or wine bowls comes at such intervals that there is no reason for the thirsty to complain or for the intoxicated to refrain. To sum up, you can find there Greek elegance, Gallic plenty, Italian briskness, the dignity of state, the attentiveness of a private home, the ordered discipline of royalty. But as to the luxury of the days of festival I had better hold my tongue, for even persons of no note cannot fail to note it. ...

The royal supper interrupts afternoon activities and the bustle fades away distributing itself among the various courtiers whose patronage this or that party enjoys. Thus they keep watch till the night watches. Occasionally the banter of low comedians is admitted during supper, though they are not allowed to assail any guest with the gall of a biting tongue. In any case no hydraulic organs are heard there, nor does any concert party under its trainer boom forth a set performance in chorus. There is no music of lyric, flutist or dance conductor, tambourine girl or female citharist. The king finds a charm only in the string music that comforts the soul with virtue just as much as it soothes the ear with melody.

When he rises from the table, the night watch is first posted at the royal treasury and armed sentries are seen at the entrances to the palace, who will keep guard through the hours of the first sleep....
Farewell. "[16]

King Theodoric did not die of natural causes. Insidious events followed. Many of his subjects, especially his brother Euric, objected to the Visigoth royal court's imitation and adulation of Roman courts. Euric murdered the king of the Toulouse Visigoths and brought the nationalist party of the Visigoths to power, instituting a vigorous anti-Roman policy.

The Visigoths[17] then pressed their advantage, besieging Clermont again and again. Sidonius urged his populace to endure. They teetered on the edge of starvation. Clermont residents ripped grass and plants from the cracks in walls for food. Some patricians began to think that the future of imperial Rome lay in alliance with the Visigoths, following through with military aid and helping them to wage a war. The Visigoths pushed all contenders from Spanish soil and took command of that country.

In the end, Rome ceded Clermont to the Visigoths in a treaty designed to permit Roman retainage of a small portion of Provence. Sidonius seethed. He had fought hard to preserve Roman glory, and was traded without consent.

"Our freedom has been bartered for the security of others," he lamented. "Is this our due reward for enduring want and fire and sword and pestilence, for swords fed fat with gore and warriors emaciated with hunger? ... We were often poisoned by noxious grasses, which, being green, with nothing to distinguish their leaves or sap, were often plucked by a hand that starvation had made as green as they."

He wrote to one of the treaty's authors, "We pray that you and your colleagues may feel ashamed of this fruitless and unseemly treaty.... Soon our ancestors will no longer glory in the name of ancestors...."[18]

Victorious Visigoths entered the town with an ex-Roman general in the Visigoth service and spared Clermont from pillage, but incarcerated its count, Bishop Sidonius.

Clermont survived Visigoth management very well. The Goths were not all that bad. They practiced Arian Christianity, but permitted a degree of religious freedom never experienced since before Constantine in the Roman Mediterranean. Pagans, Jews, Catholics, Arians, and other small sects co-existed with minimal friction. In Clermont, at least one Catholic faction continued the tradition of friendly relations with Jews that Sidonius had encouraged. Catholics could run for office. Some bishops in campaigning for office preached friendship with all faiths and received Jewish contributions[19] If only that spirit could have continued, but the Roman Imperial ghost continued to haunt the Catholic Church.

While in a Visigoth minimum security prison, Sidonius found old Roman friends who had defected to the Visigoth side and achieved great power within the king's court. These friends helped in his re-education so he could leave prison and join them in serving the Visigoths.

Due to his wide fame and previous relationship with the court of Toulouse, Sidonius was able to gain entry into a comfortable life under the rule of his former enemy. He had only to express his regrets and proclaim his loyalty. He determined to achieve the good graces of the new King Euric and apologized.[20]

Sidonius won his release from prison and the Arians permitted him to resume his duties as Clermont's bishop. The nobility of Rome continued to adjust, survive, and maintain political power. They did not accept an age of toleration with grace, but plotted to reinstitute dictatorship.

476 C.E.

By the end of the fifth century, another German tribe inhabited Gaul. This group, the Franks, swept down into the heart of Gaul and soon seized parts of Gothia. The presence of the Franks in Europe brought the new name of "Frankia" (France) to much territory and the land supported three competing powers: Goth, Frank, and Roman. If the Romans could somehow gain alliance with the Franks, perhaps they could rid themselves of the independent Goths and gain power again. Sidonius passed frequently from one regime to the other.

In passing from Frankia to Gothia, Sidonius exited the jurisdiction of Salic Law, based on the traditions of the Franks to the authority of Visigoth Law. These two bodies of law contrasted with the Roman law of the time. Roman law was embodied in the Theodosian code.[21] Both the Frank and Goth regimes allowed Romans, when interacting with each other in their own community, to utilize their own laws. Goths and Franks imparted this privilege also to Jews.

In Frank Salic law, the murder of a Frank noble cost the perpetrator 600 gold pieces, while the cost to murder a Roman gentleman rang in at 300 gold pieces. The party accused could absolve himself by producing an adequate number of friendly witnesses, and so the production of seventy-two friends could free a man charged with assassination.

Manipulation and perjury abounded with the Franks, leading to the widespread use of trial by ordeal and combat. In this way, a strong and brave man could always prevail over an acknowledged coward.[22]

Goths flexed their power, as they now controlled the vast majority of Italy, France, and Spain. This put pressure on the careers of the Roman aristocracy. A number of Roman nobles avoided the ranks of the landless and the tragedy of unemployment by the simple mechanism of joining the Catholic Church, which served as an employment agency and club for nobles. Sidonius' brother-in-law Agricola, the son of former Emperor Avitus, to whom Sidonius had addressed the letter describing the Goth king, joined the ranks of the priesthood, after a political career in which he had risen to Prefect of Gaul[23] For such a nobleman, the Roman hierarchy did not require religious credentials, and the Roman Theodosian code reserved the ranks of Catholic clergy exclusively for the highborn.

A new Visigothic King Euric of Gaul and Spain, with his seat of power in Toulouse, undertook the codification and assemblage of the set laws eventually known as the Visigothic code. It paralleled the laws of the Burgundians and Lombards in its reliance on Judeo-Christian heritage.

The issue regarding vast estates and slaveholdings of Romans arose early. When Goths first invaded Roman territory, they assigned parts of the Roman estates to their own leaders. This portion could amount to up to two thirds of each estate, but rarely exceeded half. The Goths placed their own warriors in ownership. This did not happen to all estates, as politics entered the fray. As a result, the new law needed to recognize the rights of the new Goth landlords.

Entered into law by the Visigothic Royalty:
Concerning the Division of Lands Made Between Goths and Romans. A division of arable lands or forests made between Goths and Romans shall under no circumstances be interfered with, provided said division shall be publicly made. No Roman shall take, or claim for himself, any part of the two thirds of said land allotted to a Goth in said division. No Goth shall dare to seize, or claim for himself, any of the third part of said land allotted to a Roman, unless it should have been bestowed upon him by our generosity. Any division made between parents or neighbors shall not be disturbed by their posterity.
Concerning Forests Still Undivided Among Goths and Romans.

There are forests still undivided between Goths and Romans. Where any Goth or Roman has appropriated a portion of the same, and placed it under cultivation, we hereby make a decree. The party that made the cultivation shall make compensation to any injured party with woodland of equal value. Where Goths have appropriated any of the third part of land belonging to Romans, they shall restore the entire amount to the Romans, under order of court. Romans must make their claims within fifty years.[24]

With the problem of land division solved to the satisfaction of the Goths, if not the Romans, Goths reviewed other aspects of the Roman Theodosian code. Some features of Roman law and society proved extremely incompatible with Goth welfare. For one thing, Romans considered their new neighbors to be barbarians, and the Arian Christianity of the Goths heretical.

Entered into law by the Roman royalty (In opposition to traditional Catholic values):

3.14.1 *Theodosian* No Roman shall presume to have a barbarian wife of any nation whatever, nor shall any Roman woman be united in marriage with a barbarian. But if they should do this, they shall know that they are subject to capital punishment.

16.1.1 *Theodosian* It is our will that all ... shall practice that religion which the divine Peter the Apostle transmitted to the Romans.

We command that those persons who follow this rule shall embrace the name of Catholic Christians. The rest, however, whom we adjudge demented and insane, shall sustain the infamy of heretical dogmas. Their meeting places shall not receive the name of churches, and they shall be smitten first by divine vengeance and secondly by the retribution of our own initiative.

16.5.6 *Theodosian* Crowds shall be kept away from the unlawful congregations of all the heretics. The observance, destined to remain forever, of the Nicene (Catholic) faith, as transmitted long ago by our ancestors (Constantine) shall be maintained.

16.5.8 *Theodosian* We direct that none of the Eunomians and the Arians or the adherents of the dogma of Ethius shall have the right to build churches...

16.5.12 *Theodosian* The vicious doctrines hateful to God and man, namely, the Eunomian, the Arian, the Macedonian, the Apollinarian, and all other sects which are condemned by the sincere faith of the true religion, according to the venerable cult of the Catholic discipline, shall not arrogate to themselves the right to assemble congregations or to establish churches.

16.5 *Theodosian* The madness of the heretics must be so suppressed, that the churches which they have taken from the orthodox, where-ever they are held, shall immediately be surrendered to the Catholic Church, since it cannot be tolerated that those who ought not to have churches of their own should continue to detain those.[25]

So Visigoths rejected Roman law and looked to Hebrew law and Judeo-Christian tradition for a new judicial system. This was quite natural as the bond between Arians and Jews was especially strong. Religious founder Arius conversed with rabbis and his religion celebrates

Jewish holidays including Yom Kippur, Rosh Hashanah, Sukkot, and Passover. Roman detractors called Arians "modern Jews."

Here we see the influence of Israelite laws in their Talmud and Torah on Visigoth code:

From the *VISIGOTHIC CODE:*[26]

THIEVES AND STOLEN PROPERTY

VISIGOTHIC CODE	*TALMUD/ TORAH*
A freeman who steals the property of another shall pay to the owner nine times the value.	If a thief is convicted…he has to make a four-fold or a five-fold payment --Bava Kama 62b, 70a
Not only he who actually commits a theft, but also he who was aware of it or knowingly received stolen goods, shall be a thief.	If partners commit the theft, they should be liable. --Bava Kama 68b
Where anyone, ignorantly, buys stolen property of a thief, he must restore the property to the owner after having received from the owner half the price.	One who unknowingly buys stolen goods must return them to the rightful owner upon reimbursement of the price paid. --Bava Kama 115a
Where anyone damages property or does injury, he shall pay full value to the owner.	If a utensil is trod on and broken, full damages must be paid. --Bava Kama 17a

NUPTIAL CONTRACTS

VISIGOTHIC CODE	*TALMUD/ TORAH*
Marriage shall not be entered into without a dowry When a dowry is reduced to writing, it shall not be contested.	A father must outfit his daughter and provide a dowry. -- Ketubot 52b committment to a dowry must be fulfilled. --- Ketubot 67a
A widow must wait a year to remarry or forfeit half her property to her children to protect the unborn. No divorce.	A widow must wait three months for remarriage to protect the unborn. --- Yebamot 42a A divorcee may marry after two and a half months. -- Yebamot 42a
No person shall pay more than a tenth of his property as dowry.	Marrying a daughter without setting a dowry mandates a dowry of at least 50 zuz.

WOMEN

VISIGOTHIC CODE	TALMUD/ TORAH
A widow shall have an equal portion of the inheritance with her children.	A widow may keep or sell that which came to her as a result of a marriage contract. -- Bava Kama 89a
The wife shall inherit from the Husband.	A widow may be maintained from the estate of her husband -- Ketubot, Bava Metzia
One who rapes a betrothed woman gives up his property or, if he has little property, is sold as a slave and punished.	A man who rapes a betrothed maiden shall die. Deuteronomy 22:25

CONCERNING COURT MATTERS

VISIGOTHIC CODE	TALMUD/ TORAH
Royalty and the entire body of people are subject to the majesty of the law.	Law applies to both rich and poor, *Iruvin* 47a Kings of the House of David may judge and be judged. *Sanhedrin 18a*
Only one book of law shall apply.	Ye shall have one law. *Yebamot 9a*
A judge not sanctioned by the law shall hear no cause.	No man may take the law into his own hands. *Bava Kama 27b*
False testimony shall be an offense with other penalty.	He who falsely alleges theft may have to make double payment. *Bava Kama 63b*
A perjurer shall be arrested, given 100 lashes, banned from testimony, & separated from a fourth of his property to the defrauded.	A perjurer becomes liable for all accidents, or principle, for a fifth, and for trespass, double. -- *Bava Kama 105b*
A witness shall give testimony orally.	Witnesses shall state in front of judges and be examined. -- *Sanhedrin 18a*
A judge may compel a party to court.	One may command another to testify. -- *Shevuot 30a*
A fraudulent judge shall pay the defendant.	A judge may be judged and testified against. -- *Sanhedrin 18a*
Judges decide criminal and civil cases.	The Sanhedrin hears all cases. *Sanhedrin 2a*
Ignorance of the law is not an excuse.	Ignorance is not excused. -- *Harayot 7b*

51

INJURIES TO PROPERTY

VISIGOTHIC CODE	TALMUD/ TORAH
Where anyone destroys another's garden or tree, a judge shall compel him to make restitution.	Where he damages several furrows he must pay for the best. *Bava Kama 6b*
If one entrusted with the property of another loses it, but saves his own property, he shall render full satisfaction.	When under an obligation of controlling property, one is responsible for any damages that result. -- *Bava Kama 9b*
If gold, silver, or money entrusted for safe keeping should be lost or consumed by fire along with the trustee's property, he shall incur no liability.	If even without him co-operating the fire would have spread, what, if anything at all, has he perpetuated? - *Bava Kama 10b*
Where animals belonging to any person injure the vineyard or garden of another, the owner of the animal shall pay	If my ox committed manslaughter on A or killed A's ox, a liability is established. -- *Bava Kama 15b*
A person who kills or wounds the animal of another shall give one of the same value.	A person borrowed an axe and broke it. He came before the Rabbi who said, "Go and pay." *Bava Kama 11a*
He who sets fire to the house of another in a city shall be burned alive and property taken.	Arson causing death is a possible capital case. *Bava Kama 26a*

CONTRACTS, MISC.

VISIGOTHIC CODE	TALMUD/ TORAH
Where a person plants a vineyard on the land of another without permission, he shall lose the vineyard.	A person built a villa on land of orphans. Rabbi Nahman ordered the villa for the owners. -- *Bava Kama 21a*
Whoever rents land under a lease, shall occupy as much of said land as the owner permits and o more.	A sound lease confirmed by legal documents is enforceable. Iruvin 62a.
Anyone at the point of death, may liberate his slaves by an instrument in writing or with witnesses.	A deed of slave liberaton by the master is delivered to the same. -- *Bava Metzia 19a*
The last will of a person, properly drawn, shall be valid in law.	Wills legally drawn dictate the distribution of property. -- *Bava Metzia 19a*
Contracts properly and lawfully written shall be unalterable.	If one contacts to supply flour at four he must supply at four .-- *Bava Metzia 57b*

The Early Years

With a legal code soundly based on biblical Mosaic principles, Arian Gothic Europe took off on a sprint towards renaissance. This is because Hebrew laws result in advances in medicine, philosophy, science, and other areas of human advancement. Leaders like Goth Euric of Toulouse; Frank Catholic Chilperic of Soissons; Arian Goth Leo (Leogivild) of Spain; and Charles Martel (grandfather of Charlemagne) with his dynasty from Soissons, France practiced harmony among religions. They corresponded with the Persian empire in Baghdad, traded around the world, and tolerated intellectual thought and science.

These are the principles dear to all Judeo Christians, including Catholics. However, looking to crush all opposition and free thinking, imperial Rome and Byzantium considered these developments as setbacks. About the time Soissons, Arles, Toulouse, Narbonne, Lyon, Rouen, Troyes, Mainz, Clermont, and Tours experienced a resurgence of enlightenment, Roman nobleman Gregory of Tours used his privileges to slide into the bishop's office in Tours. Noble heritage still meant everything in the Roman hierarchy.

573 C.E.

As a man of protected special rights under Roman law, Gregory took his position as bishop in charge of Tours, an office that included maintenance of the cult of Saint Martin, a job he took seriously. He embodied the thrust of Roman rule.

Gregory of Tours proudly defended many of the practices that outlined the nature of the Dark Ages. He himself, possessing a sickly body, carried dust from the tomb of Saint Martin, which he drank in potions.[28] Gregory sneered at Jewish doctors who prescribed medical cures for cataracts and the like. According to Gregory, praying and fasting in the presence of the tomb of Saint Martin brought better results.[29]

He used the strength of healing from the cult of Saint Martin as a powerful tool in his competition against the monarchy, local counts and magnates, the Jews with their medicine and knowledge, and other sects or gods. Thousands came for cures, to touch the holy tomb, to drink potions from its dust, and to donate money. Yes, plenty of money.

Gregory grew skilled in extending the healing arts into the realm of jurisprudence. Constant wars and famine pushed many into slavery, and the poor sold themselves and their family members to the highest bidder. Gregory presided over miracles. The woman unjustly sold into slavery became crippled and therefore not useful to her master. He promised freedom if a miracle cured her. At the church of St. Martin she recovered both her health and her freedom, and then went to work for Gregory. His administrators and fellow clerics were often drunk.

One of his administrators set out drunk with wine from his dinner. *"He was thrown from a high cliff when a hostile demon pushed him. This cliff was almost two hundred feet high. As he tumbled through this vast fall and soared downward without any flapping wings, he called for the assistance of St. Martin at each moment of his descent. Then, as if he had been knocked off his horse by others' hands, he was thrown on top of the trees that were in the valley. In this way he descended slowly, branch by branch, and without the threat of death he finally reached the ground. ...He injured one foot. But upon coming to the church of the glorious Lord Martin he knelt in prayer and was relieved of all the force of his pain." (History of the Franks)*

Not everyone believed in the miracle cures. Kings, popes, bishops, and counts used Jewish doctors while discouraging the masses from doing the same. When a priest from Bordeaux, so severely afflicted with fever that he could not eat or swallow, preceded the morning rush to the Church of St. Martin, he met one of the Clermont Jewish community. The priest described his intention to seek the power of the saint to cure the illness.

Unimpressed, and wishing to grant advice, the Hebrew man replied, "Martin will be of no use to you, because the dirt pressing down on him in the tomb has made him into dirt. In vain do you go to his shrine. A dead man will not be able to provide medicine for the living."[30]

Part of Gregory's arsenal consisted of his ability to promise life in another world, both to the wealthy who willed gifts and to the poor who needed hope. Gregory relied on a promise of resurrection to provide a nice donation to the church and guaranteed entry into heaven.

Arian Christians and Jews, however, presented serious reminders of alternative ideas. These presented difficulties in controlling the flock and received condemnation by the Church as heretical peoples.

Chilperic, King of Soissons, received emissaries from around the Mediterranean. Much to the dismay of Gregory, Arians and Jews held great sway in the court. King Chilperic introduced a model of a Catholic king that flew in the face of imperial dictates. Chilperic maintained that a king could faithfully follow the Catholic religion and at the same time work with other religions, other philosophies and other ideas of business. He suppressed Roman Theodosian law.

Gregory entertained an envoy of the Spanish Arian king together with Chilperic. The Arian wanted to talk about religion, and so asserted, "How can the Son be equal to the Father, when He says: My Father is greater than I am? ... He complains about the miserable manner of His death,...and commends His spirit to the Father... Surely it is quite obvious that He is less than the Father, both in power and in age!"

Gregory retorted, "He said that My Father is greater than I only in the lowliness of the flesh. Elsewhere He says, I and my Father are one."

The envoy remained unconvinced, "The Son is always less than the Father because He does the will of the Father, whereas there is no proof that the Father does the will of the Son."

Gregory pointed out, "Christ said, "And now, O Father, glorify thou me with thine own self with the glory which I had with thee before the world was made..." Therefore the Son is equal in the G-dhead."

The envoy continued, "The Holy Ghost is less than either, for He was promised by the Son and sent by the Father. No one promises anything not in his power, and no one sends any person who is not his own inferior."

Gregory grew angry, "As I have said already, you are absolutely wrong about the Holy Trinity and, what is more, the way your founder, Arius, met his end shows just how perverse and wicked your sect is."

But the envoy disagreed. "You must not blaspheme against a faith which you yourself do not accept. You notice that we who do not believe the things which you believe nevertheless do not blaspheme against them."

Hearing this, Gregory felt the man was a fool, and claimed, "May the Lord never permit my religion or my faith to grow so tepid that I waste His blessing upon dogs, or cast the sacredness of His precious pearls before filthy swine!"

The envoy walked out, disgusted, saying, "May my soul leave the confines of my body before I ever receive a benediction from a priest of your religion!"[31]

Hardly had the Trinity discussion ended when one of the king's Jewish friends, Priscus, came to visit. Priscus had just aided the king in the purchase of real estate.

The king put his hand on the head of Priscus in a friendly manner, and instigated a religious conversation by asking if Priscus saw that the mysteries of the Church were foreshadowed in Jewish writings.

"G-d has no need of a son. He said that there is no god but me," stated the Jewish merchant. "How should G-d be made man, or be born of woman, or submit to stripes, or be condemned to death?"

Gregory took up the king's argument, "Your own scriptures say that 'He is both G-d and Man, and that Behold, a virgin shall conceive and bear a son, and shall call his name Emmanuel,' which being interpreted is, G-d with us…. 'Even David says that the Lord hath reigned from the Cross.'"

The Jew replied, "G-d could send prophets or apostles to recall man to the way of salvation, without being Himself humbled in the flesh."

The general population seemed unimpressed with the announced differences between Christianity and Judaism. On the Sabbath, Catholics often preferred to attend synagogue rather than church, especially when the rabbi delivered more interesting sermons. They required physical force, laws and intimidation to keep them away from the synagogue. Perhaps the more sermons reflected the Bible the better.[32]

But each congregation by its actions promoted certain attributes. The Jew relied on medicine. Catholics strained under Roman edicts pronounced against math and science, while Arians and Jews practiced both.

Chilperic limited Church acquisition of property, returning some of it to the general population. The king lamented, "Behold, our treasury has remained poor. Behold our wealth has gone to the churches. No one reigns if not the bishops. Our office will perish and be transferred to the bishops of the cities."

Chilperic favored Frank saints over Roman, patronized moderate Catholic clerics such as Fortunatus; used Jewish doctors, not dust from the church; liked local artists instead of those promoted by Byzantium [33;] had a Jewish mint master, similar to Iacotus at Orleans and Chalons, Ose at St. Lizier, Ius at Macon, and Iaco at Viviers.[34;] He composed poetry heretical to the Church, such as his ode to the Frank Saint Medard·

"We sing and praise you, O Medard, from the depth of our hearts. It is good for the faithful to elevate praises with one voice.

"As a holy and pious bishop, you performed many good deeds, and were never tired of caring for your flock.

"You were always committed to your pastoral duties, protecting the poor, the widows and the children, and admonishing the slothful.

"You were exceptionally holy and generous to the needy, and with the divine word, you enlightened the minds of many people.

"The faith of a little mustard seed, planted in your hearth grew into a giant source of miracles and virtues.

"With your many prayers, you obtained sight for the blind, and a cure for the lame and for the cripple.

"In the name of Christ, you delivered many people affected with demon possession, restoring health to their bodies." " [35]

Gregory of Tours hated King Chilperic and conspired against him by giving refuge in his church to a co-conspirator who had murdered the son of Chilperic. Gregory hated moderate Catholics like Chilperic and Chilperic's favorite poet Fortunatus.

Gregory favored the Roman plan, such as:

Theodosian 6.30.15 Commoners are barred from Imperial service. The trustworthiness of birth status shall be investigated.

Theodosian 16.1 All must practice Catholicism.

Theodosian Nval 35.1.3 Persons of ignoble birth cannot join the Church as clerics.

Theodosian 2.1.1 Prisons shall hold the scoundrels when they are convicted. Tortures shall tear them in pieces. The avenging sword shall destroy them. For in this way the license of the inveterate lawlessness of desperadoes is restrained, if they understand that they must live with one and the same aspiration as do all others.

Theodosian 5.17.1 Fugitive serfs, sharecroppers, and slaves shall be immediately returned to their birth status.

Theodosian 7, 10-14 People engaged in trades including armorers, miners, purple dye collectors, minters, ship makers, imperial weavers, bread makers and animal drivers shall not desert their trades. Their heirs shall continue in their ignoble trade. Those who harbor them while in flight from their trade shall be punished. Tradesmen shall devote a portion of their time in compulsory service to the state. Imperial weavers, armorers, and soldiers shall be branded on the arms in order to keep track of them.

Theodosian 6.27.5, We command that all the ancient privileges shall be preserved with respect to any ex-member of the secret service who was chief of an office staff. He shall be a senator and shall deservedly be grouped with the consulars. (The secret service or secret police reported disobedience of the high and low, and the super secret police reported on the activities of the secret police.)

The Roman secret service, already with some 500 years of duty behind it at the time of Gregory of Tours, reported on the private lives of citizens and nobility to the Emperor. There is reason to believe that Gregory was a secret service member.

The Roman secret service took an active role in promoting the narrow interests of its nobility. With many tolerant regimes in France and Spain, the service seized an opportunity in Spain with a new king there.

Lacking its former military might, Romans admitted to the Church plied the trade of politics. The Catholic bishop of Merida told the Arian king about the Arian religion.

"Be it known to you that I shall never soil my heart with the sordidness of Arian unbelief, never shall I sully my mind with the foulness of its perverted doctrine."[36]

In Spain, the Arian Visigoth King Recared married a Catholic, who teamed up with agents and convinced Recared to convert to Catholicism, the Radical Catholicism of Roman nobility rather than the more enlightened version of Chilperic in Soisson. His bride was from a family that attempted to overthrow the government of Spain against his father and encouraged the conversion.[37]

589 CE

In 589 when Gothic King Recared converted from Arianism to Catholicism, the radical Catholic party won a great victory and the Church rapidly became the largest landowner after the king. Bishops appointed by nobles administered both law and religion, and governed to vast areas of land with many slaves and subjects. The fusion of the Church and the Roman nobility in Spain was formalized.

Recared proposed severe penalties against his Gothic Arian Christians and lesser problems for Jews. Revolts erupted immediately.

Arians and their friends, principally Jews, staged dangerous sorties, but superior arms enabled the king to subdue the rebels.[38] *Dux* Claudius the Roman magnate proved his worth to Recared and crushed them all, in the south and in the north. The Arian Bishop Sunna, who had just worked so hard to regain his churches in Merida, participated in one of the most deadly revolts. Claudius moved with a great force against this city, fighting not only Sunna, but also Witteric, who later, in 603, ascended to the throne in a temporary setback for the radical Roman Party. But the nobles ultimately prevailed. This system brought about no renaissance, no burst of trade, no intellectual advancement, and certainly no freedom. That was the point. Aristocrats split up the spoils and owned the slaves. The population of Spain shrank. Trade diminished.

"The Jewish community, which had been well established on the Iberian Peninsula for centuries before the foundation of the Visigothic Kingdom, was, large, and dedicated. It is even likely that Jewish aristocrats continued to hold the rank of senator into the Visigothic period. Jews seem to have been very successful in their missionary activity as well, especially in the period after 589, despite the severe penalties to which both the missionary and the convert were liable under law. Many Goths who were forced to give up their Arianism by Recared may have found it more desirable to become Jews than to become Catholics and in that manner remaining more faithful to Judeo-Christian heritage."[40]

Spain, once a stalwart friend to all religions, teetered back and forth in a type of civil war between the Roman and Gothic factions. The same situation prevailed in France, where moderate Catholics in places like Soissons, as well as Arians, Romans, and others, vied for power.

Romans laid out their programs very plainly:

"If any peasant should be found so perfidious and obstinate as to refuse to come to G-d, he must be oppressed with the heaviest and most burdensome payments, until he is compelled by the very pain of the exaction to hasten to the right way."[41]

"Against idolaters, soothsayers, and diviners, we vehemently exhort your fraternity to be on the watch with pastoral wakefulness, … If, however, you find them unwilling to amend and correct their ways, we desire you to arrest them with fervent zeal. If they are slaves, chastise them with blows and torments, whereby they may be brought to amendment. But if they are free men, let them be led to penitence by strict confinement, as is suitable. Then they who scorn to listen to words of salvation that reclaim them from the peril of death, may at any rate be brought back to the desired sanity of mind by bodily torments."[42]

While in Spain, political and military setbacks dealt to Goth powers by

Romans brought about a more dangerous society, but events coalesced that would bring about a refreshment of liberty to the north, in France. There in Soissons, the "mayor of the palace," Pepin forged the elements of a dynasty.

620 CE

Pepin started to figure out how to coalesce power in the midst of a vacuum by using political acumen, marriage, military skills, and intrigue. The children of Pepin and his allies married, thus initiating the effective reign of Charlemagne's family, a dynasty that did not successfully declare its kingship until King Pepin I, grandson of Pepin the Elder usurped the crown.

As mayors of the palace, the family of Pepin dealt with all matters of the realm. They appreciated the power of the Church, but also dealt with others including Jewish advisors and suppliers, such as the many mint masters. In short, they continued the policies of Chilperic. By means of advice from Jews, the experience with the Arian Visigoths from Spain, and interaction with traders from afar, the palace avoided subjugation by Romans.

Hence, in casting about for land grants to vassals helpful in war, Pepin surmised that expropriating lands from the Roman Church could serve them well. When they needed land to pay soldiers, they took some from the Church. At the same time, a chaotic situation existed in Spain. Toward the end of the century a particularly oppressive radical Catholic king gained power.

673 CE

The revolution of 673 began in the Basque provinces resulting in the Catholic Goth King Wamba rapidly leading an expeditionary force into the northwest. No sooner had he arrived than the Count of Nimes, way over on the eastern side of Spanish Territory north of the Pyrenees launched a revolt to coordinate with the Basque action. Arian organizations, and Judeo-Christians like the Catholic Bishop of Mauelonne joined in the fray to defend against attacks against their garrisons. The king sent the Jewish *Dux* Paul with a large force to quell the insurrection.

As the *dux* hastened eastward on a path just south of the Pyrenees, he changed sides and joined the revolution. Rebels acclaimed his army and encouraged him to lead their forces. He put himself at the head of the rebellion rather than crushing it. The *dux* of the Tarraconensis in northern Spain joined him.

The rebel leader Paul headed towards Narbonne, and with good reason. Arian and Jewish forces there mustered their armed forces, seized control of the city, and drove out the radical Theodosian Catholic bishop and his followers.[43]

At Narbonne the population elected Paul king. The rebels of Nimes and Maguelonne embraced his cause.

Many nobles joined also joined, including Bera, Count of Razes.[44] This remarkable member of a prominent Jewish family had learned well how to survive the changing political climates of southern Europe.

Overtures to Jewish Berbers in North Africa proved premature, as the

Berbers had their hands full with intrusions by Arabs. This caused Bera to turn to the northern kingdoms. In France, the ancestors of Charlemagne struggled to retain power as mayors of the palace and could not help.

Nevertheless, even without a strong ally, Rebel leader Paul wrote a jeering letter to his former lord, opening with the words, "From Flavius Paulus, anointed king of the East, to the Southern King Wamba." Paul separated Provence from Spain. The revolt, however, failed in the end.[45] Paul's confidence proved premature.

Paul's rebellious forces hoped for relief from the Franks; however, the Frank leadership remained paralyzed, with ancestors of Charlemagne angling for power against other factions. A forced march of the king on the secessionist parts of Spain reduced Barcelona and Girona to obedience. He then advanced in three columns into Narbonne, taking that city, along with Beziers and Maguelonne. Nimes fell in September. [46]

The oppression of the newly Catholic Visigoths against the independently minded Basques, Arians and Jews did not succeed in its stated aim. Rebel leaders, frustrated that the Franks to the north could not help, turned elsewhere, across the Mediterranean to Africa, for help. In 687 Jews from Spain and Africa plotted to overthrow the Gothic rule of Spain. That plot also failed, and the oppression became more gruesome.

Jews, Arian Christians, moderate Catholics, and others looked for another solution.

As the era of enlightened Visigoth leadership drew to a close, the inevitable violent clash between the freedoms of the Judeo-Christian legacy and autocrats intensified.

However, the continuing Jewish German revolution had firmly planted Mosaic Law in Europe. The laws of Moses had such appeal to advocates of freedom and civil society that even the might of imperial Rome could not dislodge them. Before Europe could breathe again, Roman and Byzantine control of Spain needed to end.

ISLAMIC LIBERATORS

MUSLIMS, CATHOLICS and JEWS SWEEP
IMPERIAL ROME

The Jerua, an African warrior Berber tribe, converted to Judaism before the Common Era, and proceeded inland to the plateau west of Carthage (Tunis). Pressure from Roman soldiers over the previous 500 years suggested the prudence of this movement. In this circumstance the Berbers and Hebrews came together. Since ancient times, Jewish traders had made their way through this region en route to the Berber homeland in Numidia.

Profiting from the help given by the Vandals, the Jerua rose to a position of dominance in northeast Africa, supplying Berbers with royal dynasties. Berbers played prominent roles in the Vandal armies that sacked Rome. In the late seventh century, a Berber queen named Dahia, the *Cohena*, כוהן from the Hebrew word Cohen for denoting Jewish priest, rose to an eminent position among the Israelite Berbers.

They wore colorful sesert garb with flowing robes and headwear of wrapped cloth. They possessed a fierce military with camels and horses, enabling them to control the area of Algeria, Mauritania, and Tunisia.

The Cohena decided to oppose the powerful Arab Muslim thrust into Africa. She valued indepence and did not hesitate to display her military prowess. Should Jews, African tribes and Copts throw their weight with the Cohena or with the Arabs? The question produced divisiveness.[1]

As Arabs pressed their conquest of the Mediterranean, the cohena gathered her forces in an attempt to put off the invaders, but the Arabs prevailed, at great cost. As a final battle loomed, Cohena Dahia consoled her sons, "She who has commanded the Rum (Christians), the Berbers and the Arabs can die only as a queen."

She fell with sword in hand during a great battle in the year 704. The Berbers both suffered and meted out massive slaughter, but ultimately reached accommodation with the Muslims, many of them converting under threat of death.[2]

After watching thousands of their compatriots killed, the sons of Cohena acquiesced to joining the Arab expeditionary force. Her son Tarik immediately distinguished himself by taking Tangiers.

As Tarik and the Berbers looked across the water to Spain, they realized the richness of the land. Jews and moderates fleeing the persecutions of the radical Catholic Goths lived in Africa with Berbers and attempted to organize Africans to help a Spanish rebellion. Spain, or, as they called it, Andalusia, contained many riches.

Arabs also knew about Spain, They later commented, "Andalus (Spain) has been compared by many authors to a terrestrial paradise. For indeed by what other name can we designate the countries which the Catholics inhabit from the gulf of Constantinople to the ocean of Andalus."

But "Muslims conquered Andalus... by their sanctity and virtues, as firm supporters of religion… engaged in perpetual battle with the (Christian) enemy of G-d, defeated him morning and evening, never resting from the fatigues of the holy war…. The conquerors sallied out, trod on the necks of the impious Catholics, and brought down their pride."[3]

Tarik, a Berber king, descendant of the Jewish Berber queen and new vassal of the Muslim caliph in Damascus, received permission from his commander to conduct an exploratory raid against Spain.[4]

His brother joined him. They assembled a small army with largely Jewish Berbers, but under the suzerainty of the Arab commander, who expected to stay in Morocco because the success of the plan appeared dubious. Also in the invading army marched the Jewish Berber chief Kaulan el Yehudi and General Tarik, a Jew of the Simeon Berber tribe[5]

711 CE

As per Ashtor:[6]

"On a particularly warm, pleasant spring evening on the slopes of the promontory later known either as the Mound of Tarik or Gibraltar, the sky displayed a new moon and a dark sky. "The pale gleam of the stars hardly broke through the clouds that scudded across the sky. No sound or movement was heard on the slope of the promontory, and the waves rolled up and broke on its shore as from time immemorial, covering the sea with white foam. The darkness enveloped the straits like a cloak that enwrapped the world. But a discerning eye could make out two dark masses that moved speedily to the other side of the promontory, and after a while it became apparent that these were two galleys. As they came nearer, they slackened their pace because of the many sharp rocks jutting out of the sea. The darkness hid the men who crowded these battered boats being driven to the western shore of the promontory. Everyone was silent. Even the oarsmen allowed themselves little movement.

With one strong pull they brought the first boat to a tiny landing, and at once the passengers sprang out and quickly went ashore. They brought a few mules and containers filled with drinking water up with them. The second boat came near, and its passengers also alit. They mounted the mules, clinging three or four bundles to a saddle, like clusters of grapes. They urged the mules on toward the crest of the hill, where guides showed them a big cave in which they could easily hide during the day. The road was difficult and full of pitfalls. Mules were almost brought to their knees.

At long last the column reached its destination; the men unloaded the burdens and took them into the cave. They began to chop down branches to fortify the mouth of the cave against any eventuality. While these men were thus engaged, three more ships came to the shore, and their passengers hurried to a nearby cave, which they began to fortify. At daybreak the two groups entered their caves and hid throughout the day. Meanwhile, the ships returned to the southern end of the straits from which they had come. The following day this scene was reenacted, without the inhabitants of the town near the landing being aware of what was happening. This time a few boats came in a group, and when the passengers had hurried ashore, the boats immediately returned that very night to bring additional groups of invaders. Again the men climbed up the rocks, remaining there. Within less than four days an army gathered on the rock.

A man stepped forth from one of the last boats; by his bearing and demeanor it was evident that he was the leader of the invaders. His skull was large, his hair black, and his face swarthy. His expression was one of energy and strong will. He wore a cloak that fit his body tightly and was fastened from within. A large entourage stood about him and paid close heed to every word he spoke. When he reached the top of the hill, a stir went through the camp. He looked about him with a probing eye, then ordered the various groups to return to their places while he, together with his staff of officers, withdrew to a corner to plan strategy."

"Tarik had arrived on Spanish soil to gain land for his master the Muslim Caliph in Baghdad, to free his compatriot Jews, and to gain glory. He wasted little time taking the city of Carteya at the end of the bay."

A frightened Roman/Goth general forwarded a message to his king:

"This our land has been invaded by people whose name, country, and origin are unknown to me. I cannot even tell thee whence they came, whether they fell from the skies, or sprang from the earth."[7]

Tarik met the Visigothic king on the shores of Lago de Janda, won a splendid victory and killed the king. He then for a second time routed a Catholic army, and the whole of Spain flew into a panic.

"At the end, The Almighty was pleased to put the Catholic idolaters to flight and grant the victory to the Muslims. So great was the number of the Goths who perished in the battle, that for a long time after the victory the bones of the slain were to be seen covering the field of action.

"The spoils found in the camp of the Catholics surpassed all computation. Tarik collected all the spoil, divided it into five shares and then, after deducting his one-fifth, distributed the rest.

"Peasants and serfs rose up to join the foreign forces defeat the oppressors, while nobles and clergy fled north. Tarik's army grew day by day with dissatisfied lower classes and the disaffected from the Gothic military. Tarik aimed for Cordoba.

"One night in Cordoba the skies became overcast and the rains came, followed by hail. The guards on the wall sought refuge from the weather and abandoned their rounds. The Africans took advantage of the darkness, crossing the river at a shallow point. The southern wall of the city was built some fifteen yards or less from the river's edge. When (Berbers) arrived at the northern bank of the river, they hastened to a point where there was a breach in the upper level of the wall. A fig tree grew near the breach. Quickly they climbed the tree and sprang onto the wall. The first man drew the second one up after him, and within moments a group of men stood on the wall. Immediately they dropped down inside, fell on the surprised guards of the nearest gate, and slew them. They opened the gate, and through it, with drawn swords, streamed the forces of Islam"[8]

Hearing the news of impending disaster, many towns chose to surrender. They received favorable terms. The ruler of Murcia did just that:

"Followers (of Murcia) will not be killed or taken prisoner, nor will they be separated from their women and children. They will not be coerced in matters of religion, their churches will not be burned, nor will sacred objects be taken from the realm, so long as they remain sincere and fulfill the conditions we have set…. You will not give shelter to fugitives, nor to our enemies, nor encourage any protected person to fear us, or conceal any of our enemies. You and each man shall pay one dinar every year, together with four measures of wheat, four measures of barley, four liquid measures of concentrated fruit juice, four liquid measures of vinegar, four of honey, and four of olive oil. Slaves must each pay half of this amount."[9]

718 CE

By 718 Islamic armies had crossed the Pyrenees and conquered Narbonne, and then concluded an alliance with the count of Aquitaine. In 731 the governor of Moorish (Muslim Berbers) Spain pushed through France to capture and burn Bordeaux, then to advance along the old Roman road to Poitiers and Orleans. Churches, towns and estates yielded rich booty. Advancing towards Tours, he met the forces of Frank hero Charles Martel in the wide valley between the Clain and the Vienne.[10]

Martel prevented Islamic rule over France with his brilliant military organization, financed by expropriation of the bloated amounts of Roman aristocrat Church land. Ecclesiasticals censured Charles Martel, falsely claiming that he had died a horrible death for the sin of appropriation, and circulated stories of Charles sightings in hell.[11] He was Catholic, but not subject to the emperor.

The forces of Islam did not aspire to further incursions into Europe. There were more interesting places in the world. In trade, Muslim realms looked elsewhere, to more civilized lands. From the Jewish Khazars came armor, helmets, and suits of chain mail. From India came tigers, leopards, elephants, leopard skins, rubies, sandalwood, ebony, and coconuts. From China came aromatics, silk, porcelain, paper, ink, peacocks, horses, saddles, felts, cinnamon, and rhubarb. Byzantium delivered silver and gold vessels, imperial dinars, embroidered cloths, copper, locks, water engineers, marble workers, and cultivation equipment. As often as not, Jewish traders supplied these elements. Little more than temporary raiding parties ventured into the realm of the Franks. [12]

With new rulers, the prosperity of Spain exceeded that of all previous times, and the population, having receded under the later radical Catholic Goths, increased quickly. The population not devoted to the Muslim religion paid taxes but did not suffer any attempts at conversion.[13] Spain, or Andalusia, entered into another time of enlightenment and freedom, this time under Muslim rule rather that Arian Gothic.

France followed suit. The time had come for Pepin, great-great grandson of Pepin the Elder and father of Charlemagne, to install himself as King of Frankia. The Roman establishment had little choice except to welcome this change. The reason for the reluctance hinged on the preference of Charlemagne's family for Moses over Constantine. Pepin continued the family habit of expropriating Roman Church property and redistributing it to counts and barons.[14] Some of those counts and barons were Jewish, who received a welcome, as did the Catholic nobles.

Pepin assumed royal power in 749, after which the pope commented, "Better to call him king who has the royal power than the one who did not." So did Pepin receive honor from the Church. The Byzantine emperor, recognizing the importance of the power change, sent presents to Pepin. [15]

Isaac the Jew served King Pepin as royal ambassador. Isaac's appointment came in an era when the royal Frank household, although Catholic, relied on Jewish advisors and traders. The tendency to appoint Jewish advisors started in the Chilperic kingdom and continued during the successive regimes of Pepin and his family. This same arrangement brought Muslim

Spain out of an economic and intellectual decline. Basically, German Catholics then in power to the north were steeped in Mosiac law and Muslims to the south tolerated it.

The Frank royal family relied on the Jewish community for personal services from the time of Chilperic. These services included medical treatment such as those from the royal physician Dr. Farragut in the time of Charlemagne; delicate negotiations between foreign states; procurement of foods, wines, and art works; and merchant expertise to procure Christian holy relics and to evaluate religious property.[16]

Churches purchased wine for their services from the Hebrews, who had started the wine industry in France, and used Jewish vessels for transportation. Jewish doctors attended the clergy, especially those high in standing, such as Archbishop Arno of Salzburg.[17]

751 CE

The Kingdom of Pepin and his son Charlemagne practiced traditional Catholicism and suffered as a result of the Roman Empire's branding of religion as a matter of state. Byzantine monarchs decreed bans on association and trade with the Islamic government that had recently seized the greater part of the empire. Muslims reacted with a reciprocal ban. Frankia, at odds with the Byzantine rulers in Constantanoble, needed better access to the Mediterranean.

Paper and papyrus all but disappeared, as did spices and international foodstuffs, and Carolingian nobles made due with a rustic menu of fowl, domestic wine or beer, and pork. Rich cardinals had to reduce their gifts of incense and perfume. Silk and various other commodities commanded high prices.[18]

Jewish friends of Catholic France were able to ease the situation, as a group tolerated by each of the opposed religious dictatorships. The centers of Islam and Judaism both resided in Baghdad. The Jewish king-in-exile from Jerusalem possessed a seat on the Muslim council of state, with each group friendly to the other, to the point that intermarriage occurred between leading families. Hebrews of Narbonne could offer a natural bridge between Frankia and Baghdad. Because, Pepin and Charlemagne favored Mosaic law and Islam tolerated it, Catholics, Muslims and Jews could unite.

Politics in Baghdad affected the government under Pepin's France. The animosity between Islam and Constantinople need not bother Pepin if he could forge an alliance with Baghdad and bypass the Roman-Byzantines. France wanted independence from Byzantium. Since Jews greatly aided Pepin's court in France and also Islam's court in Baghdad, Hebrews could provide a contact point between France and Baghdad and enable France to ally with the most important world power, the Caliphate in Baghdad.

Ambassador Isaac traveled to Baghdad on behalf of King Pepin, and sealed a partnership between Baghdad and France. Each party had problems. France desired independence from Roman Byzantine control. France could thereby increase its trade and gain an important ally.

Baghdad always looked for friends, and a friend on the other side of arch-enemies in Constantinople could prove most interesting. In addition, the Baghdad Muslims had split from those in Spanish Andalusia and wanted a chance to regain influence in that wealthy country. The first venture of mutual benefit concerned the port city of Narbonne. If France was to engage in crucial trade and politics in the Mediterranean, plus protect its southern flank, it needed Narbonne.

Pepin and his father had attempted sieges aimed at taking Narbonne for two generations. Pepin needed control of Narbonne, and he needed it fast. Spanish Muslim forces controlled the area. If Andalusian forces from Cordova sent relief columns to Narbonne before Pepin defeated that city, the Spanish enemy would control Provence and Pepin would need to cede the area for the foreseeable future.

Narbonne was the major purveyor of goods arriving from the East and destined for Frankia. Thus did silks, dates, ornaments, clothes and tools find their way into all of the houses of the assembled rulers.[19]

Inside the Narbonne fortress, the Andalusian Arab garrison represented only a small part of the population. Large numbers of Jews and Arian Goths resided within the walls. These residents were the same ones who had engineered the rebellion against the repressive Byzantine Catholic King Wamba of Spain before the Muslim invasion. Now, with offers of friendship coming from both Andalusia and France, the residents needed to take sides. At that time, even though Andalusia was begining to prosper, Baghdad was the obvious choice as it possessed more power, controlled Mediterranean trade, offered sanctuary to the most important Jewish community, (that which had penned the *Babylonian Talmud)*, and could present a long history of stability. Baghdad swore enmity to Andalusia.

In this environment Isaac the Jew pondered the fate of Narbonne, the important fortress city in the south of today's France. He talked with the leaders of the Jewish population and their group of Arian Goth partners. The Goths in Narbonne had opposed the past conversion of Spain away from Judeo-Christian values. This Jewish-Goth group could look back on almost 400 years of cooperation that had resulted in a code of laws, close working relationships in war or peace, intermarriage, and conversions in both directions. Jews had only survived the Theodosian radical Catholic Goth years thanks to the help of their Arian friends and vice-versa.

Now, with Pepin at the gates of Narbonne, the Jews and Goths of Frankia faced a complex dilemma. Their friends in Spain started to prosper under a promising new Muslim regime. A different Muslim regime ruled a large land from a capital in Baghdad with centuries of favorable ties between Islam and Judaism. The two Islamic regimes were sworn enemies.

Jews in the border areas of Zaragossa and Barcelona, leaned, for the time, towards Spain in the south, where a civilization superior to that of Frankia existed and where the Spanish emir held a tight grip. So did Amoroz,[20] Jewish governor of Zaragossa. Other Jews looked to the north and leaned towards the Frank side, particularly those who lived north of the Pyrenees.*

A sizeable Frank army under the command of Pepin remained stationed outside of Narbonne, continuing a siege. Pepin's advisor Isaac traipsed between the forces of the Franks and the delegations of Jews and Goths within the walls.

----

* Some names of those in Narbone leaning towards the Franks included Chaim, or Aiim, or Aimeri, who fought on the side of Pepin as a reliable Jewish general with past experience in his service. Milon, also Jewish, joined the group.[21] Ansemond, a Goth general, sided with the Franks as well.

THE FIRST CATHOLIC MUSLIM - JEWISH ALLIANCE

*750-777 CE Pepin and Charlemagne's deal
to capture Narbonne and befriend Baghdad.*

Charlemagne accompanied his father Pepin on the Narbonne campaign. Lessons learned there helped later to unify western Europe in a manner the earned him accolades as "father of Europe." As a Frank, he continued the German dominance of Europe and the close relationship of Christians and Jews.

"Charlemagne was large and strong (well over 6') *and of lofty stature, though not disproportionately tall; the upper part of his head was round, his eyes very large and animated, nose a little long, hair fair, and face laughing and merry. Thus his appearance was always stately and dignified... His health was excellent, except during the four years preceding his death...*

In accordance with the national custom, he took frequent exercise on horseback and in the chase, an accomplishment in which scarcely any people in the world could equal the Franks. He enjoyed the exhalations from natural warm springs, and ofter practiced swimming.

He used to wear the national, that is to say the Frank, dress - next to his skin a linen shirt and linen breeches, and above these a tunic fringed with silk; while hose fastened by bands covered his lower limbs, and shoes his feet, and he protected his shoulders and chest in winter by a close-fitting coat of otter or marten skins. Over all he flung a blue cloak, and he always had a sword girt about him, usually one with a gold or silver hilt and belt; he sometimes carried a jeweled sword, but only on great feastdays or at the reception of ambassadors from foreign nations."

"He most zealously cultivated the liberal arts, held those who taught them in great esteem, and conferred great honors upon them."

Charlemagne included his friend Einhard in his learned circle, a man who wrote a biography of the king, including the description above. And he most certainly proved expert in the arts of war, diplomacy, and national strategy. Charlemagne and his father Pepin unfolded a plan for Frankia. that included a Mediterranean strategy dependent on cooperation with the Muslim Caliph of Baghdad rather than his enemy the Muslim emir of Spain. The emir's forces held the fortress city of Narbonne, but with a small contingent that depended on the cooperation of Goth and Jewish residents.

The forces of Pepin, King of the Franks, surrounded Narbonne. Unsuccessful sieges over the previous twenty years had given the Frank king and his father Charles Martel nothing but frustration. Nothing but frustration lay ahead.

Isaac the Jew, resident of Narbonne, knew that the city would fall in due time. True, the Narbonne fortress had frustrated the forces of the Franks in their interminable most recent siege for some seven years, since 752. Outside the walls, Frank troops conducted their daily routines. Since they controlled the generous farmland surrounding the city, an extended

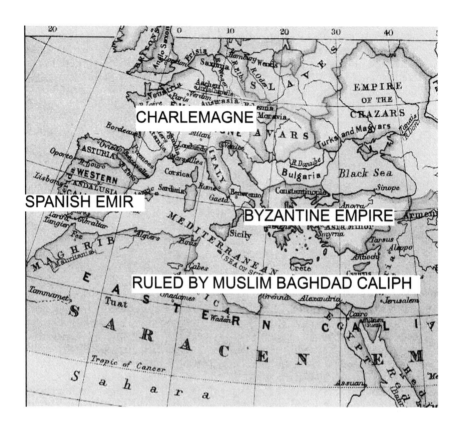

EUROPE & MEDITERRANEAN SEA IN 800

Of the four Mediterranean powers at the time, the Baghdad Caliphate controlled the most territory, the greatest army, the most advanced intellect, and the prime trade routes all the way to China and India. In choosing an ally, Charlemagne and his father did well with their Baghdad connection.

Dutton map produced in 1910

stay did not pose an impossible problem from a provision point of view. But the Spanish Emir dispatched soldiers to aid certain Catholics in Aquitaine rebelling against the Franks. Also, wars against Saxons across the Rhine would sooner or later require diversion.

Isaac and some of the leading Jews of Narbonne attempted to convince the Goth-Jewish garrison to relinquish control to the surrounding Franks. In order to promote this suggestion, he led a delegation of eleven men outside the fortress walls to speak with Pepin and his son, Prince Charlemagne. Some interesting dynamics unfolded. The ambitious King Pepin realized he could benefit from international allies that could help restrain the designs against the Franks hatched in the Byzantine capital of Constantinople. The Byzantines had just had just lost Africa, Spain, and the Middle East to Islam and those two empires maintained no relations. Wars of Byzantium caused by the rise of Muslims distracted Byzantium and enabled the family of Pepin to grow in power unchallenged and to control Italy. Otherwise, Byzantium would never have permited such a competitive power to survive.[1] Scholarly, religious, and political leaders of the Jewish community in Baghdad maintained extremely friendly relations with the Muslim caliph and his Baghdad court.

An alliance between the king of the Franks and the caliph in Baghdad could give the Franks access to the Muslim Mediterranean free trade zone and additional independence from Constantinople. Baghdad effectively controlled the Mediterranean Sea lanes and regularly raided Sicily and southern Italy in preparation for occupation. That same alliance could give the caliph help in his effort to retrieve Spanish possessions and to challenge Constantinople.

A Jewish royal ambassador like Isaac could engineer this alliance. Jews could deliver Narbonne to the Franks. In return, Pepin, King of the Franks, could formalize and expand the existing rights of Jews, give them self-governance in the Narbonne area, enlarge their participation in the affairs of France, and grant them an independent judicial process.

A policy of Jewish cooperation with the Franks did carry risks. Andalusian reprisal could bring disaster if the Franks could not sustain a military presence. Franks might reintroduce the radical Theodosian Roman nobility, which had been completely dispersed from Narbonne.[2] Isaac, Aimeri, Milon and other Jewish leaders decided to take those risks.

Jews therefore would gain stronger rights so they could own land in an allodial fashion, with rights to sell and inherit. They also wanted complete independence in matters of law and culture, similar to other subject kings and peoples who pledged loyalty and tribute.

Isaac brought the noble sum of 70,000 marks for the Frankish king. "Whatever we have will be yours," promised Isaac. Goth and Jewish leaders arranged for the capitulation of the Narbonne garrison and allowed the Franks entry into the city. This accomplishment met its objective. Only minor shedding of blood took place. The Hebrew general led the charge, planted the flag, and killed the resisting Andalusian garrison, thereby earning exceptional praise and rewards. This was the noble Don Aimeri.[3]

The understanding between Pepin and his son Charlemagne with Isaac and Jewish subjects of the realm grew in scope and value.[4] Increased shipping between French and Muslim Baghdad ports improved the economy of both dynasties. Besides Narbonne, Lyons, Arles, and Marseilles had also established Jewish trade with the Orient since early Roman times.[5]

These ports flourished.

Pepin and Charlemagne then launched a new attack on the uncoopera-
tive Duke of Aquitaine [6] from the city of Narbonne with the help of Jewish
forces. These forces included counts and other nobles. In a dramatic example of how politics sometimes overshadowed differences of religion,
this interesting war featured odd twists. The Catholic duke of Aquitaine
formed an alliance with the Muslims from southern Spain. He faced allies
comprising the Catholic Frank King Pepin, Jewish forces, Goth Arians and
aid from Baghdad Muslims.

In order to promote French interests, Isaac departed on a mission to
Baghdad on behalf of both the citizenry of Narbonne and the king of
France. He found success in meeting with the highest of officials in Baghdad. Jewish hierarchy had established itself there from the days when Neb-
uchadrezzar of Babylon had conquered Jerusalem. Having settled there,
they created a thriving community that developed many notions in law, hy-
giene,and trading as written in the *Babylonian Talmud.*

Isaac returned with a Jewish king, or nasi, for Narbonne. named
Makhir Kalonymos who packed his possessions, including books, for the
journey across the Mediterranean.

An international power axis evolved that pitted the interests of the
Franks and the Baghdad caliph against Byzantium and the Spanish Muslims.[7] The help of Isaac and Narbonne Jews in connecting the caliph and
the king helped to earn Jews and Goths territorial rights in Narbonne and
the coveted pledge of *fidelis* to Charlemagne.

770 CE

During the trip to Narbonne, Nasi Makhir Kalonymos visited North
Africa, stopping at Kairwan, the capital city that had replaced Carthage, to
visit the great African Jewish schools.[8] With ambassadors and gifts from
the caliph to Pepin and Charlemagne the entourage departed for Marseilles,
led by Isaac and accompanied by the Nasi Makhir Kalonymos.[9]

The father and son, Pepin and Charlemagne, kept their promises to their
Jewish allies, who formally received at least one third of the land in Narbonne from the king.[10] To Nasi Makhir Kalonymos he granted extensive
holdings and authority, including land in Narbonne, as well as holdings in
the surrounding area. The holdings presented consisted of alodial estates,
not subject to ordinary restrictions, but allowing the right of taxation and
with an oath of *fidelis* to the king, just as a it would be with a count or a
subjected minor king.[11] The loyal Don Aimeri made out very well, receiving great tracts of land for himself and his heirs. This guaranteed prominent
positions for the family for generations.[12]

In addition to the grants of land, Pepin guaranteed the ability of the Jews
to administer their own laws and gave them the unhampered right of appeal
directly to the king himself. These magnificent rights, were granted only
to certain chieftains or vassals within the realm, such as those granted to
Glascony, Barcelona (later), and various Slavic kings.[13] Franks lived under
Frankish law, Saxons under Saxon law, and Jews would live under *lex Ju-
daeorum,*[14] with their king, or nasi, as the final arbitrier for matters within
the Jewish community as outlined in a capitulary of the crown.[15]

"Then King Charlemagne sent to the Caliph of Babylon requesting that
he dispatch one of his Jews of the seed of the royal House of David. The

caliph harkened and sent him one from there, a magnate and sage, Rabbi Makhir Kalonymos by name. Charles settled him in Narbonne, the capital city, planted him there, and gave him great possessions in the city at the time that Charles captured the city from the (Spanish) Ishmaelites. And Makhir took to wife a woman from among the magnates of the town... The king made him a nobleman and designed, out of love for Makhir, good statutes for the benefit of all the Jews dwelling in the city, as is written and sealed in a Latin charter. The seal of the king thereon bears the name Charlemagne, and it is in the possession of the Hebrews. This Prince Makhir became chieftain. He and his descendants were related to the kings and all his descendants. Anyone who came to molest him because of his hereditary land holding and his high office was himself molested by the power of the King of France." [16] Upon his arrival, the new Nasi of Narbonne formed the first part of a Jewish legal system that shortly featured another Nasi centered in Mainz,[17] and one in Rouen. the formal study of the Talmud arrived in France. Nasi Makhir Kalonymos quickly established Jewish schools, and the dissemination of democratic ideas.

The Rabbi's offspring included many of the name Todros, a name associated with poetry in the early French tradition.[18] A revival of Judeo-Christian principles took place for all religious groups. Students who knew the Bible's original language and intent could best sustain arguments and understanding of Biblical commentary. "People like Peter the Chanter championed the virtues of knowing the plain sense of scripture...

Torah, Deuteronomy 16:19 You shall not judge unfairly: You shall show no partiality; you shall not take bribes, for bribes blind the eyes of the discerning and upset the plea of the just.

Talmud : What is the reason for the prohibition against a judge receiving a gift? Once he receives a gift from him, his opinion draws closer to his, and he becomes like him, and a man cannot see guilt in himself. What is a gift? He is one with the giver. A person should not judge a case of someone he loves, nor of someone he hates, for a loved one – one does not see his faults; a hated one – one does not see his merits.[19]

Isaac the Jew became a member of Charlemagne's court and carried out diplomatic missions such as one to the Baghdad Caliph Harun-al-Rashid. Jewish traders linked the kingdom to the trade routes of the world, bringing spices, metals, textiles, and foodstuffs. Narbonne and Marseilles remained important ports.

"His (Charlemagne's) relations with Haroun, King of the Persians, who ruled over almost the whole of the East, India excepted, were so friendly that this prince preferred his favor to that of all the kings and potentates of the earth, and considered that to him alone marks of honor and munificence were due." [20] stated Charlemagne's friend Einhard.

Muslims, Jews, and Catholics traded ideas and enjoyed things like a spice connection from the East that came in unison with knowledge of medicinal treatments the world over. Charlemagne employed numbers of both Catholics and Jews in his court, as had Frank kings and mayors of the court for hundreds of years before.. Charlemagne relied on the Jewish physician Farragut for the health of his family.[21] The idea that a doctor looks after the health of a community as well as the health of patients evolved into a stream of court physicians who also advised nobles and royalty on other issues.

From Baghdad eastward, traders entered both India and China. To the

Alliance

north they entered Khazaria, and then Europe, or traveled more directly to Europe through the Balkans and Ukraine or travelled by ship to Italy, Marseilles and Narbonne. Finally, there existed the route along Africa either by land or sea to Spain.[22]

In cases between Chirstians and Jews, Charlemagne endorsed an alternative form of secular trial in cases between Christians and Jews that did not involve ordeals such as combat or dunking. The Jewish community, however paid higher taxes, but received special independence as a master of Jews, *magister judeorum*, administered central administration of Jewish law.

The Jewish Narbonne allies of Pepin and Charlemagne needed to show their support in the subjugation of Aquitaine where the truculent Catholic duke dared to ally himself with the Arab Spanish ruler in order to preserve his independence from Frankish domination. (Counts Berenguer, Mermenald, de Berry, and Childerane reported for duty with armed escorts.)[23]

In the same season that the nasi committee arrived on European soil with the new nasi for Narbonne, Frank forces succeeded in their attacks against the rebellious Duke of Aquitaine and assassinated him in the forest of Perigord. Pepin and his son Charlemagne disbursed rewards aplenty to their allies, installing many counts, rebuilding forts, and appointing judges. This was accomplished by the issuance of the Capitulary for Aquitaine, written in Saintes during the year 768.[24]

At this time King Pepin died a natural death, and Charlemagne inherited the rulership of the realm. Rapid changes in the Frank kingdom necessitated promotions. The court of the Carolingian rulers, Charlemagne's family, continued many traditions of their predecessor, the family of Chilperic. One tradition involved the dispersion of responsibilities among a diverse group. Goths and Jews got their share of honors as well as Franks.

In a show of the cooperation between the two Biblical peoples, in addition to the Catholics in court positions, Jewish names also sprang up in positions of influence: Bera, Count of Razes; Bera, Count of Barcelona; Ansell, Count of the Palace; Berenguer, warrior and eventual count; Curson, Count of Toulouse; Aznar, Count of Aquitaine; Count Solomon; Count Echter or Itiel of Auvergne; Count Zigun or Siguin of Bordeaux; Aimeri, noble and general of Narbonne; Milon, first Count of Narbonne,[25] Count Chaim or Haimo in Albi, Count Abba of Poitiers[26] and others Some descendents of these early personalities in later generations, converted to Islam, Arian Christianity or Catholicism. Later the names Anselme and Berenguer, spawned some Catholic relations, and there also developed Berenguer support of Arianism or the Cathar sect. These counts generated descendants who married into the European aristocracy.

Inspired by Jewish intermediaries such as Isaac, the Jewish governor of Barcelona, Solomon, his son Joseph, and his son-in-law decided to co-operate with Charlemagne against the Andalusian Muslims.

Solomon ruled Barcelona and its environs out to Zaragossa as governor during a time of revolution and uncertainty. As the Muslim wave spread over Spain northward, the credentials of Solomon would face scrutiny. He could attempt to make peace with them or seek help. Solomon approached Charlemagne. The king of France decided that next year's campaign would not take on the usual foes: Aquitaine, Saxons and, Bretons, but instead Solomon looked to Spain and the city of Zaragossa, the control of which would stop Muslim ambition and curtail the ability of the Gascons to harass Aquitaine.

Solomon returned to Zaragossa to welcome the Franks. Charlemagne thought he had two friendly routes into Spain. One of those routes wound through Aquitaine, recently defeated with its rebellious duke killed. Now the son of that duke secretly plotted his revenge.

Preparations for the invasion force took some time and involved the call up of soldiers from far-away places who had to convene and form a long marching line with a large baggage train behind. Observation and tracking of this process would not involve much effort on the part of enemies.

In 778 a massive Frank army moved through the Pyrenees in two columns. One marched down the east coast of Spain to Barcelona, and turned west, and the other marched southwest of Toulouse through Aquitaine and into the narrow western Pyrenees mountain pass by the village of Roncesvalles. They emerged near the city of Pamplona, controlled by Andalusian Muslims and possibly a staging ground for raids within Aquitaine. Catholics and Jews marched together.

The two attacking legions targeted the city of Zaragossa, where the Barcelona governor had promised to offer no resistance. With Zaragossa in hand, the Franks could control northern Spain.

Before joining in the pincer about Zaragossa, the western column arriving in Spain after its journey through the mountains picked up hostages from the Barcelona governor to prove his good intentions, and then pounced on Pamplona as an easy mark. This assumption proved a gross error as the defenders put up significant resistance. The Franks moved on to their objective city.

Zaragossa found itself surrounded, but the promised easy surrender did not occur. The governor could not deliver because the Andalusians governed well. The Muslim government in Cordoba had achieved control of Spain and began to show signs of great tolerance and promise. Many in Zaragossa made peace with Emir Abd al-Rahman, and his Spanish unity government. Those elements friendly to the Cordoba government prevailed. They did not view the Franks as desirable overlords. The Frank force laid siege and plundered the countryside, and the long wait began.

But then another turn of events occurred. The unruly Saxons to the west of the Frank empire rose up again. Charlemagne had expended all the time he could in Spain, and he needed to lift the siege of Zaragossa and return to the Saxon battlefield with his entire entourage intact, through the Roncesvalles pass in the Pyrenees.

They again passed the city of Pamplona. Many there deplored the presumptions of the French in laying claim to Spanish and the area of northwest Spain known as Basque or Gascon territory. Perhaps the Gascons could better preserve their independence with scattered rulers: Aquitaine to the north, Franks to the north and east, Muslims to the south. However, if the Frankish program succeeded, one great country would rule Gaul and Spain, leaving the Gascons to fend for themselves or submit to the greater power. So when the Franks appeared again in Pamplona, the resistance increased. Franks razed the town[27]

Big mistake. For centuries, imperial rulers had underestimated and misunderstood the Basques. Before the Roman and Muslim conquerors came, Basques had roamed the hills and mountains of the western Pyrenees. They continued after all those conquerors had melted into dust, never totally submitting to any of them.

Charlemagne thought the territory his, but his friend and biographer observed that, "In the midst of this vigorous and almost uninterrupted struggle with the Saxons, he marched over the Pyrenees into Spain at the head of all the forces that he could muster. All the forts and castles that he attacked surrendered, and up to the time of his homeward march he sustained no loss whatever; but on his return through the Pyrenees he had cause to rue the treachery of the Gascons."[28]

The Spanish resistance to the incursion of Charlemagne inspired elaborate Spanish literature and poetry on the subject. The troubadours of Spain did not like northern Basque King Alfonso because of his close association with the Franks and treated him accordingly.

Songs of Spanish Troubadours:
Romance the Sixth. Bernardo Prevents King Alfonso from Yielding His Kingdom to Charlemagne

Bernardo del Carpio gathered together the best and bravest knights of Asturias and all of Galicia, then proudly marched from the City of Leon. He stirred the citizens to the verge of war in order to prevent France from usurping the throne at the request of Alfonso. They would not stand by while King Alfonso cavorted with the French. The people shouted praises as the brave ones departed. Farmers threw up their hands, plows, sickles, and hoes. The shepards and young people showed their elation, and all shouted "Freedom. Freedom."

Before leaving the kingdom the men boasted openly. Raising his voice, Bernardo said to them, "Listen to me, men of Leon, those of you that boast of being born of free parents. To King Alfonso you pay what you must for his divine mandate. Because God does not want the decrees of foreigners to obligate our children, the fruits of your lives, we draw a line. Let the king give his gold to the French, but not his vassals, because the king does not have the power to diminish the liberty of his subjects. You will not permit foreigners to come and subjugate us. Those of you that refuse to fight the French on the battlefield, stay here, and even though we are fewer, we will be equal to the fight."

His speech over, Bernardo pushed forward with the fury of conviction, saying, "Follow me all of you who would be free men."

The valiant Bernardo then went forward on his blood red horse. He and his men dressed in the style of the Moors, in order to disguise themselves in front of the opposing French forces. Bernardo rode towards Zaragossa where a Moorish king waited to join them.

Romance the Seventh. The Battle of Roncesvalles.

The French, Moors, and ersatz Moors began the battle. The resolution of the Moors allowed the French no quarter.

"One French knight shouted, 'Listen to me my friend. This day goes badly! My wounds ache so that I want to give my soul to God. My horse and my sword arm tire. Let us plead with Roland (our leader) to sound his horn so that the emperor riding ahead will hear and return, because we are worth saving.'

'Then, my cousins, we Spanish entered the fray, ready as requested. The French still fought on. Ah! Rather death than to endure such suffering.

'The French held the line for some while. Roland, that famous paladine, made such a valiant effort. For he led them well, as they grew dismayed and fled, but he regrouped and they prepared to die with sword in hand. To live otherwise would bring dishonor, and so the French return to battle with heart, charging the line of Moors, and killing more than one can count. The blood from wounds painted the very grass the color of red.

'Bernardo, our hero, the center of troubadour stories, always fought to the advantage of the Spanish Army. He outflanked Roland, charged the French with the Moors and his compatriots from Leon at his side. With this charge did Bernardo kill Roland, the leader of Charlemagne's cavalry." [29]

Note: The defeated French army had included soldiers from across the entire spectrum of Frankia: Burgundy, Austrasia, Bavaria, Provence, Provence, and Lombardy [30] – Catholics, Jews, pagans, possibly Baghdad Muslims or their materials, and other Christians. The Christian - Jewish army was impressive.

The portion of the French army commanded by the famous and loved Count Roland, a favorite nephew of Charlemagne, brought up the rear and was devastated. Before entering a narrow Pyrenees mountain pass, Roland donned his gear, consisting of a lance, a favorite sword given him by Charlemagne named Durendal, and a shofar, the ram's horn used by the Hebrews since ancient times to sound alarms in battle and for religious ceremonies. He rode with nobles like Oliver, Bera, Berenguer, Aton, Turpin and Samson. Many knights and nobles came from Jewish families, like Bera.. An earlier Bera had fought along Jews, moderate Catholic and Arian rebels with General Paul against the Catholic Goth King Wamba back in 673. Also in Roland's contingent marched Turpin, who rose to the rank of archbishop in the Catholic Church.

Alliance

Just as Spanish troubadours recorded the events of the battle at Roncesvalles, so did Todros, son or grandson of Rabbi Makhir, Nasi of Narbonne. His effort later circulated as the *Song of Roland.*

"Charlemagne has devastated Spain,
has seized its castles, ravaged its walled towns.
The king now says that his campaign is ended,
and toward sweet France the Emperor rides out.
Count Roland has attached his battle pennant
and raised it skyward, high upon a hill.
In the countryside the Franks pitch camp.
The (Basques) ride down the broader valleys,
Their hauberks (mail) on and gorgets tightly shut,
Their helmets laced, their swords upon their hips,
shields hung from their necks, lances ready.
They hold up in a thicket in the hills:
Thousands wait for break of day.
God! The French know nothing! Aoi! ׳ I א

"A Basque from East of Zaragossa stands nearby:
His flowing hair sweeps down along the ground.
While playing, he will lift more weight for fun
Than four pack-mules can carry, fully loaded.
It's said that in the land from which he comes
No sunlight shines, the wheat cannot mature,
No rain falls, and there's never been dew.
No rock is there that isn't solid black –
Some say it is the devils' habitation.
He says, "I've strapped on my good sword;
I'll tint it blood red there at Roncesvalles,
And if I find proud Roland in my path
Don't attack him; take my word no more.
I shall conquer Durendal (Roland's sword).
The French will die, and France will diminish."

...

"The day was bright, the sunshine beautiful;
No piece of armor failed to catch the light.
A thousand trumpets sing, to add more splendor.
So deafening their noise, the Frenchmen hear it.
"My lord companion," says Oliver,
I think we'll have some Saracens to fight."
And Roland answers, "Grant us this, oh G-d!"
It's fitting we should stay here for our king."
Oliver has climbed to higher ground,
Looks down a grassy valley to his right,
And sees that horde approaching them.
He calls out then to Roland, his companion,
"From Spain I see a dreadful glare approaching,
They'll cause us French enormous suffering.
That fraud, that traitor Ganelon knew this,
Appointing us before the Emperor."

...

Oliver says, "There are many Basques,
And, it seems to me, we Franks are few.
Companion Roland, sound your shofar." שופר
Count Roland answers, "I would play the fool!
Throughout sweet France my glory would be lost.
I'll strike mighty blows with Durendal (my sword)
Until its blade is bloody to the gold.
These Saracens err in coming to the pass;
Promise to mark them to death." Aoi! א ו '
...
"Companion Roland, sound your shofar שופר
Charles, who's going through the pass, will hear.
I promise you, the Franks will soon return."
"May God forbid," flung Roland back at him,
"that it be said by any man alive
I ever blew my horn because of Basques!"
...
A Moor champion
Rides well out in advance of all the host,
Hoes shouting words of insult to our French,
"French villains, you shall fight with us today,
For he who should protect you has betrayed you.
The king who left you in this pass is mad.
This very day sweet France shall lose her fame,
And Charlemagne the right arm from his body."
When Roland hears this, he is enraged!
He spurs his horse and lets him run all out
And goes to strike the chanter with all his force;
Roland breaks his shield; lays his hauberk open
Pierces through his chest and cracks the bones.
Cuts the spine completely from the back and with
his lance casts out his mortal soul, then impales him
well, and hoists the body up; throws him dead
A spear's length from his horse. Aoi! א ו '
...
The duke Samson attacks the enemy. שמשון
Samson breaks his gilt, fleuron-emblazoned shield
The well-made hauberk gives him no protection
And cuts him to the liver, lights, and heart,
Then will-nilly throws the man down dead.
The archbishop says, "A baron struck that blow!"

Next Anseis allows his horse to run,
And goes to strike a Moor of Tortelose.
Anseis breaks his shield beneath its golden boss,
Tear through the double thickness of his hauberk,
Then puts his good spears head into his body,
Impales him and drives the steel clear through
And tumbles him to earth a spear's length off.
Then Roland says, "A hero struck that blow!"

And Engelier, the Gascon from Bordeaux,

First spurs this horse, then, slackening his rein,
Goes out to fight with Escremiz of Valterne.
He cracks his shield and knocks it from his neck
And rips into his hauberk at the gorget
And hits his throat between the collarbones;
He throws the corpse a spear's length off.
And tells him, Now you're in hell!" Aoi   א ו י

Aton   then hits a pagan, Esturgant,   אטון
Upon the upper border of his shield,
Cuts down clear through the crimson and white.
Rips into the skirting of his hauberk;
Drives his good, sharp lance into his body,
Then throws the corpse down off his horse.
He tells him afterward: "You won't be saved!"

Relief Moors and Basques advance
Numbered in twenty columns.
Light flashes from those golden studded casques
And from those shields and saffron yellow flags ....
"Oliver, friend, brother," Roland says,
"False Ganelon has sentenced us to die."
...
Count Roland sees the slaughter of his men.
...
Count Roland realizes death is near.
His brains begin to ooze out through his ears.
He prays to God to summon all his peers,
and to the angel Gabriel, himself.
...
The Emperor has come back home from Spain,
...
Look: Alde, a lovely girl, comes up to him,
She asks the king; "Where is the captain Roland,
Who promised he would take me as his wife?"
...
The traitor Ganelon, in chains of iron,
...
The Franks above all other have agreed
That Ganelon should die in awesome pain.
And so they have four war-horses led forward,
Then tie him to them by his feet and hands.
The horses are high spirited and fiery,
And at their heads four sergeants urge them on,
Down toward a stream that runs across a field.
Now Genelon has gone to his damnation.
His ligaments are horribly distended,
and every member of his body broken.
Bright blood comes spilling down upon green grass.
Thus Ganelon has died a renegade.
A man should never boast that he's a traitor.
...The story that Todros son of Rabbi Makhir tells ends here."[31]

A generation passed before France invaded Spain again. Solomon, left to defend Zaragossa against the Muslim forces, went down in defeat and met his death. Baghdad Muslims, for a time, parted with the idea that they could reclaim the country of Spain from the Cordoba Muslims.[32] Basques enjoyed a period of respite from French attack.

French literature began with the Song of Roland and other songs celebrating the ventures of Charlemagne's court, both Catholic and Jewish.

Charlemagne's apologists struggled to depict the rousing defeat. They admitted trickery at the hand of the Basques.

"On his return through the Pyrenees he had cause to rue the treachery of the Gascons. That region is well adapted for ambushes by reason of the thick forests that cover it. As the army was advancing in the long line of march necessitated by the narrowness of the road, the Basques, who lay in ambush on the top of a very high mountain, attacked the rear of the baggage train and the rear guard in charge of it. They hurled down battle to the very bottom of the valley."[33]

785

Finally it happened. In a small campaign, some small area south of the Pyrenees came under the control of the Franks through the efforts of their Narbonnese allies. The Jewish Count Borell took control of the area in 785 in a clever maneuver. This outpost put troops within easy striking distance of Barcelona, enabling a point to stock supplies and project a campaign.

This gain did not result in rapid follow-up. The defeat at Roncesvalles so demoralized the French and Narbonnese that a full generation of recovery needed to pass before they could muster another attempt. However, the successes of Borell and others encouraged Charlemagne to grant continuing civil rights to his Hebrew subjects.

On the side of legal administratiion, royal charters granted Jewish communities the right to a separate legal system, a right also granted other constituencies. Numerous *capitularia sanctionum*, which the king signed to define the Jewish legal system, disappeared when under the supervision of later radical Roman dominated regimes. They provided for a *magister Judacorum* to supervise in Narbonne, Cologne, and Rouen. These magistrates protected the rights granted against infringements while punishing internal criminals.[34]

The activities of Borell continued south of the Pyrenees, to the point where Charlemagne decided to strike out again, and he issued a call to arms.

"Be it known to you that we have arranged to hold our general assembly this year in Saxony, in the eastern part, on the River Bode, the place called Stassfurt. Wherefore we command you that you must come to the aforesaid place with all your troops, well armed and equipped, on 17 June, which is seven days before the mass of St. John the Baptist. And you are to come with your troops to the aforesaid place equipped in such a way that you can go from there with the army to whichever region we shall command – that is, with arms, implements and other military material, provisions and clothing. Each horseman is to carry shield and spear, long-sword, bow, quivers and arrows, and your carts are to contain implements of various kinds – axes and stone-cutting tools, augers, adzes, trenching tools, iron spades and the rest of the implements which an army needs. Place provi-

sions in the carts for three months following the assembly, weapons and clothing for half a year. This we command in absolute terms, that you see to it that whichever part of our realm the direction of your march may cause you to pass through you proceed to the aforesaid place in good order and without unruliness...

"Every freeman seen to have five mansi as an aloid (90 hectares as private property) is likewise to come to the army; and he who has four mansi is to do likewise; and he who is seen to have three is to act likewise. But wherever two men are found of whom each is seen to have two mansi, one is to equip the other; and he who is the more capable is to come to the army....

"And all our principal fideles (vassals) are to come to the assembly that has been announced with their troops and carts and gifts, as well equipped as possible...."

——— *Karlos Magnus (Charlemagne), Emperor of Frankia*[35]

A man who held twelve *mansi*, (about 180 hectares or 445 acres), needed to arrive fully armed and on horseback, ready for war. He carried a coat of mail, a helmet, a shield with a boss, mail leggings, spear, sword, and short sword. Not just Franks, but also Visigoths, Basques, and Jews within the domain of Frankia met this obligation. The historic heroes of the Carolingian army emphasized the ancient Hebrew leaders Moses and Joshua, with special veneration to King David. This they did with songs, references to Israeli battles, and comparisons of Charlemagne to David.[36]

Charlemagne set his sights on Barcelona, Spain, ruled by the Andalusian Muslim regime, but also where Jews had established themselves in the El Call neighborhood, receiving refugees disbursed early on, even from the fall of Jerusalem in 70 CE. In those beginning days Barcelona remained a small town. [37] Charlemagne assigned the mission of capturing Barcelona and chasing out the Andalusian garrison to his Jewish troops. After a time, they were ready for victory.

801 CE

Victory came in the year 801, the same year Isaac the Jew returned from another trip to Babylonia to visit Harun, Caliph of the Persian Muslims. He returned with gifts including a great elephant. He wintered in Italy and delivered the animal to Charlemagne the next spring in the capital of Frankia, Aachen.[38] Charlemagne used the elephant in many later battles as his personal steed.

It was a success year for the Jewish contingents. The city of Barcelona fell to the army of Charlemagne after a two-year siege and the capture of its Muslim governor.[39] Count William "of the curved nose," son of Aimeri, the Jewish general who had aided in the capture of Narbonne, coordinated the campaign.

Count Borell, the vassal of Charlemagne installed just south of the Pyrenees, continued to maintain an aggressive presence that protected the area around Barcelona. One of his associates urged him to go forward and claim all the land he could. "I will have spread many a brain of that people who do not love Israel."[40] The activity of Borell aided William.

William spoke both Hebrew and Arabic, and he often addressed his nobles in Hebrew.[41]

Count William formed three military divisions to achieve the submission of Barcelona. One remained as back-up in Roussillon with Louis of Aquitaine, son of Emperor Charlemagne. The second, commanded by Count Rostagnus set up the siege, while the third under William drove south to defeat enemy forces attempting to lift the siege. Counts Bera[42] of Razes and Borell participated.

Count Bera was a descendant of the Count Bera who fought with other Jews and moderate Arians under the leadership of Duke Paul against the radical Roman Catholic Spanish Goth King Wamba. That incident occurred after the Roman take-over of the Spanish government that replaced a tolerant Goth regime with repression. The failure of that rebellion encouraged moderates to support the Arab – Berber invasion of 711.[43]

When the Muslim defenders of Barcelona offered to surrender on a Saturday, William declined to enter on holy Sabbath, and entered the next day. Louis, the son of Charlemagne, and the military majority retired to France for the winter, leaving Bera in charge with his soldiers from Gothia, i.e. Jews and Goths.[44]

Inscribed in the Royal Frankish Annals is the following:

"The city of Barcelona in Spain that had previously revolted against us was returned to us by its governor Zatum Said. He came to the palace in person and submitted with his city to the Lord King."

After commending William, commander of the attack on Barcelona, and the other heroes, Prince Louis departed for home, leaving Count Bera in charge of Barcelona, and Count Borell in charge of Ausona (Vich), Cardona, Casseres and other deserted towns.[45]

In one of the very next campaigns, Prince Louis sent his victorious troops back to capture territory south of Barcelona. Count Bera led the campaign.[46] Louis's friend tells what happened:

> "They held a council among themselves to see how they might be able to take the enemy by surprise with a clandestine attack. They hit upon the following method: boats would be built to serve as ferries. Each would be divided into four sections in such a way that each part could be carried by two horses or mules and the whole could be easily assembled using ready prepared nails and hammers. Then, as soon as the river was reached, the joints of the structures could be sealed with ready prepared pitch, wax and tow. Equipped in this fashion, the bulk of the troops then marched with the liege Ingobert, upon Tortosa.
>
> "But those who were assigned to the task, Ademar, Bera and others, traveled a journey that took them three days without pack-saddles. During this time they had no roof save the sky, did without fires in case the smoke gave them away and traveled as best they could at night while hiding in the woods by day. On the fourth day the troops crossed the Ebro River. Men and equipment used the assembled boats, but made the horses swim.....
>
> "The Moors immediately sent two of their number off on horseback to scout, and these men saw ours and reported the facts to their leader. Impelled by fear, the Moor garrison took to flight, disregarding and abandoning all the property in their camp. Our men took possession of everything they had left behind and spent

that night in the enemy tents.
"On the following day, the Moors advanced to do battle.
They gathered a large force and our men were heavily outnum-
bered. Yet despite this, trusting in Divine aid, we forced the foe
to flee and filled the fugitives' path with a mass of their corpses.
We proceeded to slaughter until, with the light of the sun and the
day receding and shadows falling upon the earth, the shining
stars were rising to illuminate the night.[47]

With important new lands conquered,[48] Charlemagne again could grant favor by naming his friends and allies to important posts in Barcelona and environs, which he then called the March of Spain. Those in the thick of the campaign came up for honors first: Jewish counts. The appointments included Bera, first Count of Barcelona; and William, son of Aimeri and Count of Toulouse.[49]

Bera captured the prize of political trophies. He accepted the post as the first French Count of Barcelona. Borell stepped into the position of count in Ausona. He immediately repopulated the countryside with Jewish individuals.[50]

As Borell repopulated Ausona with Jews, he enjoyed tremendous powers. He could grant empty lands from the crown under personal royal protection, free of any rents, payments or duties, and, except for reserved offenses, under their local jurisdiction separate from that of the count. They received the absolute right to pass on land to their heirs or to sell or dispose of them between themselves in any way.

Note: Other recipients of political trophies were Count Curzo who preceded William at Toulouse; Count Leibulf; Count Heribert, brother of William and also adversary of Amoroz from Zaragossa; Count Gisclafred; Count Odilon; Borell, Count of Ausona and others.

The recipients of these generous grants earned the appellation "Hispani."

"Thus it is not surprising that certain counts and the less favored indigenous landowners often attempted to harass or dispossess these Hispani, especially in periods where the central authority was temporarily weak, as in the later periods of Louis the Pious' conflicts with his sons... and the civil wars. Charlemagne, Louis the Pious and Charles the Bald, the latter in a capitulary issued at Toulouse on June 11, 844, all took steps to protect the Hispani and to force the counts to make restitution of lands illegally seized from them... As the lands and special privileges of the Hispani were inheritable there grew up an increasingly large body of landowners, especially to the south of the Pyrenees, who looked directly to the king for title to their lands and for the protection of it."[51]

In the Spanish March, Hebrew became a common language of the court system set up by the Nasi Makhir, and responsa (Jewish legal opinions) of the period refer to the exclusively Jewish population of Ausona. New settlers came from as far away as Egypt.[52]

The Barcelona area, devoid of Catholic activity for over two centuries, did not change. The archbishop of Narbonne took over titular religious control of the territory, comprised of virtually no churches.[53] The Jewish nobles in charge brought in mostly Hebrew settlers. Muslims had eliminated virtually all Christians, who did not appear again as a measurable group until almost the year 900.[54]

The changes in alliance of the Barcelona area lead to ripples along the Pyrenees. In 802 Basques from the Pamplona area revolted against the Cordoba Muslims (Umayyads) in alliance with a rebel Muslim group,[55] and with support from Charlemagne's Barcelona possession.

Franks attempted to create a march in the western Pyrenees as Charlemagne prepared to turn over power to Louis in 813, by placing Aznar as the first count of Pamplona. Later, in the waning of Frank power in 824, a second major battle in the Pyrenees took place, where Aznar suffered a coup and the western march came to an end as the usurper brought total independence to Pamplona. Aznar's son died in that turmoil, and so Aznar himself invested with the counties of Cerdanya and Urgell in the eastern Pyrenees march. A surviving son, Galindo Aznar, subsequently recovered his father's county of Aragon and formalized Jewish participation in the government. However, the son did not reconnect with the Frank Empire, but instead married the daughter of the Pamplona king and founded a line of counts named Galindo and Aznar who ruled for 100 years.[56] Thus the continuation of Jewish presence and leadership would account for the use of Jewish symbolism in seals of state such as the lion of Judah, the fortess castle of Simeon, and the four stripes of Passover.

812 CE

With the degree of military campaigning undertaken by Charlemagne, a great deal of pressure bore down upon the ordinary foot soldier, expected to leave his residence on a regular basis and subject himself to the vagaries of war. The Emperor issued a memorandum on military matters:

"Reasons why men are wont to neglect their military obligations:

1. That poor men complain they are deprived of their property and make this complaint equally against the bishops, abbots and their advocates and against the counts and their hundredmen.

2. They also say that if a man refuses to give his alloid (land grant) to a bishop, abbot, or count, or to a judex (magistrate of the Jewish legal system) or noble, these seek opportunities to harm that poor man. They make him go on every occasion to the army, until he is impoverished and hands over or sells his alloid, like it or not. Others, who have handed their's over, stay at home without any trouble.

3. The counts say that some of the people in their counties do not obey them and refuse to fulfil the orders of the Lord Emperor.

4. Above all, the people in the counties are becoming more disobedient to counts."[57]

The Emperor took military discipline seriously. Bishops and abbots in possession of landed estates, and many with other privileges, needed to honor obligations for armament. Charlemagne followed Judeo-Christian Catholicsm and had no time for imperial Rome's Theodosian privileges.

"Those bishops and abbots who have either benefices or such alloidal estates as render them well capable of going to the army in accordance with our order... must pay us a fine, and also the lord must pay, if the clerics stay at home or buy an exemption."[58]

Charlemagne's conflicts with the Emir of Cordoba made him a continuing close ally of the Caliph of Baghdad, Harun al Rushid. This connection, provided by the Jewish community, served him well.

Charlemagne's "relations with Harun, who ruled over almost the whole of the East, were so friendly that this prince preferred his favor to that of all the kings and potentates of the earth, and considered that to him alone marks of honor and munificence were due. Accordingly, when the ambassadors sent by Charlemagne to visit the most Holy Sepulchre and place of resurrection of our Lord and Savior presented themselves" in Jerusalem, Harun sent them back with magnificent gifts and perfumes.

This alliance allowed Charlemagne to act independently of Constantinopl, and establish the freedom of the western empire, namely, the separation of the pope in Rome from the emperor in Constantinople. Hence the Byzantine proverb, "Have the Frank for your friend, but not for your neighbor."[59]

With the friendship of the Caliph Harun, Charlemagne felt sufficiently powerful to rescue Pope Leo from the Italians and street mobs, thereby directly asserting French supremacy in Rome over the power of Byzantium in Rome. As a reward for saving Rome and the Pope, Leo crowned Charlemagne Emperor of the West by sneaking up on him during Christmas worship and dropping the crown on his head. Although uncomfortable with the nomination to protect the Catholic Church, Charlemagne did not return the title.[60]

This move formalized the split with Constantinople. In Constantinople, the eastern emperor held absolute power over both secular and religious matters, as head of both the state and the state church. In western Europe a slight change occurred due to the inconsequential military prowess of the Roman Catholic Church. In western Europe, the Pope directed the Church and Charlemagne, the western emperor, directed military and secular concerns. This separation of powers, long present in Hebrew affairs, introduced a new order in the affairs of Europe. However, the problem immediately ensued that Charlemagne wanted to direct religious affairs. However, the Roman Church wanted to supercede Charlemagne on the military and secular side. Each desired absolute power. The conflict between national sovereignty and Church power lasted centuries and led to armed hostilities.

Charlemagne opposed the rule of Constantinople, effectively splitting imperial Rome into an eastern empire ruled from Constantinoble, and a western one, ruled by Charlemagne (with a religious center in Rome and the true center of power in Charlemagne's Aix-la-Chapelle). He did not present a codification of laws as complete as either Rome or Euric's Visigoth Code, but he favored the Visigoth and Hebrew presentation over the Roman Theodosian oppression.

This manifested itself in many ways. Local laws abounded, one for Romans, one for Jews, and one for Franks, all networked with his capitularies.

One capitulary established reforms such as jurata enquiry procedures, a simple form of decision by jury. Another established traveling judges, interpreted as a relinquishment of power by the sovereign. Many established the priority of the Catholic Church, but curtailed its powers in favor of the monarch. Many Hebrew concepts received explicit favor such as the prohibition of false witness, the honoring of parents, contract law, making sorcery illegal, the reestablishment of a ban on murders, making incest illegal and admonishing judges to follow written law.

Charlemagne did not, however, go as far as Hebrew culture's dictates. He did not, like King David, live under the same law as his subjects, nor did he agree to any separation of powers, keeping even ecclesiastical decisions to himself. The rights of women, slaves, and minorities were severely limited.

So Charlemagne made a giant step towards outright Mosaic law. Later Catholic kings in Northern Spain such as James, Pedro, Alfonso, and Ferdinand, would accomplish that. But the progress of Charlemagne was greatly resented by a later resurgent imperial Roman sentiment and quashed by the likes of later popes and French kings.

Parts of Charlemagne's capitularies:

"Since it is our concern that the condition of our churches should always advance towards better things, we strive with vigilant zeal to repair the manufactory of learning. This was almost destroyed by the sloth of our forefathers. We summon whom we can, to master the studies of the liberal arts.

~To all: Those excommunicated by their own bishop by reason of their faults are not to be received in communion by other ecclesiastics.

~Fugitive clerics are not to be received or ordained by anyone.

~Usury is forbidden.

~He who lends money is entitled to receive it back.

~Priests must partake in the sacrament.

~Bishops do not dare to innovate without permission.

~Clergy shall not interfere with the legal affairs of the crown.

~Monks and clerics shall not enter taverns to eat and drink.

~The Lord's Day shall be observed.

~Only the angels Michael, Gabriel and Raphael shall be pronounced.

~Women must not go to the altar with men present.

~A monk may not abandon his calling. (And therefore a political figure tonsured may not return.)

~The doctrine of the Holy Trinity and of the incarnation and ascension into heaven of Christ is to be preached to all.

~Those not of good conduct with reprehensible lives shall not dare to accuse bishops or men of higher birth.

~False names of martyrs and uncertain shrines of saints are not to be venerated.

~A wife cast aside by her husband is not to take another during her husband's life nor the husband another wife during his first's life.

~Persons of low status have no right of accusation.

~The Catholic faith will be taught and preached to all by the bishops and priests.

Alliance

~*There shall be peace and concord among Christians.*
~*It is written, "You shall not swear falsely," and therefore perjury is forbidden.*
~*It is written, "Do not practice augury," and sorcery is forbidden.*
~ *"Honor your father and mother."*
~*Bishops shall examine the doctrinal beliefs of priests.*
~*Clergy must lead laudable lives.*
~*Writings contrary to the Catholic faith shall be burned. (Not interpreted to include Jewish texts.)*
~*Clergy must preach about the three persons of the Father, how the Son of God was made flesh from a virgin, about resurrection, about sin, eternal punishment, feuds, jealousy, wrath, heresy, killing, drinking, and suchlike.*
~*Bishops must control church sextons from stealing as Jewish merchants have told us that sextons sell whatever a person orders from the vestry."* [61]

And on the subject of begging,

> *"Each of our vassals shall provide for his own poor and not have them go begging elsewhere. No one is to presume to give them anything unless they do manual labor."* [62]

The waning years of Charlemagne were recorded in the Royal Frank Annals as follows:

806 The Huns finally submitted themselves to subjugation, considering that they could not defend themselves from the Slavs, and Charlemagne ravaged the Slavs through Bohemia. In October Isaac returned from Africa with an elephant.

The Franks plunged deep into the Balkans with attacks against the Bulgars and Slavs along the Danube.

Pamplona and Navarre were placed under Frank authority with Aznar as count.

The Franks' new navy engaged the (Andalusian) Moors for control of Mediterranean islands (off the coast of Spain).

Military engagements with the Vikings boded poorly.

Count Aureo, commander of the Spanish March, died .

810 Amoroz was expelled from Zaragossa by Abd al-Rahman, the founder of the Umayyad dynasty in Spain, and forced to enter Huesca. Governor Amoroz assumed the count's position, placed garrisons in his castles, and sent an embassy to the Emperor Charles with promises of submission.

814 Charlemagne died. Louis succeeded him.

Charlemagne insured a smooth succession of his title. His son Louis did not have to worry about brothers or cousins. Charlemagne placed his nephews in prison, and they never again reappeared. In 811, when Charlemagne approached death, these two cousins and potential rivals of Louis to the throne suddenly and conveniently died in prison, leaving Louis the clear choice, as attested by a coronation conducted by Charlemagne himself.

Louis, upon ascent to the throne, threw out rooms of concubines used regularly by Charlemagne, his friends, and many clergy such as Alcuin. A new moral standard replaced loose women and the misappropriation of government funds.[63]

The court of Louis the Pious gleamed with grace, and the flowering of culture and the arts, plus peoples of every description. Foreigners of every sort visited. Muslims with flowing garments and burnooses, riding on fine Arabian horses and bearing exotic gifts as the Jewish connection with Baghdad brought representatives of the Caliph; Byzantines contemptuous of western crudity but in need of peace with Louis; Russians first entering the West; and Jews from all corners but mostly regular members of the court entourage.

Louis repaid Jewish loyalty and help to the crown. Most of his proclamations and court records concerning Hebrews later under the supervision of Roman Catholic clerics, but some reconstructions exist:

"- Let no one presume to keep a Jewish community from building a new synagogue.

- Let no one presume to deprive a Jew of the right to purchase, possess, employ, or sell pagan slaves.

- Let no one presume to punish a Jew for converting a pagan slave to Judaism.

- Let no one presume to punish a Jew for circumcising a pagan slave.

- Let no one presume to baptize a Jewish-owned slave without the owner's permission.

- Let no one presume to stop Jews from employing Christian laborers.

- Let no one permit a market to be held on Jewish Sabbath." [64]

Jewish doctors enjoyed public recognition far and wide. Emperor Louis himself and his son Charles retained a Jewish doctor, Sedechias. They treated kings, princes, and members of the aristocracy. Catholic and Arian clergy also made use of Jewish doctors, to the extent that the majority of medieval and Renaissance popes used them in their medical retinues. Catholic officials, however, forbade the Catholic population at large from availing themselves of Jewish medicine. The common folk, however, did not hesitate to defy these regulations[65]

Bishop Agobard wrote a letter about the situation:

"The Jews are especially popular at the court, and it is said that the Emperor values them highly because of the patriarchs. Important people at the court seek the prayers and the blessing of the Jews and they wish that they had such people to support them as those who favor Jews. The Jews say that the Christians at the court are angry because Bishop Agobard has prohibited the use of Jewish wine. The Jews make a great deal of money from these sales. Indeed, according to the canons, Christians are forbidden to eat and drink with Jews. All the time the Jews go around showing people the imperial orders that they have been given under the imperial name and seal, which protect the privileges granted to them. They are permitted to build synagogues against the law. Indeed, the Jews brag about the glory of their ancestors. Their wives show off clothing that they claim to be gifts from royalty and from the ladies of the palace. Some Christians even say that the Jews are better preachers than are the priests." [66]

Alliance

Agobard's complaint to King Louis, to clerics, and to the pope only served to notify the larger community that the Jewish dedication to work had founded the wine industry in France, and had created a highly desirable approach to religious assembly. Other Roman clerics schemed to exclude Jews from professions while imitating those professions and forming exclusive guilds.

Agobard possessed a sharp tongue and complained also of his exclusion from Catholic inner circles. Few could stand the man. The palace clergy continued to come from the ranks of the privileged, and like other Carolingian kings and emperors, Louis had to work within the framework of an exclusive group of aristocrats.[67]

Louis continued to use the title of "Emperor," which his father had first assumed as a result of the proclamation of the pope. Of course, this meant the world needed to contend with two emperors, the western Holy Roman Emperor in Germany and France, plus the imperial eastern Byzantine Emperor in Constantinople.

Several years later, Empress Judith gave birth to a son. This upset the previously planned division of the empire between the older three sons of Louis. The new son of Judith and Louis, Charles, named after his grandfather Charles the Great (Charlemagne), needed an inheritance and Judith strived to create and protect one. She also gave Charles an affectionate Hebrew name of Benjamin used in personal situations.[68]

The three sons of Louis, anointed kings of Germany, Italy, and Aquitaine under the umbrella of the western emperor Louis, started a revolution in order to reverse the inheritance of their half-brother Charles, and nobles aligned themselves according to their grievances and alliances. The powerful count of Jewish Provence, Bernard, son of William and grandson of Aimeri, gave his unstinting support to Louis and Judith.[69] This sealed the strong Jewish relationship of the court with Louis and sent the Roman radicals to the side of the sons.

Even among the Jewish nobles of Barcelona, some dissent occurred. While France floundered, Spain flourished. Count Bera and his son Willenund grew exasperated with France and attempted to secede and rejoin Muslim Spain. Bernard out-maneuvered Bera and Barcelona remained French with Bernard as its new count. Bernard then assumed the title of chamberlain to the king and second in command, controlling access to the crown and the distribution of monies.

Bernard and his wife Dhuoda, a scion of a noble and wealthy Provencal family, became the closest of friends to Emperor Louis and Empress Judith. Bernard was a grandson of Don Aimeri, the Jewish general who had helped deliver Narbonne to Charlemagne's father Pepin.

Lothar, the eldest son of Louis the Pious, took to open revolt. He conspired with the pope and brought the pontiff across the Pyrenees to interfere with the royal fight. Emperor Louis forbade his bishops to meet with the pope, and most obeyed.

The pope fumed, "Do you not know that the rule over souls, committed to us as pontiff, is higher than the rule of an emperor, which belongs but to time? If I did not declare the Emperor's sins against the unity of his realm, I should be committing perjury."[70]

And so the pope jumped again, visibly, into royal politics.

The radical Romans of the Catholic Church worked for the end of the Carolingian Empire, and the creation of a replacement that would abide by the pope's orders, and punish Jews for not obeying Rome.

By the end of 826, Andaulsian Muslims from Cordoba threatened the March of Spain and set siege to Barcelona with Bernard ensconced therein. Louis ordered his son, King Pepin of Aquitaine, to hold his Spanish possessions together with two magnate allies of his other sons. The three dallied with their armies while the Muslims had their way in Barcelona. An angry King Louis redistributed the lands of the older three brothers into the inheritance of Charles.

This act precipitated the most serious revolt of the three older sons. A palace coup ensued pitting the armies of the three sons against the king. Malcontent barons in league with the rebellious sons captured Queen Judith and placed her in a monastery. Bernard fled to Barcelona, and son Lothar assumed the daily command of the empire while Louis performed figurehead duties. Emperor Louis, after a short time, outmaneuvered his sons and regained the empire. He did not, however, remove their kingdoms, a sign taken as weakness. His sons planned further revolution.

Sensing instability in France, in 825, a Basque army threw the Franks out of Navarre and Pamplona, parts of the French owned borderlands that Jewish forces had held for some dozen years.

Entries from the Royal Frank Annals:

816 Basques revolted and cooperated with the Spanish Muslims.

817 Revolts began against Louis, who was perceived as weak, the first instigated by his nephew Bernard, King of Italy. Louis ordered the conspirators blinded, including his nephew, who died in the process. Basques continued their revolt.

The title count of the palace, or major domo, for Louis at the time went to Count Bertrich.

826 Revolt began in the Spanish March, when Count Asseo (Azio) entered Vich, outside of Barcelona, destroyed the city of Roda, fortified the stronger castles of the country, and allied with the Moors.

(Counts Aureo, Asseo, and Bertrich were probably Jewish. At this time, the Frank empire disintegrated and the Spanish Umayyad Empire from Cordoba coalesced into a tolerant world power sympathetic to Jewish rights.)

827 This year describes constant battles and destruction of the countryside as Muslim forces engaged Frankish counts.

The tempestuous nature of Louis' reign resulted from the military strikes between family members, and also from forays from the spectrum of ecclesiastical interests. A number of ecclesiastical battles erupted. Differing interpretations of scripture surfaced, causing the Catholic interpretation unwanted competition.

Roman Catholics wrote many commentaries on biblical subjects. The use of Hebrew references, admitted or not, was prevalent. In his commentary on the Book of Kings, one cleric admitted to consultations with a "Hebrew of our own time learned in the knowledge of the Law." The work in fact reflects in its entirety the Jewish treatise *On Hebrew Questions in the Books of Kings and Chronicles.* Various Church authorities had tried previously to pass this Jewish work off as written by Jerome.[71]

Bishop Felix of Urgell, backed by the eminent archbishop of Toledo and others, gathered together masses of parishioners to preach liberalized Christian thought reflective of the old Gothic Arian practices. Felix brought down upon himself wildly bitter accusations, and life imprisonment.

Felix so horrified the Church establishment with the possibility that the unapproved doctrine might reach a mass of people and that they might prefer different versions of Christianity, that the Church prevailed upon the emperor to issue a capitulary on the subject.

> *"All the bishops and sacredness of the Kingdom of the Franks and of Italy, Aquitaine and Provence being present in synodal council, the most gentle king graced the assembled with his appearance. Whereupon under the very first heading there arose the matter of the impious abominable heresy of Elipand, bishop of the See of Toledo, Felix of the see of Urgell, and their disciples who, with wicked opinion, asserted adoption in the Son of God. All the present most holy fathers rejected and unanimously denied adoption and decreed that this heresy must be wholly eradicated from the Holy Church."*.[72]

The culture of Spain flourished under toleration. In northern Europe, the family of Charlemagne could not institute lasting freedoms because the Roman aristocracy would hear none of it. In Spain, however, the continuing dynasty of al-Rahman permitted all faiths to practice openly, businesses to operate independently, and authors to write without censorship. Perhaps the largest paper factory in the world sat on the Spanish Mediterranean coast by Valencia as a result of the Hebrew trade that connected Chinese goods and ideas with the rest of the world. The results spoke loud and clear: Spain rumbled towards its golden age and northern Europe relapsed into dark age.

Certain Catholic clerics feared the exposure of their flocks to Jewish ideas. Some Christians shifted their market days from Saturday to Sunday so they could attend a synagogue service instead of Mass. Catholics at times neglected fasts to observe Jewish celebrations.

Politically, French Jews in Provence faced two enemies: the aggressive and successful Muslim force in Spain allied with a protected Jewish population within, and the revolution in France. William, Count of Barcelona, fought pitched battles against Muslim invasions without the help of the Frankish military. In addition, he sent forces to help Louis. His son Bernard accepted the position of *major domo* to try and save the power of Louis against his warring sons, but Louis died and the wars continued..

845 CE

The Jews of Barcelona - Catalonia faced a quandary. They needed an allay in a time of peril. They could look to the Muslim regime in Cordoba, or to the one in Baghdad. France was weak. The strongest nobles decided to look for help from the Babylonian Muslims of the Baghdad regime.

The old ally of the Jews, the one that Isaac brought to the table of Charlemagne, the Caliph of Babylonia, sent reinforcements to Barcelona. The Barcelona rebels cut ties with France and produced a new country.

Diplomatic ties, established directly between Barcelona and Baghdad, brought a vast increase in communication between the Middle East and Spain. A new Jewish state of Barcelona was born.

Rabbis from Babylonia sent prayer books and copies of the *Talmud,* plus written *responsa* to answer questions of law and give legal guidance. Jewish immigration to Barcelona picked up its pace.

The son of Louis, King Charles the Bald's regime grew increasingly unstable. Solomon the Jew, Count of French Roussillon and Count of Confluent, stepped into the picture as ally and friend of both the Barcelona Jewish community and King Charles. Charles sent Solomon, his intimate friend, his *familiarissimo,* to Spain on an important mission.

Upon the return of Solomon, the king restored peace with Barcelona, and the March of Spain returned to the French fold.

The grateful king sent a personal thanks to all of Barcelona, carried by the king's *fidelis* Judah the Hebrew.

"To all in Barcelona, our own special subjects, greetings.

Know ye that we are enjoying fitting prosperity by gift from on high. That the same may be among you is our own strong desire. Very many are the thanks we offer you that you have always ended toward fidelity to us in every way. There has now indeed come to us Judah the Hebrew, our fidelis. He had described your faithfulness to us at length. For this faithfulness we are prepared to offer fitting remuneration and proper reward."

Solomon assumed the title Count of Barcelona and the Jewish enclave continued as a French vassalage.

But as the Carolingian dynasty disintegrated, alliances formed for what would become the next military and economic power of the Mediterranean: the State of Catalonia in the March of Spain, blessed with cooperation between Jews and Catholics.[75]

In the meantime, with Barcelona back in his empire, Charles isolated the kingdom of Aquitaine from its alliances with his enemy brothers and won tentative control. He entered into treaties with the Muslim Lord Musa and Christians in the Pyrenees desirous of separation from Aquitaine. Charles also battled the meddling of the pope on the side of his brother the King of Italy. After Charles had scored a few successful counterattacks against the invading Vikings, Aquitaine swung totally to Charles, and a magnate delivered one of his nephews to Charles, who applied tonsure and banished the nephew to a monastery. When his brother the king of Germany sought to undermine the Aquitaine victory, Charles bribed Slav and Bulgar tribes to open a front from the east, and convinced his brother to back off.

Charles, like his father Louis and most of the Carolingians before him, did not enjoy the support of the pope. He recognized an enemy when he saw one and implemented a policy to appoint soldier friends to important church positions and bishoprics. the heritage from the old court of Chilperic still influenced the Carolingians.

When Charles' brother Lothar, King of Italy, passed away suddenly, the pope and the remaining brother pressed for the heirs of Lothar to step up to rule. Charles brushed them aside and, with the persuasion of force, crowned himself emperor over Frankia, Aquitaine, and Italy. Charles set his sights on his last brother, the king of Germany.

875 CE

Italian magnates and the pope rapidly built up reverence for the rising star of Europe. With no choice, the pope presented an enthusiastic triumphal march and received Charles in Rome to crown him Emperor in Saint Peter's in 875.

The grand plan of Charles fell into place. His last brother, the King of Germany, cooperated by dying the next year, and Charles prepared an army to claim the remnant of Charlemagne's old empire. Charles departed Italy in order to secure his easy victory and the rule of Gaul, Germany, and Italy. He fell violently ill in route. What appeared to be strong poison took hold rapidly, and he quickly passed away. Someone with access to a strong secret service redirected history. Lacking a central authority figure, the former lands of Charlemagne fell into disarray with the Church, magnates, and various heirs vying for power.[76]

Lack of central rule in France brought a series of local rulers and constant skirmishes to the landscape. An era of power in central Europe came to an end and the dark ages for France, Germany and Italy deepened, while Spain and North Africa prospered. The property of the Church came under pressure from many sources. The wealth of churches and monasteries caught the eye of Viking raiders, who singled out these establishments. The entire Gascon Church vacated the Pyrenees.

Local magnates, realizing the political nature of the Church, did not hesitate to usurp its property when possible. Whenever the monarch could exert effective power over the magnates, expropriated Church property usually came back. In order to survive, however, the Church acceded even more to the wishes of the magnates.[77]

By the year 900, Frank monarchs lost all effective control over southern France and Catalonia. Real authority over the Spanish March, Gascony, Provence, and Aquitaine lay in the hands of noble warlords.[78]

With the end of rule by Charlemagne and his family, France lost its grip on tolerance and, again, the inevitable violent clash between the freedoms of the Judeo-Christian legacy and autocrats intensified. However, during that reign, much was added to our modern civil society by many individuals possessing military, intellectual, and faith-based wisdom. Those mentioned here are but a fraction of all who should be remembered. A seemingly unlikely candidate became the protector of civil values.

Lion's Court at Alhambra Palace, Granada, Spain,
Home of the Andalusian Muslim Emir and one of the
Architecural Wonders of the World.

MUSLIM RENAISSANCE

PART OF THE WORLD PROSPERED

Constantinople continued to hold on to its wealth and position as a great city, but the greatest cities, Baghdad and Cordoba, grew because Muslim leaders of the tenth and eleventh centuries created open and tolerant societies. They permitted trade to flourish and expand. Rome and France, treating trade as a cow for milking and freedom as a scornful heresy, continued to languish accordingly.

"The Lord spoke unto Moses, saying: "Take thou also unto thee the chief spices, of flowing myrrh five hundred shekels, and of sweet cinnamon half so much, even two hundred and fifty, and of sweet calamus two hundred and fifty, and of cassia five hundred, after the shekel of the sanctuary, and of olive oil a bin. And thou shalt make it a holy anointing oil."[1]

Since Moses knew about cinnamon and cassia (cinnamon bark), trade with China already existed. What did the Mideast have to trade in exchange? Something persuaded the Chinese to part with their spices. What goods might also bring their silk and jade to the West?

As it happens, the Chinese did express interest in a product from the West just as unusual as their silk, jade, and spices. That product was glass. The Chinese were burying their precious collections of glass beads, glass animals, glass cylinders, and glass artifacts with their corpses long before the great Silk Road coalesced into a definitive route. All along the routes into the heart of China, vast collections of glass materials accumulated.

4,000 or 5,000 years ago the first crude glass furnace fired up in Akkadia, the home of Abraham and his father Terach.[2] Hebrew products such as glass found their way to China, and Chinese silk found its way to Mesopotamia. Minerals, jewels, spices, tools, wool and cotton followed as traded commodities. Businesses introduced the products, first as traders and then as settlers.

The prophet Isaiah, writing in 700 BCE thought they would return:
"And I will make all My mountains a way.
And My Highways shall be raised on high.
Behold, these shall come from far;
And lo, these from the north and from the west,
And these from the land of Seenem."
(Seenem is China. Hebrew has no "ch" and the land of Chin becomes the land of Seen: Seenem is plural)[3]

When Romans destroyed Jerusalem and spewed destruction over North Africa, a number of Hebrews fled to Europe, while the larger number went east. For hundreds of years they migrated to Central Asian cities like Samarkand and Bokhara; to Khazaria; and to India or China. They continued the old traditions of shepherding, farming, learning, producing, and trading.[4]

Using the ethics of the *Talmud* and submitting to the religious courts, Jewish traders linked the world. A Muslim official in northern Africa observed:

"These merchants speak Arabic, Persian, Roman, and the Frank, Spanish, and Slav languages. They journey from West to East, from East to West, partly on land, partly by sea. They transport from the West slaves, (for Christian and Muslim nobles), brocade, castor, marten, and other furs, and swords. They take ships from France, on the Western Sea, and make for Pelusium. There they load their goods on camel back and go by land to Suez, a distance of 25 parasangs. They embark in the Red Sea and sail from Suez to the Port of Medina and Mecca, then they go to Sind, India, and China. On their return from China they carry back musk, aloes, camphor, cinnamon, and other products of the eastern countries to Suez and bring them back to Pelusium, where they again embark on the Western Sea. Some make sail for Constantinople to sell their goods to the Romans; others to the palace of the King of the Franks to place their goods. Sometimes these Jewish merchants, when embarking in the land of the Franks, on the Western Sea, make for Antioch; thence by land to al-Jabia, where they arrive after three days' march. There they embark on the Euphrates and reach Baghdad, whence they sail down the Tigris, to al-Obolla. From al-Obolla they sail for Oman, Sind, Hind, and China...

"These different journeys can also be made by land. The merchants that start from Spain or France go to Morocco and then to Tangier, whence they walk to Kairouan in Africa and the capital of Egypt. Thence they to ar-Ramla, visit Damascus, Al-Kufa, Baghdad, and Bassora, cross Ahwaz, Fars, Kirman, Sind, Hind, and arrive at China. Sometimes, also, they take the route behind Rome and, passing thought the country of the Slavs, arrive at Khanlij, the capital of the Khazars. They embark on the Jordan Sea, arrive at al Balkh, betake themselves from there across the Oxus, and continue their journey toward Yurt, Toghuzghuz, and from there to China."[5]

The trade tended more towards the precious than the bulk. Spices, incense, silk, pepper, enamels, and paper dominated the overland routes. Grain and lumber required shipping and so took place more between seaports.[6]

Aristocrats of Greek, Roman and Muslim persuasion disdained the trades, especially tanning and dyeing. The Talmud mandates the teaching of a trade. Jews monopolized many crafts low in social esteem such as dyeing.[7]

As Muslims swept Romans out of the Middle East and North Africa, they selected craftsmen rather than slaves for certain trades. In populating the new capital of Tunis, the caliph ordered a thousand Jewish or Coptic Christian families from Alexandria, and thereafter his city, Kairuwan, became a notable seat of Jewish learning.[8]

A tenth century caliph might change his prime ministers fifteen times, but he retained his Jewish court banker from the beginning of his reign to its very end. Even in the early twentieth century, the Iraqi minister of finance, Hezkiel Sassoon, continued this traditional service.

Benjamin of Tudela, Spain, visited Baghdad (later, in 1168):

"The great city and the royal residence of the Caliph...(is in)

Baghdad three miles in extent, wherein is a great park with all varieties of trees, fruit bearing and otherwise, and all manner of animals. A wall surrounds the whole, and in the park there is a lake whose waters are fed by the River Hiddekel. Whenever the caliph desires to indulge in recreation and to rejoice and feast, his servants catch all manners of birds, game and flesh, and he goes to his palace with his counselors and princes. There the great... Caliph holds his court, and he is kind unto Israel, and many belonging to the people of Israel are his attendants. He knows all languages, and is well versed in the law of Israel.. He reads and writes the holy language (Hebrew)...

"He does not issue forth from his palace save once in the year, at the feast that the Mohammedans call Ramazon, and they come from distant lands that day to see him. He rides on a mule and is attired in the royal robes of gold and silver and fine linen. On his head is a turban adorned with precious stones of priceless value. Over the turban is a black shawl as a sign of his modesty, implying that all this glory will be covered by darkness on the day of his death. He is accompanied by all the nobles of Islam dressed in fine garments and riding on horses, the princes of Arabia, the princes of Togarma, Gilan, Persia, Media, Ghuzz, Tibet, which is three months journey distance, and westward of which lies the land of Samarkand. He proceeds from his palace to the great mosque of Islam that is by the Basrah Gate. Along the road the walls are adorned with silk and purple, and the inhabitants receive him with all kinds of song and exultation, and they dance before the great caliph...

"Jews dwell in security, prosperity and honor under the great Caliph, and amongst them are great sages, the heads of the Academies engaged in the study of the law. In this city there are ten Academies...

"Daniel the son of Chisdai, who is styled Our Lord the Head of the Captivity of all Israel...has been invested with authority over all the congregations of Israel.

"And every fifth day, when he goes to pay a visit to the great Caliph, horsemen, Gentiles as well as Jews, escort him. Heralds proclaim in advance, "Make way before our Lord, the son of David, as is due unto him." ....Then he appears before the Caliph and kisses his hand The Caliph rises and places him on a throne that Mohammed had ordered to be made. All the Mohammedan princes who attend the court of the Caliph rise up before him." [9]

In France, a different situation prevailed. After the demise of Louis the Pious, son of Charlemagne, southern France, Aquitaine, the Pyrenees, northwestern Spain, and the Spanish March all removed themselves from the control of monarchs, and paid little heed to either the King of France, the Emperor of Germany, or the Caliph of Spain. Heads of the families that ruled called themselves dukes, counts or kings. Whatever their title, the power they held equaled that of royal monarchs, and the territories controlled matched the power of many a nation.

The castle and the noble family were the basic building blocks in the French system. Knights forming permanent militias served the noble families, not as land-owning proprietors, but as professional military forces.

A harsh age came to roost in France, Italy, and Germany, the Dark Age of feudalism. Nobles launched campaigns against each other and they felt free to stage raids into what remained of French territory and the March of Spain. A center of *Reconquista*, or military conquest arose in Galicia. A center of *Convivencia*, or cooperation took hold in Catalonia.

Northern Europe could not escape the grip of its own despoiling hands. The lords disliked the power of the king, as he was weak and his rule interferred with their own plans of glory. The Duke of Normandy had a much better army than the king, whose only control was around Paris. Especially independent were the Dukes of Normandy, Flanders, Aquitaine, Champagne, Toulouse, and Anjou.

During the tenth century, the center of world activity moved west, from Baghdad to Spain and not north to France. In Spain and North Africa, a lively sense of freedom and opportunity produced a modern, diverse region in the Mediterranean basin. Old trade routes rich in spices, gems, and silk originated in China and India and then extended across North Africa and into the heart of Europe. Grain, metals, sugars from Egypt; paper from Spain and Damascus; and foodstuffs, potions, manufactured items, and textiles from everywhere circulated about the Mediterranean basin.

The countries and independent states that participated were a wide-ranging lot. Stretching from Spain, across northern Africa, and clear to India lay various competing Sunni and Shiite Muslim dynasties. Byzantine control shrank to the area around Constantinople, while ever-changing states in Europe remained to the north. Towards Central Asia stood the large Jewish empire of the Khazars, largely out of the Mediterranean picture, except as inspiration to minor Jewish bastions.

920 CE

Rahman III, the grand Caliph of Spain, ruled after concluding the brilliant unification started by Rahman I, who had started the Arab (Umayyad) dynasty in Spain a century and a half before. Years of tolerance and cooperation among the Spanish under Muslim leadership yielded the jewel of Europe. The cooperation between the black Moors, Arabs, Christians and Jews still held. Kings from afar sought advice from Rahman III, including Otto, King of the Germans and son of Emperor Henry I.

Under Muslim and Berber rule, increased tolerance caused a flowering of Spanish trade and thought. For a long time, the area flourished, the population increased, and culture expanded. The Muslim-Jewish combination produced the most advanced society of the Mediterranean. While France remained a back-woods area, Spain possessed the two largest cities in Europe, Cordoba and Seville, plus a third of all European cities with populations over 10,000. An Arab free trade zone opened much of the world to unfettered business.[10]

The capital city of Cordoba showed the world all of the possibilities. The Golden Age of Muslim Spain brought its genius to full front. This age featured superiority in military, culture, knowledge, tolerance, science, literature, medicine, law, and architecture.

The city's Great Mosque amazed travelers who stood among the forest of columns that opened to endless vistas on all sides. Glistening porphyry, jasper, marble, and glass mosaics sparkled like jewels. The sanctuary featured fantastic crossed arches, with stretched acres of oranges in many directions.

Moorish culture blended Hebraic monotheism in its focus, Hellenism in its rational inquiry, and a unique tolerance that opened doors of all persuasions. Cordoba grew into the home of European culture, and attracted the brightest from the continent. The city gave birth to many artists and thinkers, including the Jewish leaders, Averroes, Chasdai ibn Shaprut. and Maimonides.[11] These men pulled together ideas that, centuries later, created the northern European Renaissance. Chasdai, special envoy to the caliph, assembled intellectual substance from the world over. He imported writings from Persia of the Jewish naturalist and astronomer Mashallah.

Mashallah's instructions on the construction of spherical astrolabes provided a major leap from the older flat versions. His instructions were still the standard of the world when Chaucer and Pelerin de Prusse, among others, copied it in the 14th century and Cristannus de Prachaticz used it as a basis for the first printed book on astrolabes.[12]

Mashallah produced many works. His *De Scientia Motus Orbis was* continuously read, translated, and used as a basic text on astronomy and natural science into the 16th century and beyond. Albrecht Durer created an engraving for a 1504 publication translated by Gherardo Cremonese. Other translators published the work throughout the century.[13]

The young of Andalusia learned Arabic, and in that language could read the greatest of writers, forbidden to northern regions across the Pyrenees in France and Rome. Plato, Aristotle, Euripides all constituted regular reading fare.

Muslim scholars achieved internatinal fame. Ibn Hazm produced 400 works of anthropolgy, jurisprudence, logic, history, and ethics. Ibn Khayr, in his *Farasah*, noted, "There is nothing greater in the eye of G-d than a man who learned a science and who taught it to people."

The court poet earned high praise as the society revolved around poetry, exemplified by Ali ibn Nafi, or Zirjab. Zirjab helped Seville rise to a center of musical instrument production and himself introduced a fifth string to the lute. He could also converse in the subjects of science, history, astronomy, and art, a precise example of the widespread veneration of knowledge that prevailed in Andalusia.

Christians garnered a share of the glory, as the then bishop of Elvira served in the highest levels of diplomatic corps as the caliph's envoy to the German court. Some Catholics resented the dominance of Islam and the learning of Arabic:

"The Christians love to read the poems and romances of the Arabs. They study the Arab theologians and philosophers, not to refute them but to form a correct and elegant Arabic. Where is the layman who now reads the Latin commentaries of the Holy Scriptures, or who studies the Gospels, prophets or apostles? Alas! All talented young Christians read and study with enthusiasm the Arab books. They gather immense libraries at great expense. They despise the Christian literature as unworthy of attention. They have forgotten their own language. For every one who can write a letter in Latin to a friend, there are a thousand who can express themselves in Arabic with elegance, and write better poems in Arabic than the Arabs themselves." [14]

As regimes to the north remained stagnant, Muslim chroniclers filled vast libraries and engineers provided running water. At a time when the largest library in Roman Europe held about four hundred manuscripts, the library of Cordoba held some four hundred thousand, and it was but one of seventy libraries in the city. The vigorous international trade fomented by the caliphate added to the ideas considered by the population. Material and intellectual trade flourished and added manuscripts to the collections. Catholics converted to Islam by the score.[15]

Women such as the accomplished Lubna, as learned as she was lovely, wrote grammar, verse, arithmetic, and other sciences. The Caliph of Cordova entrusted her with his private correspondence. Also, in Seville, the admired Maryem ran a school that taught letters to the young girls of the leading families.[16] Just north of the Cordoba Caliphate, nascent Catholic kingdoms sparred with each other.

Castile fought Leon for its independence. Armies of the Caliph took advantage of the situation and picked off the outlying parts of Leon. Edged into an impossible situation, Leon sued for peace from all sides. Castile won the civil war and Leon received negotiators from the Caliphate of Cordoba lead by the Jewish Inspector General of Customs, Chasdai ibn Shaprut. He did not take long in arranging concessions agreed to by the king of Leon, Sancho in 955, including the relinquishment of certain fortresses.

Sancho, however, did not manage his nobles well, and in fact arrogantly usurped their powers and privileges to the point of causing hatred. At the same time his girth grew to such an immense size that he could no longer mount his horse and needed to lean on an attendant for support. The meddling king of Castile aided the disaffected nobles in replacing Sancho the Fat with his hunchback cousin.

This all caused great distress to Sancho's grandmother who ruled Navarre and supported her grandson Sancho the Fat. Sancho required military help from a formidable ally and medical help from one of the best physicians in the world. These requirements brought her back to Cordoba and back to Chasdai.

The grandmother was determined to seek the council of her enemy, the infidel with whom she had fought for thirty years, and who regularly devastated her valleys and burnt her villages: the grand Caliph Rahman III in Cordoba. She could not seek help from France, for even though the countries shared a religion, they shared no peace.

The population of Castile Jews aided the queen in her decision. This population stemmed from the time when Jewish counts ruled some of her territories including Aznar of Pamplona. These Hebrews maintained relations with the Jews of Spain under the Muslim caliph, and could trust the caliph.

In return, the caliph sent the esteemed Chasdai the Jew as his representative, and could not have made a better choice. "Chasdai united in his own person all the qualities necessary for such a mission. He spoke the language of the Catholics fluently, and he was at once a physician and a statesman. Praises of his judgement, his talents, his erudition, and his vast ability were in all men's mouths. Not long before, an ambassador from the further end of Germany had declared that he had never met with such a master of diplomatic subtlety.

"*Upon his arrival at Pamplona, the Jew soon gained Sancho's confidence by personally undertaking his treatment and promising him a speedy cure. He then informed him that the caliph, in return for the service he was prepared to render him, demanded the cession of ten fortresses. Sancho promised to make them over as soon as he had regained his throne. But this was not all: Chasdai had also been instructed to extort the queen's consent to visit Cordoba, accompanied by her son and grandson.*

"*The caliph, desirous of gratifying his own self-esteem, while at the same time regaling his people with the unexampled spectacle of a Catholic queen and two kings humbly prostrating themselves at his feet and craving his assistance, had strongly insisted on this condition. It had been foreseen that the proud queen would resist the demand. To make a journey to Cordoba would be, indeed, a greater humiliation for the queen than that to which she had already subjected herself in entering into friendly relations with her inveterate foe. This was accordingly the most delicate and thorny part of Chasdai's mission. Even to make such a proposal, still more to induce the queen to agree required extraordinary tact and ability. But the Jew justified his reputation of being the most adroit of men. The haughty Queen of Navarre was subjugated by the charm of his words, the ripeness of his wisdom, the power of his cunning and his manifold wiles, to use the words of a contemporary Jewish poet, and believing that her grandson's reinstatement could be obtained at no less a price, she consented, after a powerful exercise of self-control, to undertake the proposed journey.*

"*Spain then saw a strange sight. Followed by a long train of nobles and priests, the queen of Navarre journeyed by easy stages to Cordoba, accompanied by her son and the luckless Sancho, whose health was not yet much improved, and who walked supported by Chasdai. Delightful as the spectacle was to the national pride of the Muslims, it was yet sweeter to the self-esteem of the Jews, seeing that it had been wholly brought about by a man of their own faith.*"[17]

Jewish poets sang praises in celebrating Chasdai's return:
"*Bow down, O ye mountains, to Judah's chief!*

"*While he was not therein, the famous city with its fair wall was sorrowful and in darkness. The poor, who saw no longer his countenance shining as the stars are in affliction. The proud held dominion over us and we were bought and sold into slavery... God hath given him to us as our chief. He standeth at the right hand of the kin, who calleth him prince, and hath exalted him above the mighty....Without sword or arrows, by the words of his mouth alone, he hath taken by storm the fenced cities of the devourers of accursed flesh!*"[18]

Muslims gathered and marched against the kingdom of Leon, accompanied with a Sancho much slimmed down as a result of remedies prescribed by Chasdai. By 960 Sancho ruled over the kingdom, and he sent an envoy to the caliph, thanking him for the aid and pledging support.

Chasdai carried on correspondence with other kingdoms, such as that of Khazaria:

"To the King of the Khazars:

I, Chasdai, son of Isaac, son of Ezra, belonging to the exiled Jews of Jerusalem live in Spain, a servant of my lord the King (al-Rahman). I bow to the earth before him and prostrate myself towards the abode of your Majesty from a distant land....

"Spain is a fat land full of rivers, springs and stone cut wells. It is a land of grains, wines and purest oils, right in plants, a paradise of every sort of sweet. It contains gardens and orchards where every kind of fruit tree blossoms, including those with silkworms in their leaves....

"Praise be to the beneficent God for His mercy towards me! Kings of the earth, to whom al-Rahman's magnificence and power are known, bring gifts to him, conciliating his favor by costly presents, such as the King of the Franks (Lothar, descendant of Charlemagne) the King of the Gebalim, who are Germans, The King of Constantinople, and others. All their gifts pass throughout my hands, and I am charged with making gifts in return. Let my lips express praise to the God in heaven, who so far extends His loving kindness towards me, without any merit of my own, but in the fullness of His mercies!"[19]

955

Other international escapades followed. With the Islamic world split, the caliph of Spain, Rahman, shifted about for protective alliances. The Catholic world also split, with Rome going a differing direction than Constantinople. Spanish dignitaries Chasdai and Racemundo, the Bishop of Elvira, shared duties as representatives of the caliph in forming an historic alliance between Muslim Spain and Catholic Constantinople against incursions from Rome, North Africa, or Baghdad.

This treaty counteracted the old axis of power that united Charlemagne and his progeny with the caliph of Baghdad.

Rahman III died shortly thereafter, leaving the treasury of Spain, managed by Chasdai, in an overflowing state of wealth. Agriculture, manufactures, commerce, arts and science flourished. Well-cultivated fields irrigated by scientific principles fed the population and provided exports while security held in the land. Cordoba, the jewel of the West, found itself excelled only by Baghdad. Hakam II succeeded his father, Rahman.

Sancho made new alliances with Castile; Galicia, his cousin, king of Navarre; Count Borell and Count Miron from Catalonia. He then hesitated to honor his pledges to the new caliph. The appearance of a large Muslim army that had inflicted losses on all of Sancho's allies rendered a decisive end to the equivocation. Sancho of Leon sought terms in 966, while his allies lost forts and made other concessions. By 985, a successor to Hakam so devastated Leon and Castile that he undertook a sacking of Barcelona as well.

1000 CE

The dynastic descendants of Rahman did not hold the paradise of Andalusia forever. Dissension prevailed after one weak ruler and the immense caliphate of Cordoba fractured into mini-states. These smaller morsels attracted the predatory attention of the Catholic northern states, which alternately allied with the small Muslim kingdoms and preyed upon them. Catalon counts looked to the weakened southern kingdoms as potential sources of loot. 1009 witnessed the count of Barcelona siding with one of the many Muslim factions in the Spanish civil wars. Raymond Berenguer of Barcelona and Ermenegild of Urgel entered the fray looking for loot and land. They won no lasting benefit as the Moors struck back and Ermenegild lost his life.[20] Successors like Raymond Berenguer II interceded again and again.

As a result, holes appeared in the armor of Muslim Spain. Smaller and smaller kingdoms prevailed. One small state, however, appeared impregnable. The Kingdom of Granada dominated southern Spain early in the eleventh century. A family of Berber kings controlled the kingdom under King Badis, under whose leadership the kingdom grew in importance and overshadowed the great kity of Cordoba, by then reduced to minor status. Berbers continued to remember their Jewish heritage and rely on the Hebrew population for advice and support.

King Badis employed many of the same families that had propelled Cordoba to prominence. No family could rival the Halevi family, whose head, Samuel, rose to the title of nasi, or nagid, leader of the Jewish community. Samuel Nagid Halevi also rose in the ranks of the diplomatic core to the position of vizier to the king.

In Granada Hebrews lived in such great numbers that people called it the City of the Jews. Indeed, they took an active role in politics. The choice of Samuel met the approval of all factions, including Arabs, as Samuel commanded respect throughout the land with his knowledge of many languages, mathematics, logic, astronomy, and scholarship.

He typified the movement of the educated from the war-torn former capital of Cordoba to the outlying capitals of new kingdoms. A golden age continued in the tradition of the Greek city-states.

Samuel also contributed to the Hebrew community, publishing an introduction to the Talmud and many other works. He generously provided an education to impoverished Jews in Spain, Africa, Sicily, Jerusalem, and Baghdad.[21] All of these cities, especially in northern Africa, had large communities in touch with Spain.

Tripoli, the great city in North Africa, accounted for large amounts of trade with Spain. Since its founding, Tripoli served as a tremendous trading city. The Hebrew Talmud and Midrash mention donkeys and silk worms that come into Palestine from Libya. Caravans of Jews traversed the desert in every direction. Hundreds of caravans each year headed for the Sudan, bringing richly embroidered robes of velvet, caftans, girdles, slippers, perfumes, ornaments, salt, apparel, hardware, and arms. Returning, the long camel train carried ostrich feathers, ivory, precious skins, and tropical products. The ostrich feather trade alone supported many family groups.

Olives, barley, pelts, leather, rugs, saffron, dates, date wine, ivory, feathers, corn, salt, and tin headed out across the Mediterranean and came back transmogrified by trade into cloth, hardware, metals.

Muslims prohibited Catholics from this lucrative trade just as Catholics had prohibited those of other faiths for so many years.[22]

In the days before aggressive military men like El Cid and Alfonzo of Castile, all the nobles of northern Spain paid homage to Muslim Cordoba.

Great lords, including those of Castile, relied upon the caliphs to direct politics and settle quarrels. It did not stop there. Money for weddings and vendettas might have to be borrowed or requested from the caliph, and so these lords curried the favor of the caliph.

The universities and learning centers in Spain continued to thrive. All these activities continued to place Spain at the pinnacle of leadership in the world. Interaction with the Catholic states to the north increased, but the less cultured north acted more as the trader and student.

1039 CE

Vizier Samuel Nagid led the king's forces into battle. His title included duties as commander-in-chief of the army, a position he executed with brilliance. Seville fell to the Granada military. Also the little kingdom of Almeria down on the coast fell to the Granada forces.

In fifty consecutive campaigns, another minister from Cordoba struck at every opposition Catholic center in Spain, burning monasteries and destroying castles. Kings of Navarre and Leon surrendered their daughters to caliphs as slaves or wives. Long lines of prisoners and trains of carts, filled with the heads of the vanquished, crosses, holy vessels, and rich booty poured into Cordoba. The prisoners set their hands to work constructing impressive mosques.[23]

Then something turned and the golden age of Islam in Spain melted. The Muslims of Andulusia splintered when the central governments grew incompetent, quarelling and especially corrupt. This came at a time when fundamentalist jihadist Muslim forces gained power in north Africa and put an end to rational discussion and tolerance. The power vacuum in Spain attracted the fierce military fanatics from Africa, who entered Spain and changed the whole picture. The Christians and Jews who had lived peacefully in Andalusia scattered before invaders who put dissidents to death. Many refugees came to northern Spain where Catholic monarchs resurrected the old Judeo-Christian regimes along the lines of those that had been tendered by the Visigoths. The ancient Visigoth spirit survived.

Abu Muhammad Ibn Hazm, 933 - 1064, statue in Cordoba

CATHOLICS AND JEWS AS ALLIES

BROTHERS WITH A MISSION

From the northern city of Barcelona, capital of Aragon and Catalonia, a more complicated and dynamic structure of policy evolved. A solid base of urban industry and trade offset an undue reliance on military quest. A tolerant society allowed differing groups access to business, religion, and thought.

The Borell and Berenguer families, with both Catholic and Jewish members, continued the Visigoth vision for Europe, and in so doing, represented the only federation in Europe at the time to unite into a great nation. Count Raymon Borell III Berenguer and Countess Ermissende inherited the throne of Catalonia. They made Catalonia the era's paragon of leadership.

They made Catalonia into a fledgling nation by uniting the nobility through persuasion, military action, and grants of money. Ramon Berenguer I the Great defeated one of the last holdouts, his cousin.[1] This family tended more and more to profess Catholicism, while remembering their Jewish roots.

1045 CE

The next Berenguer, Catholic Count Ramon Berenguer I of Barcelona, worked on legal codes, called *Usatges,* from the Hebrew word usot. וסות

This legal document simplified and extended the ancient Visigoth Code. It subjected the monarch to the rule of law and provided equal protection for all citizens while ignoring Roman Theodosian Code. Count Ramon needed to insure and protect the continuing existence of his *Convivencia.*[2]

The family conducted raids into Spain as far as Cordoba, setting the Muslim leadership reeling. They coalesced the legal system into a revitalized and simplified version of the *Talmud-Goth Code* and at the same time exerted control over errant castle lords. The countess continued ruling after the death of the count.

1068 CE

Count Ramon Berenguer the Elder pushed greater Barcelona, or Catalonia, in nationhood and greatness. He continued the formalization of the old Goth - Hebrew legal code, then called Usatges, and extended the control of Barcelona.

He used money from raids into Spain to purchase support from his barons. For 20,000 solidi, the Count of Urgel decided to subject himself to the inevitable, and his cousins in other counties followed suit. Impetus galvanized for peace in Catalonia in the name of a Truce of God, or Peace of God.[3]

When Ramon the Elder pronounced the Usatges the law of the land, he used the words of the Hebrew writer Simon (also used in Ecclesiasticus) for his preamble: "*An unwise king destroyeth his people; but through the prudence of them which are in authority the city shall be inhabited.*"

The laws in Catalonia reflected neither the Muslim laws to the south, the mixture of Roman and Frank to the north, or the heterogeneous mixture of the emerging small kingdoms to the west. These laws reflected a Judeo-Christian understanding, and each regulation, called an usot, added to a compilation referred to as Usatges.

The Usatges evolved from old Visigoth law and continued Jewish texture paralleling work done by Talmudic scholars in Babylonia and Jerusalem. Ramon Berenguer signed the Usatges, a written code defining the reciprocal rights and responsibilities of the sovereign and his subjects in 1068. Laws were approved by a council of eighteen persons of high rank, one of whom was a cleric.

The most striking and immediate parallel between the Usatges and the Talmud consists of the complete reliance on the written word, and the application of an extensive and detailed outline suitable for a sophisticated society and business environment. Panels of judges arbitrated justice, sitting with the count or his deputy, who served as president of the court. Pleas, judgements, sworn statements, extensive use of witnesses, and renunciations of claims made by losing parties, made this legal system unique in Europe.[4] The Catholic monarch was only following Judeo-Christian tradition and rejecting the Roman Theodosian model of dictatorship.

In a tragic turn of events, northwest Africa and southern Spain fell under a strict fundamentalist Muslim ruler, Yusuf, who killed the culture of renaissance and sullied the Muslim reputation. Creative individuals such as Maimonides, who formed the nucleus of Andalusian renaissance fled to Catalonia, Castile, Alexandria, and Baghdad. The Berenguers in Catalonia and Saladin in Alexandria kept the flag of freedom alive.

The famous warrior El Cid and his armed detachment rode to the Emir of Seville and Cordoba to collect the annual tribute due the Catholic Emperor Alfonso VI of Castile. Generally, Alfonso put some of his trusted Jewish advisors in charge of the actual collection.[5] El Cid mounted his loyal steed Babieca. Islamic Spain stood in tatters as petty nobles fought among themselves. Catholic nobles from the north simultaneously hired themselves out as mercenaries to some Islamic lords and extracted protection payments from others.

The Muslim nobility knew El Cid well, both as an ally and an enemy. They called him "Cid," from the Arabic word meaning lord.[6]

1071 CE

As the Cid, a young man at the time, made preparations to receive tribute, another armed militia comprised of Granada Moors and Catholic mercenary nobles from the greater Castilian area appeared on the scene. The Cid knew these knights well, as he had fought on the same side in many battles.

The Court of Seville, derived from Yemeni heritage, despised the leadership of neighboring Granada, consisting of black Moors, or Berbers from Africa.

The Cid reacted quickly.

"Warning the mercenary nobles of the consequences of trespassing on the territory of a prince who was under the protection of the King of Castile. He reminded the Catholic mercenaries of their allegiance and requested firmly but respectfully for them to desist from their enterprise. A hint was at the same time given to

the effect that any further encroachment would be resisted to the best of the writer's power....

"In the battle that followed the Cid wholly succeeded. The number of the slain was very large ... and many celebrated warriors fell into his hands, who he held as prisoners for a short time.

"The Emir received him in triumph at Seville and paid not only the full tribute owing the King of Castile, but made his deliverer a handsome present." [7]

1085 CE

Then Alfonso, King of Castile, after taking a daughter of the Emir as one of his wives, expanded his control over his southern neighbors by marching into the city of Toledo.

This brought the petty emirs and princes of the south into complete panic. They could plainly see the consequences of *Reconquista*. As a chorus under the lead of the emir from Seville, they beseeched their brethren from Africa, where fierce and fundamental black Berbers ruled under Yusuf, a leader dedicated to the military and to spartan rule.

A fleet of a hundred ships bearing a powerful army suddenly appeared at a small town near Gibraltar. Fresh detachments arrived quickly and then Yusuf himself landed in Spain. Word spread quickly, and Alfonso of Castile, besieging Zaragossa at the time promised to leave quickly upon payment of a small bribe. The inhabitants, who also knew of the landing, refused and Alfonso departed anyway.

Alfonso quickly removed his detachment to Toledo and collected the largest army he could muster, calling knights from as far as France. The two armies camped in sight of each other, and Alfonso received a letter from Yusuf, offering him the alternatives prescribed by the Prophet of Islam, namely tribute or the sword.

Alfonso VI, King of Castile and self-proclaimed Emperor of Spain, returned a royal answer expressing surprise. He pointed out that the Muslims had for many years submitted to his demands and served as his vassals. The insolence of the African offer could only provoke a response from his army, which stood ready.

Yusuf waited while his secretary formulated long formal phrases in another letter, but Yusuf could suffer no more delay. He snatched the note that came from Alfonso and hastily wrote on the back, "What will happen, you will see."

Alfonso suggested a time for the battle, as per the custom of the day. "Tomorrow is Friday, your holy day, while Sunday is ours. Let us fight on Saturday." All parties agreed.

The force from Castile loomed three times the size of their adversaries. In addition, the Spanish emirs who contributed helping militia to Yusuf lacked aggressive combat capability, as they regularly proved inferior to the aggressive knights from northern Spain. The action received careful recordation:

"Fearing surprise, the Emir ordered his cavalry to watch the movements of the enemy while he consulted the diviners and soothsayers, on whose predictions he placed much faith. On Friday, Alfonso's forces began movements towards the contingent of knights from Seville.

"The Emir of Seville at once sent word to Yusuf, encamped on the hills in his rear, to warn of the danger and to beg for support.

"Yusuf merely replied, 'What does it matter to me that those folk be slain?'

"A battle shortly erupted and the greater part of those from Seville fled, but the emir fought courageously with a small band, aware that the whole of his fortunes depended upon this one fight. He determined to either conquer or die.

"Just as the emir prepared to retreat, suddenly the Catholic army wheeled about and left him. The Africans under Yusuf had turned on its flank, slaying those who had been left to guard the camp in the rear, and setting all tents afire.

"Thus assailed, in a direction from which he had expected no danger, by a force superior to that which lay in front of him, Alfonso executed a maneuver considered well nigh impossible on the field of battle. He faced the whole of his army and fell upon the already victorious Africans.

"Again and again the camp of the Castile army was taken and retaken, and the final issue of the battle remained in doubt. Then the Seville army that had fled at the first shock, rallied and attacked the Castillians in what was now their rear.

"Meanwhile Yusuf let loose on the main front a large especially picked contingent of his Negro guard, which he had hitherto held in reserve. This decided the fortunes of the day.

"Alfonso found himself wounded in the thigh with a dagger by a Negro who contrived to make his way to him through the struggling ranks. At nightfall Alfonso departed the field, leaving the flower of his knights either dead or dying.

"The Castile power seemed crushed by this defeat. Losses in killed and wounded counted as high as twenty thousand. Zaragossa and Valencia, only a few days earlier on the verge of surrender to Castile, enjoyed freedom. The Moors and Arabs of the south at once renounced their obligation to pay tribute. Yusuf could complete his campaign of Spain at his leisure." [8]

Yusuf saved Andalusian Spain from exterior invaders. He placed *Reconquista* on hold and then proceeded to dismantle the golden age of Spain by imposing an oppressive dictatorship. His unrelenting religious theocracy demolished the Muslim *Convivencia*, which allowed for toleration and rule of reasonable law. Moderate Muslims, Jews, and Christians came under duress and many fled. The end of freedom and the end of an economy drove the life out of southern Spain. Thus did the rule of Yusuf and his fundamentalists change Spain. The country never recovered, as one dictatorship followed another, first Muslim and then Catholic.

An age of warlords emerged, and the exploits of mercenary warriors such as El Cid punished city after city. But these petty lords did not have a large enough imagination or impact to make the final determination regarding the fate of the Iberian Peninsula.

Yusuf possessed an overriding vision, but it was one that led to poverty and misery. The king of France had a vision, also dependent on plundering the assets of his most productive subjects. That policy kept France small and ineffectual.

Feudal law prevailed in France: the law of the manor; trial by ordeal;

imprisonment as detention for trial in infested cells; stocks; ducking stools; galley slaves; flogging; branding; piercing the tongue with hot iron; mutilation of hands, feet, ears, and nose' eyes gouged out. In England, William the Conqueror advanced the status of the law by proclaiming that "no one shall be killed or hanged for any misdeeds, but rather that his eyes be plucked out, and his hands, feet, and testicles cut off." [9]

The Berenguers of Barcelona and their relatives who ruled in Aragon had a vision that included freedom for various groups. This vision meant that traders, physicians, administrators, philosophers, and even independent militia flocked to Catalonia and made it the most successful and powerful country in the Mediterranean.

One other influential person put forth a vision for the age. The pope first demonstrated his power by interfering with the religious rites used in various Spanish churches. He successfully lobbied for the country of Castile to dispense with the old rite of the Castile Catholic Church and replace it with the liturgy of Rome.

1095 CE

Pope Urban II presented a concept to rival the view of Yusuf. While Yusuf relied on the Berbers, the pope proposed to use the Franks in order to initiate an age of crusade. If the pope could harness the military prowess of those German warriors, much could be gained for Rome.

After centuries of attempts, Muslim armies finally stood at the very gate of Constantinople, and so the Byzantine Emperor Alexis implored pope Urban II to rouse leaders from Europe to send troops to help hold back their advance. This made sense to both Urban and Europe. If he helped to defeat Muslims in Constantinople, the battles would take place far from home and he could gain the status of hero. If, on the other hand, Muslims conquered Constantinople, they could next attack Rome. The memories of Germans sacking Rome were still raw.

The pope knew that Italian cities such as Pisa, Genoa, Venice, and Amalfi wanted to end Muslim ascendancy in the eastern Mediterranean in order to open markets for their trade. With the pope as negotiator for a war that brought significant business to Italian cities, those cities would willingly provide funds for disposing of Islam.

If Urban could channel the in-fighting of feudal barons toward a successful campaign against Islam, his power would excel anything in the world. In a potential reversal of centuries-old tradition, he could even bring the eastern Church under papal rule. Then, with Christendom united under papal authority, Rome would rise again as undisputed capital of the world.

He sounded out leaders. Urban, who was French, gathered a vast crowd in open fields at At Clermont in Auvergne. At Clermont, the old city of the Roman noble Sidonius in France, in the area where Sidonius had heard pledges to restore the glory of Rome, Pope Urban II stirred the crowd.

"Oh race of Franks, race from across the mountains, race chosen and beloved by God – as shines forth in very many of your works – set apart from all nations by the situation of your county, as well as by your Catholic faith and the honor of the Holy church! To you our discourse is addressed and for you our exhortation is intended. We wish you to know what a grievous cause

has led us to your country, what peril threatens you and what all the faithful throng can do.

"From the confines of Jerusalem and the city of Constantinople a horrible tale has gone forth and very frequently has been brought to our ears. Namely, that a race from the kingdom of the Persians, an accursed race, a race utterly alienated from God, a generation forsooth which has not directed its heart and has not entrusted its spirit to G-d, has invaded the lands of those Christians. It has depopulated them by the sword, pillage and fire. It has led away a part of the captives into its own country, and a part it has destroyed by cruel tortures. It has either entirely destroyed the churches of God or appropriated them for the rites of its own religion. They destroy the altars, after having defiled them with their uncleanness. They circumcise the Christians, and the blood of the circumcision they either spread upon the altars or pour into the vases of the baptismal font.

"When they wish to torture people by a base death, they perforate their navels, and dragging forth the extremity of the intestines, bind it to a stake. Then with flogging, they lead the victim around until the viscera flushes forth and the victim falls prostrate upon the ground. Others they bind to a post and pierce with arrows. Others they compel to extend their necks and then, attacking them with naked swords, attempt to cut through the neck with a single blow. What shall I say of the abominable rape of women? To speak of it is worse than to be silent....

"Jerusalem is the navel of the world. The land is fruitful above others, like another paradise of delights. This the Redeemer of the human race has made illustrious by His advent. He has beautified by residence, has consecrated by suffering, has redeemed by death, has glorified by burial. This royal city, therefore, situated at the center of the world, is now held captive by His enemies, and is in subjection to those who do not know God, to the worship of the heathens. She seeks therefore and desires to be liberated and does not cease to implore you to come to her aid. From you especially she asks succor, because, as we have already said, God has conferred upon you above all nations great glory in arms. Accordingly undertake this journey for the remission of your sins, with the assurance of the imperishable glory of the Kingdom of Heaven." [10]

"G-d wills it!" shouted the crowd.

Pope Urban started the crusades against Muslims, and other Crusades followed, even pitting Catholic against Catholic.

1100 CE

South of the Pyrenees Mountains, events unfolded differently. Count Ramon Berenguer III the Great inherited the mantle of Barcelona and Catalonia. He continued the refinement of rule by law and equality under the law embedded in the Usatges. He did this to the consternation of the Muslims to the south, whom he dominated and who paid him tribute. In doing this he ignored the wishes of the pope, who wanted tribute for himself, but did not possess the strength to oppose the count. The Berenguers represented the truly rising power in Europe.

The Usatges, reformulated under the direction of many Berenguer generations, placed certain emphases:

To protect the nobility:
—*Thus whoever kills, wounds, or dishonors a viscount in any way, let him make compensation...*
—*If anyone sets an ambush, premeditatedly assaults a knight, beats him with a club, and pulls his hair, let him make compensation...*

To provide equal protection:
— *Moreover, let townsmen and burghers litigate among themselves, be judged, and compensated as knights are...*
— *Let Jews who are beaten, wounded, captured, incapacitated, and even killed be compensated according to the ruler's will.*
— *If a bailiff who is a noble eats wheat bread daily, and rides a horse, is killed, incapacitated, beaten, or held captive, let him be compensated as a knight.*
— *Let the murder of a peasant or any other man who holds no rank besides being a Christian be compensated by six ounces...*
— *Let every woman be compensated according to the rank of her husband...*
— *If a lord wishes to unjustly oppress his knight or take away his fief, the ruler then must defend and come to the aid of the knight.*
— *And if the ruler publicly accuses one, he must put himself in his custody and make restitution according to the court, or clear himself by oath and judicial battle with one of similar rank, bearing the loss and gain incurred. We say loss and gain so he shall receive as much if he wins as he shall lose if he is defeated.*
— *This must be done in the same way between magnates and their knights.*

To protect trade:
— *Indeed, let all ships coming to and then returning from Barcelona day and night be under the peace and truce and protection of the prince...*
— *Roads and thoroughfares on land and sea are the ruler's and, for their protection, must be included in the peace...*
— *A person who has posted a guaranty must carry out the obligation, or the courts will compel him to do so.*

Freedom from discrimination:
— *An evil prince who is without both truth and justice ruins a land and its inhabitants for all time. Therefore we, the oft-mentioned princes Ramon Berenguer and Almodis, with the counsel and aid of our nobles, decree and command that all princes who will succeed us in this princely office shall have a sincere and perfect faith. They shall demonstrate truthful speech for all men. The noble and ignoble, kings and princes, magnates and knights, peasants and rustics, traders and merchants, pilgrims and wayfarers, friends and enemies, Christians and Saracens, Jews and heretics should trust and believe in the princes without any fear or evil suspicion. Individuals, their cities and castles, fiefs and property, wives and children shall remain safe...*
— *Indeed, the aforesaid princes also decreed that if a dispute occurs or a*

lawsuit arises between Christians and Jews, two witnesses from both parties shall prove their cases...

To protect the prince:
— Indeed if the prince should be besieged, holds his enemies under siege, or hears that a certain king or prince is coming against him to wage war, he must warn his land by both letters and messengers or by the usual customs. Then all men, knights and footmen alike must come to his aid.

For private property:
— Princes, magnates, and knights can likewise give their fiefs to whomever they wish...

For widows:
— If a widow lives honorably and chastely after the death of her husband in his fief, raising children well, let her possess her husband's estate...[11]

The Usatges predated the Magna Carta by almost two centuries and provided a more complete declaration of human rights. Also, the predecessor of the Usatges, the first Visigothic Code, limited a monarch's rights almost a millennium before the Magna Carta. The Usatges were used until 1716, with amendments, at which time the use of the Catalan language itself met with political difficulties, and French Bourbon conquerors attempted to reign in the area.

The Berenguers and other rulers took the Usatges most seriously, as evidenced by the oath of allegiance from citizens to Catalonian monarchs:

"*We, who are as good as you, swear to you, who are no better than us, to accept you as our king and sovereign lord, provided you observe all our liberties and laws but if not, not.*" [12]

The Usatges insured that those who did not wish to live under the harsh repression of the fundamentalist Muslims to the south or the aggressive Roman doctrine embedded in Catholic laws to the north found a home in Catalonia or its sister state Aragon.

King Alfonso of Aragon wrote in his *Cantinas* that God is

"The one who can pardon
Christian and Jew and Moor,
While they fix their intent
With all firmness on God." [13]

With their proclamations, the rulers of Barcelona, Aragon, and Castile welcomed an age of *Convivencia*. The combination of *Convivencia* and a strong national defense surely would lead to renaissance in Catalonia.

Ramon Berenguer III did not rely on the law alone to keep Catalonia strong and healthy. He needed soldiers, for avaricious neighbors did not hesitate to plunder weakly defended prizes. To the south, a vast Muslim empire ruled by fierce and aggressive fundamentalist warriors looked to expand their lands. France to the north did not foreswear its centuries' old desire to possess Catalonian territory. To the west, military regimes in Navarre and Castile did not need many excuses to attack and occupy weaker rivals. Finally, the Mediterranean to the east invited peaceful maritime commerce, but also invasion by covetous powers.

Ramon looked for a means to combine military prowess with his concept of freedom and law.

In the twelfth century world, the two great military forces consisted of fundamentalist Muslims ensconced in their North African– Spanish empire, plus the pope's army of zealous Crusaders. Religious warriors overshadowed the old concepts of Roman legions, tribal hordes, and even armies of kings.

1127 CE

In the wake of the Crusader victories in the Middle East, a new form of military order emerged: the monastic order of knights. One such order, the Templars, volunteered to protect pilgrims from Arab marauders during their journey from ports like Jaffa on the Mediterranean to Jerusalem. Along the way, attacks from Muslim bandits resulted in death and robbery. Another group, the Hospitellers, offered medical aid.

The Templars and Hospitellers received only difficult tasks and little support when they spread out into Europe seeking contributions in 1127. In Catalonia, in Castile, and in Portugal, the Templars came into the beginnings of their vast influence and fortune.

Ramon Berenguer, the Great, Count of Barcelona and thus head of Catalonia knew all too well that his neighbors on all sides desired his territory. He could not fend off a concerted Muslim attack any more than he could resist the pope's army, should he come up against it. And so Berenguer enacted the most brilliant yet obvious of all solutions.

Berenguer hired the Templars to wage battle against the Muslims, conquer their land, and add it to Catalonia. Though an old man near the end of his life, Berenguer himself joined the order.

He saw that the Templars could provide the muscle to make Catalonia strong. Used in conjunction with the forces of his nobles, Ramon could secure the borders of Catalonia against intrusion. Ramon signed a charter granting the Order of Knights Templar the castle of Granena on the Muslim frontier.

Ramon's daughter Berengaria, Queen of Aragon, and his son-in-law Alfonso, King of Aragon, mirrored his efforts. They invited the Templars to establish themselves in Aragon at great profit by allowing them to keep booty captured from the Moors.[14] This set off a trend. Military fraternities proliferated in Spain and Palestine to provide troops for continuous war against Islam.

Thus strengthened, the countries of northern Spain not only battled the Muslims to the south, but also each other, and also the lands north of the Pyrenees. Alfonso probed into Aquitaine with his ally, the Count of Toulouse. This took place in the middle of a free-for-all casting for land that involved Castile, Portugal, Galicia, Aquitaine, and neighboring states.[15]

The gifts of land, castles, and exemption from taxes combined with plundering raids that benefited both the Templars and the kings. Wealth flowed to the Templar coffers. The Templars duplicated this formula in Palestine and Lebanon, acquiring castles and subjects in exchange for contract war.

In helping to capture land, the Templars won lordship over a fifth of the individual cities of Tortosa, Lerida, Asco, and Ribarroj; land along the Ebro river, and the castles or estates of Miravet, Mequinenza, Flix, Asco, Garcia, Mora de Ebro, Tivisa, Marsa Oropesa, Chivert, Montornes, Horta, Encinacorba, Alfambra, Camanas, Malvecino, and Perales.

The Templars enhanced their income by acquiring churches, and gaining revenue from church lands by lending money to bishops. They owned entire shopping districts in many towns. Bickering did occur with some of these arrangements. When the bishop of Zaragossa leased the Church of Novillas to the Templars for only twelve pence annually, his successor renegotiated the deal for a generous increase. The Templars still could operate the religious property at a profit.

In order to till fields and maintain property, the Templars owned enormous numbers of slaves.[16] The Templars became rich. They needed help in management. In a society committed to *Convivencia*, different groups discover ways to benefit each other. The Templars could loose their franchises with poor management. Like the Templars, nobles, monarchs, bishops and archbishops requested Jewish assistance in coordinating and evaluating their estates.

Templars and Jews came together early in the cities of Zaragossa and Lerida. The Templars received grants of control in portions of those municipalities, and turned to Jews for their political, fiscal, and land management needs.[17]

In Zaragossa, the Knights Templar lent their protection to the family of Judah de la Cavalleria. The family in turn administered a tax system for the knights to enjoy income from their many properties and many lands where they received rights of tax collection. The family served nobility and Templars for many generations, some giving into conversion.[18]

These associations led to great changes in the Templars, as they learned the trade of money lending, which, once tried in Spain, spread to the rest of the Templar world. Templars began to lend money to all parties, but especially to Jews, clerics, and nobility, right on up to kings.

"In Aragon, as elsewhere, Templar houses served as places of deposit, and they were frequently used for this purpose by all classes of men. At Berdeny there was even a special house of deposits. Anything could be deposited, including Moorish prisoners or a mule, left while its owner was abroad... Gerald of Cabrera and son had gold, silver, horses, and corn in safekeeping at Bardeny. Most deposits, however, fell into one of three classes; jewelry, documents, or money."[19]

Thus Catalonia and Aragon provided the will and intellect to formulate military might by using resident forces coupled with knightly orders. These countries added the freedom of laws to attract the creative and economically oriented.

With the introduction of a theocratic state by the Muslim fundamentalists in southern Spain, writers, business-people and administrators who met with scorn and oppression escaped to Catalonia and Aragon. The golden age of Moorish Spain ended. The pope's strong influence in northern France created a similar situation, with people leaving bound for Catalonia.

The cultural life of Granada died for all residents: Muslim, Christian and Jew. Rabbi Moses ibn Ezra, courtier and poet laureate, wept.

"I grieved not for the wealth that was plundered. I cared not that it had vanished and gone. I lamented not opulence come to an end. I felt not ill over servants deserting... I can only scoff at the works of fate and laugh at its pranks. Throughout my life I

have known success. My wealth took flight like a soaring eagle, all the toil of my hands took wing, and God's mighty hand thereby became manifest.

"But the tears flow from my eyes as I seek to overcome my grief over my loneliness in my native land, without a companion at my side. I am like a stranger sojourning therein, and I see no man about me of my family and kin.

"I remain in Granada, a city of declining bustle and splendor, like a stranger in the land, like a sparrow strayed from its nest, like a bird banished and driven. Amongst this generation, wayward and corrupt, there is no refuge for me. There remains no one to remember me and inquire after my welfare."[20]

Moses ibn Ezra, together with Judah Halevi, Judah ibn Ezra, and Johanan ibn Daud fled Granada. This august group found solace in the city of Toledo, Castile. They accepted invitations and protection from the family of Joseph Ferrizuel Cidellus, physician and minister for Alfonso VI of Castile.[21]

The Catholic kings of Spain, especially Castile, appointed these learned Jews as ministers, counselors, and *major-domos*. Every king had his alfaquim, Jewish courtier, literary scribe, and personal emissary of the king.[22]

Urban life in Barcelona flourished and inspired all the Mediterranean as Cordoba and Alexandria had in earlier times. Intellect, economy, and religion of great diversity took hold. Jews minted coins for the counts, operated vineyards, smithies, and cloth houses. Kings and queens especially sought them out to administer property and medicine.[23]

Simultaneously, a situation of *Reconquista* existed between the states of Aragon and Castile against their Muslim neighbors while a sense of *Convivencia* emerged with Aragon and Castile that granted rights to Jews, Christians, Catholics, and even Muslims within the boundaries of the respective countries.

Because the fundamentalists who gained control of the Muslim part of Spain created an atmosphere of extreme repression that exceeded even the efforts of France, an exodus of Andalusia's creative and economic people accelerated.

Alfonso VI, King of Castile, regained control of the city of Toledo, preserved the Jewish quarter, and put its inhabitants in the service of the monarchy. He employed members of that community like Joseph Cidellus and his nephew Solomon as physicians, diplomatic ambassadors, associates in defeating the Muslims, and trusted representatives to collect tribute from decaying Muslim regimes.

In Aragon, Sheshet ben Shlomo served as bailiff, and in Catalonia, Abraham bar Hiyya attained the rank of steward of Count Ramon Berenguer III's possessions.

So the Jewish community, once sheltered by Islam, became victim to Islamic excesses. They scattered and affiliated with their Catholic conquerors.

When the next King of Castile, Alfonso VII, made his solemn entry into Toledo in 1139,

"All the populace had heard that the Emperor was coming to Toledo. The high officials of the Christians, the Saracens, the Jews, and all the people of the city went out to meet him. They demonstrated with tambourines, zithers, other instruments and a

multitude of musicians. Each one of them praised and glorified
God in his own tongue for having so greatly favored all the deeds
of the emperor. And they all said: 'Blessed be he who comes in
the name of the Lord.'"[24]

Smaller Spanish states like Galicia and Navarre mimicked France. The nobles of that area perhaps did not notice the successes of Castile and Catalonia, for their princes and kings could not even read.[25]

The next Berenguer of Catalonia, Ramon IV, united the states of Barcelona and Aragon. He continued the efforts of his father by enforcing the Usatges, granting castles to Templars. When the count needed co-signers for a large loan from a wealthy Catholic, many volunteered, including several clergy, four knights, the count's Jewish doctor Abraham and his Jewish minister Shealtiel, son of his father's bailiff Sheshet.[26]

"Spanish society broke up into three different hierarchies,
each independent of the others, and therein lies a major expla-
nation for the absence of a feudal society. ... In the twelfth and
thirteenth centuries Moors and Jews held castles in fief from the
king."[27]

"The Hispano-Christian, with no other horizon than his be-
liefs, could not organize within the Christian community the
whole of his system of values. He had to accept as inescapable
realities various kinds of Muslim and Jewish superiority. Thus,
the daughter of James II of Aragon, married to the highest lord
of Castile, brought up her children under the tutelage of Jews."

In the Mediterranean area on both sides of the Pyrenees, the old Jewish enclave expanded its population to include more and more French and Spanish Catholics. Provence, the old home of the Roman Seventh Legion, looked more and more like Catalonia, the emerging state.

Another trend took place in Catalonia. Unlike its neighbors, the counts of Catalonia at this time did not aspire to the designation of king. Their neighbors, with chaos in France, and the reduction of military threat from the Muslim south felt differently. Eastern neighbors in Provence and Burgundy repudiated Carolingian rule. To the west, nobles of Leon, Navarre, and others rushed to crown themselves.

Cordoba, home of European culture for centuries into the twelfth century had inspired learning, medicine, literature, poetry, and science throughout all of Europe. But in 1148, it inspired nothing but fear. In that year the last dynasty of tolerant Islamic rulers fell to the radicals from North Africa. Churches and synagogues met the torch. Citizens could either convert to Islam, emigrate, or meet their death.

Unlike many who moved to Catalonia or Castile, the family of Moses Maimonides fled from persecution through Morocco to Israel, where, for the first time, he encountered a Catholic culture. By the beginning of the twelfth century, adverse situations in France and Spain led to the eastward migration of many Jews to Egypt, Palestine, and other eastern nations.[28]

The constant display of holy statues used by Catholics shocked Maimonides, as this practice leaned more to the worship of idols than he had ever experienced under the Spanish Muslim influence. The decimation of the land and the dangers extant for non-Catholics due to Crusaders drove him to a more tolerant land, that of Egypt and Alexandria[29]

Saladin, the Muslim Caliph of Egypt, opened his gates to the creative almost as much as the Berenguers of Catalonia. As a result, Maimonides departed from southern Spain and took up residence in Alexandria. Maimonides changed many basic concepts of Christians, Jews, and Muslims alike. Others of great learning joined Maimonides in North Africa.

In Alexandria, with a quietude not previously experienced, the world began to learn of the genius of Maimonides. This first came by way of commentaries on the Talmud, and took centuries to radiate through other religions and philosophies. Maimonides pointed out that many harbored a wrong conception of the life to come. Virtually the entire religious belief of the time pictured heaven as a place where the rivers ran with wine, where people ate and drank free from toil and occupied beautiful homes, and where the righteous lived with families and loved ones in bliss.

These credulous people saw hell as a place riddled with the burning bodies of the wicked. Maimonides instructed his audience not to take the sages too literally and not to abide by incorrect teachings. He did this not by lecture, but by careful deductions from scripture, the method of exegesis. He added the equally important concept that God is not corporeal, a striking diversion from popular teaching of the day. Then Maimonides instructed his flock that spiritual and psychological illness paralleled physical illness. A person suffering from either affliction needed the care of someone trained in guiding sick bodies or souls.

After reconciling much of Greek philosophy with Jewish practice, he demolished the pseudoscience of astrology.[30]

"As regards the logic for all these calculations, we know why we have to add a particular figure or deduct it, how all these rules originated, and how they were discovered and proved. All this is part of the sciences of astronomy and mathematics, about which many books had been composed by Greek sages... and had been composed by the Sages of Israel, of the tribe of Issachar, who lived in the time of the Prophets." [31]

One could say that Maimonides studied rationalism. In a world of religious distrust, he stated that the virtuous Muslim, Christian, and Jew alike could share in the world to come.[32] So, in the collected works of one individual, religion entered the realm of modern faith more than half a millennium early. His influence on philosophy and medicine also made significant marks. With his fame ever growing, Maimonides married into a family that served the administration of Egypt's caliph, Saladin. He gave medical care to the vizier of Egypt and entered the service of Saladin.

For several hundred years, the Egyptian caliphs relied heavily on their Jewish subjects as advisors and contributing citizens starting early in the tenth century, when Paltiel rose to the rank of chief vizier to the caliph.[33]

While Maimonides advanced theology, Saladin competed with Charlemagne as the greatest military commander and statesman of the medieval age. Saladin paid strict attention to the pope and to Jerusalem. The pope could not hold Jerusalem. He could not hold Jerusalem because Saladin, Caliph of Egypt, decided to liberate that great city. He did it with masterful military precision.

The infamous "Fourth" Crusade made this all too clear as the Catholic armies, in concert with Venetian merchants, aimed not at Muslim Jerusalem, but Catholic Constantinople. In a stunning military and financial success, Catholic crusaders murdered Catholic civilians in the streets of Constantinople, looted countless churches, public buildings and private residences, and established a short-lived Latin Empire of Constantinople.

Several Italian cities that financed the Crusades benefitted greatly from the pillage of their sister Christian city. Florence finally had enough gold to mint florins.

The end of the Fourth Crusade and the exposed corruption of the entire history of the enterprise. However, it opened European ears high and low to talk of Aristotle the forbidden Greek and the rationalism of Averroes the forbidden Jew. Why did G-d allow the defeat of His defenders and grant military success to Muslims and financial success to the Venetians, who shunned the pope?

1200 CE

The Berenguers of Barcelona played games, with clever alliances, strategic marriages, use of the Templars, and military campaigns.

The king of France shivered in Paris. His empire consisted of little more than the capital city and its immediate environs. The Viking king of Normandy and England, and also the king of Aquitaine, towered over him with the French lands in their domains. The south of France ignored the north and obeyed only a group of nobles, counts, and kings. They even spoke an entirely different language, Catalan, and considered themselves part of Catalonia. The leaders of Toulouse, Aquitaine, Provence, and the Spanish March, as well as other lords, carved out petty fiefs. The magnates loved it that way - all the more power to themselves.

In northern France a Catholic population, with a light sprinkling of Jews, heretic Christians, and pagans prevailed. To the south, the majority practiced a different form of Christianity and called themselves Albigensians.

The residents of the south perhaps did not understand the danger that accompanied activities not in keeping with the dictatorial powers of the pope. Others gave newfound respect to Rome. Constantinople, that imperial city of Catholic power had succumbed to pillaging by crusaders, as the holy knights found more profits in attacking Christians than Muslims.

The depravations of the Crusades further degenerated in the unfolding of the Children's Crusade, when thousands of children paraded onto ships that promptly delivered them to the slave markets of Africa rather than the battlefields of Jerusalem.

In a display of the pope's power, King Henry II of England, excommunicated for the murder of Thomas Becket, received the pope's pardon only after a public apology and act of humiliation. France found itself under papal interdiction in 1200 as a result of King Philip II's illegal divorce. The pope intervened in the election of the Holy Roman Emperor, and caused King John of England to beg for the return of his crown when the king dared to appoint an archbishop not to the pope's liking.[34]

During this time the English drafted the Magna Carta, given much exposure in later history, but extremely crude compared with the centuries earlier Usatges or the even earlier Visigoth Code in its original form.

The picture in southern France, Catalonia, Aragon, Portugal and Castile differed. Businesses could operate with safety, and the religious, either Muslim or Catholic, could enjoy a measure of tolerance.

Jews enjoyed exceptional freedom, and made wide-ranging use of it, endowing universities, practicing professions, owning land, and writing poetry. Jewish doctors and savants received the utmost respect from the general populace throughout the cities of the area, administering Hebrew schools and offering free lectures that Catholics frequented.

Every sort of craft and art flourished in the Languedoc area of southern France. This section enjoyed independence from the Parisian king. The larger cities boasted schools of medicine, philosophy, mathematics, astronomy, and astrology. Toulouse, Narbonne, Avignon, Montpellier and Beziers developed into university cities. The course on Aristotle in Toulouse embodied various recent commentaries made by Arab philosophers. Students from France came south to learn what northern authorities prohibited.

The whole south wrote poetry, from the nobles down. Trading communities avoided the strictures of Roman totalitarianism and cautiously brought in new ideas from other sources. Leonardo of Pisa in his *Liber Abaci*, asserted the superiority of Arabic numerals over Roman.

The Catholic clergy, shepherding a flock of the minority, did not mind it, as they spent time tending to their private affairs, enlarging their properties, and maintaining earthly ties, though not to the extent of their co-religionists to the North.

Provence enjoyed its heritage and recoiled from French aspirations of domination. Hence, association with Barcelona gave them a degree of protection. However, the signigicant Albigensian population in Provence, or Languedoc, believed in Christ, but not in his divinity and certainly not in the authority of the Catholic Church, beliefs entirely consistent with Arian heritage. This posed a danger for Provence as the Roman clergy united with the French. They took aim at the Albigensians, condemning them at first with degrees and delegations. The Albigensians complained of priestly abuses.

Around Albi, near Toulouse, the center of the religious group lived. Among them, the "Cathari," or purified ones, broke their ties to perceived evil, material things. Hence the group centered in Albi called themselves Albigensians, and others called them Cathars. Albigensians denied that God ever existed in human form, and many of them extended that belief to contempt for the vanities and material side of the world. This of orthodoxy had existed in the very early pre-Christian and Christian communities.

Cathar ritual included recitations of the Lord's Prayer, the laying on of hands, and the exchange of the kiss of peace. At a regular meeting, the faithful simply said the Lord's Prayer, made a general confession of their sins, asked forgiveness, and ended with a common meal. These services extended the familial atmosphere of the very first Christian congregations.

Christian sects that adhered to their own doctrine and rejected Catholic interpretations proliferated in the southern climes. These included Arians who settled in Languedoc and Spain; Pricillian followers, who spread out through Spain, Aquitaine, and Languedoc; Coptics; and Nestorians. Only the Cathars, however, still eluded the brunt of Roman repression and elimination. Home-grown in Languedoc, the Cathars, or Albigensians traced their practices and traditions back to simple Christian rites of the first century. They fit in with Arian rulers, but dictators in Rome wished them eliminated..

The Romans of the Catholic Church labeled the Albigensians heretical because they believed, praising Jesus was not enough. "Enough" meant paying taxes to Rome, giving patronage to Rome, and following the Roman details of ritual and dogma.

The popular rumor that a brother of Jesus and other members of his congregation had fled to Languedoc to avoid capture from Roman legions fanned the flames of religious independence in Languedoc. They did not need to follow the upstart and presumptuous Rome.

Ramon Berenguer VI, Count of Toulouse, cousin to the king of France and to the king of Aragon and Catalonia, served as figurehead and ruler from most of Languedoc. He belonged to a noted and influential family with Jewish, Catholic, and Cathar heritage, which put him in a powerful position to lead the whole ramshackle, independent conglomeration of poets, universities, scholars, businesses, jobs, exports, freethinking, tolerance, and scattered authority. The man refused to condemn the endemic "heresy," and, indeed, hosted a court reminiscent of Louis the Pious, since it featured a cosmopolitan mixture of Jews, Catholics, and Cathars.

The leader of Beziers, a city near Toulouse, and chief advisor to Ramon, Simon the Jew, assumed the reigns of government when Count Ramon traveled. In Narbonne, ancient landholdings held since Isaac had served Pepin and Charlemagne still served Jews well, supporting a famous Talmudic university and several synagogues.

Open-air debates between Cathars and Catholics attracted thousands. Arguments regarding the right of women to serve in professions and as clerics came to the surface as Catholics told the women Cathars to "go back to your spinning."

The papal legate, ambassador, and envoy plenipotentiary, planned to put a stop to freedom of thought at any cost. His initial action resulted in a league of southern barons, joined for the purpose to hunt down heretic Cathars. Ramon VI was refused admission to this august group. The legate then incited the lords to rebel against Ramon, excommunicated the count, and forwarded the papers for confirmation by the pope. The legate moved on to various parts of Ramon's realm to denounce any deviation from the doctrine of Rome. Careers opened right in the center of Europe for persons talented in forcing the masses to change religion or suffer confiscation of property and torture[35]

"In the cool haze of a Provencal dawn, Monday, January 14, 1208, the legate prepared to cross the Rhone River at the great divide before the river enters the Mediterranean. The legate made slow progress astride his mule, as the sound of galloping hoofs came from behind. From out of the mist, a military lance sailed through the still air and entered the rib-cage of the man. The force of the projectile caused his arms to fly up and his body to lunge forward, catapulted through the air like a doll. It landed with a dead man's thump on the ground. The hoof beats continued their drumming until all sight and sound of the horse and assassin melted into the fog."[36]

Pope Innocent III, a charismatic and wealthy Roman baron, insisted on the rights of Romans to rule the world without limits. He came from a family that represented inherited power. His family boasted a number of popes and cardinals. Pope Innocent III dressed and acted like Emperor Constantine, wearing garments shining with gold and jewels, riding a scarlet covered horse, and accepting kisses on his feet from supplicants.

He declared the Vatican a state. Then, in an historic twist of reason, he concluded that if the Vatican existed as a state, and heresy involved defamation of the Vatican and Church, then heresy also was a crime against the state. Innocent would guide the papacy to the greatest of its temporal powers and the lowest of its moral example.[37]

He wrote to Ramon a most abusive letter.

Innocent promised that which the Church should not: a gift of property and not spirit, a present of land not the Church's to give. This was the deal:
-The property of heretics would be turned over to persecutors.
-The property of Catholics not helping would also be subject to seizure.
-The King of France could own land as far away as the Mediterranean.
-A Crusade against Christians began.
-Monks traveled north to solicit knights.
-The pope granted full remission of sins to Crusaders.
-Monks hired mercenaries.
-Child scavengers (there were plenty up north) could join.
-A moratorium on Crusader debts began.
-Money for Crusaders flowed from the Church.[38]

Everything came at a price, and all was strictly business: forgiveness of sin in exchange for breaking those of the wrong religion, teaching a lesson to those who refused to pay for protection from the powerful church. This initiated another Crusade featuring Catholics versus other Christians. The papacy had tasted the victory over Catholic Constantinople and wanted more. Other Crusades with Catholics pitted against Catholics would follow.

An army of 5,000 mounted warriors between and 10,000 and 15,000 squires, crossbowmen, priests, kitchen boys, mercenaries, prostitutes, monks, thieves, and child scavengers descended on Languedoc. They camped outside the city of Beziers. The residents inside refused the demand to hand over heretics. Troubadours criticized the Church for offering equal indulgences for a crusade against the Albigensians in France. The faithful wondered about offering the same reward for Christian blood as for that of infidels.

In an act of cowardice and stupidity, Ramon VI joined with the crusaders and feigned allegiance rather than rallying his neighbors and defeating the crusaders once and for all. He would regret that decision later. Thousands of frenzied servant boys from the crusader's army, with not a pair of shoes in the lot of them leaped defensive ditches, ignored injuries, scrambled over ramparts, and with blood lust in their veins, smashed in the city gates.

Surging knights behind the boys asked the pope's main representative monk, how to tell who was a heretic?"

"Kill them all, God will know his own!" shouted the monk.[39]

The boys swarmed the city, clubs and blunt instruments in hand, while the knights stood back. They beat and killed their way threading through the narrow streets, meeting healthy and feeble, children and adults. All died. The northern French knights rode in with swords and lances flashing. The papal legate could tell the pope "that our men spared no one, irrespective of rank, sex, or age, and put to the sword almost 20,000 Catholics, Jews, and Cathars. Divine vengeance raged miraculously."

A scramble for treasure ensued, the boys grabbing what they could. The knights turned on the boys. To share in killing is one thing, but to share loot, quite another. The crusading nobility drove out the urchins like so many stray dogs.

But the youths did not cooperate. "Let it burn," they shouted.

And so it did: houses, churches, taverns, trading stations, and all that treasure. But the valley held other cities, with Carcassonne the next to go. Other towns and villages followed the way of the sword. The Crusaders chained many a Cathar to a stake and lit him up.

As a count from Ile-de-France hacked his way through the valley, four hundred people from one village came into his custody. He burnt them all in a great meadow, and started hanging their knights until the gallows fell over. The count earned himself the lands of Carcassonne and Beziers.

But still another nobleman claimed suzerainty over large portions of Languedoc. The Catholic King Pere II of Aragon and Catalonia,[40] fresh from spectacular victories over Muslims in Spain, received bleak reports regarding the mayhem in his provinces north of the Pyrenees. King Pere of Aragon played by different rules, and fiercely defended tolerance and *Convivencia*. Refugees from the mayhem in Languedoc rushed to his protection.

1213 CE

Pere, King of Aragon, covered with the glory of victories in Spain, interceded on behalf of his bother-in-law Count Ramon of Toulouse. The king sent messages to the pope that the repression in Languedoc had gone too far:

> *"Not content with taking up arms against the heretics, you also have fought under the banner of the Crusade, against Catholic peoples. You have spilt innocent blood, and have invaded, to their detriment, the domains of the Count of Foix and those of the Count of Comminges and of Gaston de Bearn, (my) vassals, though the population of these said domains was in no way suspect of heresy..."*

The pope officially attempted to restrain his French military, but wrote back to the King of Aragon, "Would God that your wisdom and piety had grown in proportion to your renown! You have acted ill, both towards us and yourself."

The pope's legates thereupon threatened to excommunicate the Catholic King Pere, hero of the Muslim wars. The pope warned the king not to meddle, "Such are the orders which your Serene Highness is invited to obey, in every last detail. Failing which…we should be obliged to threaten you with Divine Wrath, and to take steps against you such as would result in your suffering grave and irreparable harm."[41]

The king nevertheless gathered an army and decamped outside of Toulouse. As a faithful Catholic, he knew that his religion did not sanction papal abuses. The Spanish maneuvered for a glorious battle, to once and for all teach the French a lesson. The French, knowing that their only chance against a larger force lay in guile, allowed the Aragonese to spread out and initiate a charge led by the king himself. The French anticipated this rash act, and focused a small brigade to specifically target the king. The French plan worked to perfection.

King Pere met his death on the battlefield outside of Toulouse while attempting to bring some kind of justice to extreme oppression. Aragonese and Catalan forces, demoralized by the death of their king, fled the field, confusing their replacements, who had to skirt the battle in order to avoid the retreating panic. The French won the day.

That victory started a land rush, as second and third noble sons from

France packed their gear to claim land south in Languedoc. But Raymond VI found his courage and drove the French out of Languedoc. His forces killed the pope's general, Simon de Montfort who had attempted a dynasty ruling Toulouse and Carcassonne. Celebration erupted across the Languedoc,

"Montfort
Es mort
Es mort
Es mort!
Viva Tolosa
Ciotat gloriosa
Et poderosa!
Tornon lo paratge et l'onor!
Montfort
Es mort!
Es mort!
Es mort!"[42]

The victories only postponed action until the advent of the next generation, as clerical provocation and demand for military solutions set the stage for more invasions and property seizures.[43]

The warlord pope fumed. The Muslims regained Jerusalem. Jews still lived in Europe despite his rules to the contrary; the barons of Britain had dared challenge his autocracy with the Magna Carta so he anathematized them, and, worst of all, the people preferred the Cathars to the Catholics in Languedoc. And then Pope Innocent III died quite unexpectedly.

Another generation passed, but the next count of Toulouse, Ramon VII, produced no male heir. His daughter married the brother of the king of France. In a matter of time, France could obtain legal ownership of Languedoc.

The Albigensian Crusade escalated into the Albigensian Inquisition. Rome determined to impose its interpretation of the Trinity and its demand of absolute authority.

From the Capitula promulgated by the Council of Toulouse in 1229:

"In every parish, whether within or beyond the city limits, the bishops shall nominate a priest and two or three lay persons of unblemished reputation, who shall take an oath to search out, loyally and assiduously, such heretics as may be resident.

"The house in which a heretic is discovered shall be razed to the ground, and the land on which it stands confiscated.

"Those who return to unity with the Catholic Church through fear of death or for some other motive rather than of their own free will, shall be cast into prison by the bishop.

"All faithful Catholics of adult years shall swear an oath before their bishop to preserve the Catholic Faith and to persecute heretics according to their means.

"Lay persons are forbidden to possess the Books of the Old and the New Testament, with the exception of the Psalter, the Breviary, and the Book of Hours of the Blessed Virgin.[44]

On August 5, 1234, a wealthy old lady, Madame Borsier of Toulouse, said on her deathbed that she wanted to make a good end.

One member of the household dashed across town to the Dominican monastery, then ducked into its chapel. He made his way round the darkened ambulatory and knocked on the sacristy door.

William Pelhisson, a Dominican inquisitor whose memoir of Languedoc immediately after the end of the Albigensian Crusade gives a vivid glimpse of the altered circumstances of life in Toulouse, was most probably in the sacristy that day. With Pelhisson and his fellow friars was Raymond du Fauga, the bishop of Toulouse, also a Dominican. The bishop was changing out of the vestments in which he had just said Mass in honor of the newly canonized Saint Dominic.

Raymond, William, and the other friars in the sacristy listened to their visitor's tale: A Cathar believer, in the delirium of death throes, lay helpless in her bed just a few doors down from the cathedral. The bishop sent a servant out to fetch the prior of the Dominicans back from his midday meal. Bishop Raymond was always given to the grand gesture; his inaugural act on taking over from the deceased Fulk in 1232 had been to bully Ramon VII of Toulouse into hunting down and executing nineteen Cathar perfects on the Montagne Noire. There was a chance to put on a similarly instructive show for the populace of Toulouse.

According to Pelhisson, the traitorous servant led the bishop, the prior, and the other Dominicans into the woman's house. They climbed the narrow stairs and entered her room. Her relatives shrank back into the shadows on seeing the friars arrive. The dying woman's in-laws, the Borsier family, had long ago fallen under suspicion of heresy. One of them whispered a warning to the sickbed, to tell the dying woman that the Lord Bishop had arrived.

She apparently misunderstood, for she addressed Raymond du Fauga, the Catholic bishop, as if he were Builhabert of Castres, the Cathar perfect.

Since she was too feeble to move on her own, the woman was lashed to her bed. It was carried downstairs and into the street. Raymond led the curious procession past his cathedral and into a field beyond the city gates. A bonfire had been lit in expectation of their arrival. News of the spectacle spread throughout Toulouse. A large crowd assembled, then watched, openmouthed, as a barely conscious woman, with just hours left in her natural life, was thrown into the flames.

This done, the Dominican eyewitness noted, the bishop, together with the monks and their attendants, returned to the refectory and, after giving thanks to God and Saint Dominic, fell cheerfully upon the food set before them. The situation worsened from that point. The papacy of Gregory IX began in 1277 and marked a fevered new departure in the race to silence dissent. The notion of a permanent papal, as opposed to an episcopal, heresy tribunal or inquisition began to gain ground...

The papacy remained in the family of Roman aristocrats. Like his late uncle Innocent III who launched the crusade against the Albigensians, Gregory IX wanted results, and on a continent-wide scale. This papal family insisted on pursuing extraordinary powers of Roman intervention. Special papal legates were granted wide prosecutorial powers and sent out all over Europe to put down heresy. Some of the men chosen for these posts, unfortunately, soon proved themselves to be overzealous sociopaths, so many event like that persisted that an exasperated Franciscan friar killed one papal murderer.[45]

In Languedoc, the Albigensians remained strong to the great consternation of Pope Gregory. He staffed the episcopal palaces of the area with draconian predators, offered a cash bounty to those who informed on heretics, and shared any confiscated property with the informer.

An inquisitor must get people to talk in order to continue. He would bring in a citizen and begin questioning.

"Did you see a heretic or a Waldensian?"

A negative answer could end the inquisition if it was convincing. A positive answer obviously led to other inquiries:

"If so, then where and when, how often and with whom, and who were the others present?

"Did you listen to the preaching or exhortation of heretics?

"Did you give heretics lodging or arrange shelter for them?

"Did you lead heretics from place to place or otherwise consort with them or arrange for them to be guided or escorted

"Did you eat or drink with the heretics or eat bread blessed by them?

"Did you give or send anything to the heretics

"Did you act as the financial agent or messenger or assistant of the heretics?

"Did you hold any deposit or anything for a heretic?

"Did you receive the peace from a heretic's book, mouth, shoulder, or elbow?

"Did you adore a heretic or bow your head or genuflect and say 'Bless us' before the heretics?

"Did you participate in, or were you present at their consolamentum?"

"Did you ever confess to another inquisitor?

"Did you believe the heretics to be good men and good women, to have a good faith, to be truthful, to be the friends of God?

"Did you hear, or do you know, the errors of the heretics?

"Did you ever hide the truth?"[46]

A grateful Church elected one inquisitor as Pope Benedict XII.[47] We should really say that grateful Roman imperialists defied Church teachings in order to conduct the Inquisition.

Thanks to all the confiscated land, France suddenly leaped into the status of a world power, stretching from the English Channel to the Mediterranean Sea. The Albigensian loot propelled the king of France into great wealth and power. Since France had destroyed the means of creating wealth, the loot disappeared rapidly and the kingdom ran out of money.

With the Cathars out of the way, only Jews and scattered remnants of Visigoth and Greek communities stood apart, independent and free in France, England, Italy and Germany. The Romans took the idea to exclude them from trade, property, and banking. In the area of banking and lending, the Church lent a hand to its favorites, the Lombards, on whose behalf the Roman Curia would excommunicate anyone who failed to repay loans.[48]

The appeal of the Judeo-Christian heritage remained attractive. The people who believed in them allied with Catholic kings in order to catapult the country of Aragon-Catalonia into a Mediterranean renaissance.

CATHOLIC - JEWISH RENAISSANCE
WHAT FRIENDSHIP YIELDED

People prefer renaissance to oppression. That does not make renaissance inevitable. Renaissance requires all the uplifting attributes of humans including the will to defend, to educate, to tolerate, to believe, to share power, and to excel.

Catholic King Jaime I (pronounced *Hymie)* stood down to no one, including despotic popes and threatening Muslims. He doubled the size of his Aragon-Catalonia kingdom by seizing territory from Islamic forces. At a time when other European sovereigns bowed to the wishes of the pope, Jaime refused to use only Catholic monks as royal administrators and advisors. He employed better-qualified Jews[1] as bailiffs, ambassadors, and supreme advisor, or *alfaquim*. While Europe shivered with the deprivations of medieval abominations, Jaime I grasped the concept of *Convivencia* and used it to build the only medieval empire able to rival that of Charlemagne or the culture of Muslim Andalusia.

Jaime ruled as a Catholic monarch, King of Aragon and Catalonia; conqueror of Valencia, Majorca, and various Mediterranean islands.

He brokered no compromise with those who would upset the balance of his kingdom or attempt to set it on a theological footing rather than one of rationality and lawfulness. He therefore followed the Judeo-Christian focus rather than the Theodosian Code. Jaime put together his special *Convivencia*, which relied on knights, nobles, Jewish businesses and advisors, Templars, and all major religions.

Jaime had started his life with some strong impressions. His father King Pere had died fighting the French. The battle resulted from the Catalan attempt to stop the French Crusade against the Christian Albigensians, the Count of Toulouse, and other vassals and relatives of the king. Subsequently, the Knights Templar took the young lad into their protection and raised him.

With the influence of the Templars upon him, Jaime practiced the military arts and close Catholic/Jewish relations from an early age. He entered Aragon to claim his inheritance from those loyal and from those not so loyal.

"I was not more than nine years old at the time, and for the expected battle, a knight lent me a light coat of mail or hauberk, which I put on. That gave me a beginning with the first arms that I ever used. That very day I went to Berbegal without meeting any opposition on the road. The next day I entered Huesca. Then continued onward to Zaragossa and my first time in Aragon. The people rejoiced at my coming.

Council resolved, for I had not yet judgement enough to advise myself and others, to march against our enemies who imprisoned those loyal. After our war engines had battered the enemy castle for two consecutive days, the garrison surrendered."[2]

Catholic - Jewish Renaissance
1229 CE

With the influence of the Templars upon him, the young King Jaime was determined to capture land from Muslims, starting with the island kingdom of Mallorca.
"The fleet consisted of twenty-five full-sized ships, eighteen tartans, seventeen galleys, a hundred barges, and smaller craft.

"(With their city besieged) I proceeded to establish three watches, one for the engines and lines of attack, another for the Templars to watch the main gate, and another against the other gate.... I had, from merchants in the camp, sixty thousand libres to be repaid when the town was taken....

"When all were in motion, the knights and the men-at-arms approached the breach in the walls, and then all the army with one voice began to call, 'Saint Mary! Saint Mary!' ...When the armed horsemen had entered by the breach, the cry ceased, and by the time the passage was cleared for the horsemen there were fully five hundred footmen inside the city....

"When the knights with their armored horses got in, they at once charged the Saracens. So great was the multitude of the latter, that their lances stopped the horses. The animals reared up as they could not get through the thick ranks of the enemy. So knights had to turn their steeds. By so turning, more horsemen managed to enter the breach till there were forty or fifty of them... They attacked the Saracens and drove them back. When the Saracens of the town saw that the city was being conquered, thirty thousand of them, men and women, went out through two gates and took to the hills. So great were the goods and booty that the knights and the footmen found inside the city, that they took no heed of those who went away."[3]

"I ordered Don Berenguer and others to go in a galley and tell the people of Minorca that I was there with an army and I did not desire their death. They had seen and heard what befell those of Mallorca who would not submit....

"I then had credentials in Arabic drawn up by an alfaquim (Jewish scholarly advisor) of mine from Zaragossa, named Don Solomon, brother of Rabbi Babiel, bidding them give credence to my envoys and believe that they spoke for me."[4]

The reliance of Jaime on his *alfaquim* extended a long tradition. Before his *alfaquim* obtained the experience necessary to advise a monarch on matters of state, he had submitted to a medieval curriculum of advanced Jewish and secular studies. This would include the following, not available elsewhere in Europe:
"Reading and Writing. The method of instruction must be so arranged that the teacher will begin first with the script, in order that the children may learn their letters, and this is to be kept up until there is no longer any uncertainty among them...

"Torah, Mishnah, and Hebrew Grammar. Then he is to teach them the Pentateuch, Prophets, and Hagiographa, that is the Bible, with an eye to the vocalization and modulation in order that they may be able to pro-

125

nounce the accents correctly. Then he is to have them learn the Mishnah
until they have acquired a fluency in it. The children are then taught the
inflections, declensions, and conjugations, the regular verbs...
    Poetry. The teacher is to instruct his pupils in poetry. ..
    Talmud. Then say the wise, 'At fifteen the age is reached for
the study of Talmud' (Avot 5:21).....
    Philosophic Observations on Religion.
    Philosophic Studies. Mathematics, natural sciences, meta-
physics.
    Logic. Logic presents the rules which keep the mental powers
in order, and lead man on the path of clarity and truth in all things
wherein he may err.
    Mathematics & Arithmetic. Arithmetic and geometry.
    Optics.
    Astronomy. Mathematical astronomy and the movements of
the heavens. Astrology, however, is not a real science and is for-
bidden by God.
    Music. This includes how melodies are linked, and what con-
ditions make the influence of music pervasive and effective.
    Mechanics. The studies include consideration of heavy bodies
and the principles of instruments to raise, lower, or move them.
    Natural Sciences, Medicine. This portion of philosophic stud-
ies shows the art of keeping the human constitution in normal
condition and bringing back the sick to normalcy.
    Metaphysics. Here we study Aristotle and divide the science
into being, proofs, and the investigation of forces. "[5]
The exploits of Jaime I grew. As the man who drove Muslims out of
Mallorca, the fame of Jaime quickly spread throughout Europe. In addition
to his fame as a soldier, his handsome physique brought much admiration.
Taller than most men, muscular, with a ruddy complexion, glistening white
teeth, and golden hair, he commanded both respect and adoration.

1260 CE

    Jaime I started to look about for a wife for his son, the *Infante* Pedro.
He focused on the Princess Constanza of Sicily. Sicily could provide a key
base for Aragon ships that plied the Mediterranean in search of trade and
military targets. Aragonese ruled the sea at that time, but not without competition. In addition to the attractive nature of that island, Princess Constanza's parents had started to cast about for a husband for her.
    In Europe, the simple matter of arranging a marriage contract could
have the most far-reaching international consequences, especially when the
prospective bride and groom stood to inherit kingdoms. The pedigree of
Constanza passed the most stringent of tests. Her grandfather Emperor
Frederick II of Germany had married Constance, whom Jaime I knew as
his aunt, the sister of King Pere (Peter) II of Aragon.
    Europe of the thirteenth century mirrored Europe of the sixth century.
The same political situation and delicate balance prevailed. In Spain, tolerant monarchs sat on the throne in the persons of rulers like King Jaime I
and his wife Queen Violante of Aragon and Catalonia, whose policies
closely followed those in Castile and Portugal. The Spanish King had a
soul-mate on the other side of Europe, in this case Frederick II, King of

Germany, Italy, and Sicily and Holy Roman Emperor. In addition to their similar political views, the two kings were cousins-in-law. As tolerant rulers who permitted wide-ranging freedoms of trade, religion, and government service, these kings naturally earned the enmity of the Roman establishment, which then meant the papacy. The other factor in the equation centered about a French king allied with the papacy to promote terms of totalitarian ambitions i.e. King Louis IX. Feeling strong from its pillaging of the Albigensian lands, the Church continued it's alliance with France, and looked to Frederick of Germany, then conducted another nasty little European war. Popes Gregory IX and Innocent IV excommunicated Frederick and declared a crusade, this one with the Catholic king of France against the Catholic king of Germany. Frederick won that war. He instituted freedoms for all religions, allowed both scientific and artistic exploration, and broke down feudal institutions.

Like tolerant Catholic and Arian kings and counts of the past, including Arian Leo of Spain; Chilperic of Soissons; and French Raymon of Toulouse and many Carolingians, Jaime made numerous overtures to the Roman popes. Like his predecessors before him, Jaime and his family received excommunication and crusades against their countries in return. The papal war against Catholic King Frederick II served as precedent for Vatican wars against Catholic kings and marked the beginning of the use of crusades to punish Catholic monarchs who did not believe in the resurrection of imperial Rome and insisted on secular independence.

But in 1260 Aragon stood highest among the states of Europe. When Jaime conducted negotiations for the marriage of his son Pedro to Constanza of Sicily, Constanza's grandfather, Frederick II, the enlightened ruler of Germany, Sicily, and Italy had died. Constanza's father King Manfred ruled in Sicily and Naples, much to the chagrin of Pope Alexander IV.

Hence the ambitions of Aragon, France, and Pope Alexander crossed swords over the kingdom of Sicily and opened a gash that never healed. King Manfred of Sicily ruled with a kind and cultured hand as his father Frederick had before. You might say he was a Judeo-Christian Catholic rather than a Theodosian Catholic.

Sicily represented one of the most valuable pieces of real estate in Europe at the time, offering an important center for maritime stopovers in the intense Mediterranean trade, a large granary, and a contributor to industrial output. Sicily remained an important source of papyrus, which contributed to the export of paper products. The influence of Sicily extended into Italy, where the powerful Ghibelline family allied themselves with Sicily and Germany, all from the Judeo-Christian Catholic heritage. Shakespeare's Romeo came from Ghibelline stock. Juliet, on the other hand, came from the Guelph family, which pledged its allegiance to the pope against the Sicilians and Germans. Shakespeare, however, did little to reveal the true depth of the conflict including its international drama and the vast armies of knights and cavalry involved. The story of the Guelphs and Ghibellines extended to the countries of France, Aragon, Sicily, and the Vatican.[6]

King Jaime of Aragon wanted his son Pedro to marry the beautiful Constanza of Sicily. Her father, King Manfred agreed wholeheartedly. Pope Alexander warned Aragon and Sicily in the most threatening terms that he would not condone the marriage. The kings and queens of Aragon and Sicily did not bend, but proceeded in the best interests of their countries. Ambassadors fixed the dowry at over a ton and a half of gold and a large number of precious jewels. As the marriage contract acquired the needed signatures in Barcelona on July 28, 1260,[7] King Manfred tended to the future fortunes of the engaged couple.

He sent troops to Italy in order to defend the Ghibelline family from a final attack by the Guelphs, allies of the pope. The Guelphs (think Juliet) wanted to insure their own control over northern Italy with papal blessings. As Guelphs moved an enormous army of some 35,000 in for a rout, Manfred's royal German cavalry prepared an aggressive defense, together with a network of compatriots within the enemy forces.

Just five weeks after the signing of the marriage contract for Pedro and Constanza, the pope's allies launched their assault. Combat of the most vicious variety had not determined a victor by the evening hour, although the assailants seemed to gain strength. The defending German cavalry and Ghibelline nobility launched what seemed like a desperate counterattack that would end in their slaughter.

But the counterattack signaled the Ghibelline allies inside the offensive forces to act quickly on a secret plan. An inside spy rushed to the standard bearer of the Guelphs and severed the bearer's hand, which dropped to the ground with the flag. This action, performed in the middle of a quick maneuver confused the Guelphs at the worst possible moment. 15,000 of them died.

King Manfred and his Ghibelline forces declared victory, and the kingdoms of Sicily, Germany, and Aragon celebrated.

Tolerant Catholic kings like Manfred also ruled in Castile, Portugal, Germany, and Aragon. These kings professed the Catholic faith and at the same time ruled governments that promoted various freedoms for and tolerance of all faiths, including Islam. Muslims, who previously occupied and ruled throughout the Mediterranean and parts of Italy were free of persecution and even served in the military of King Manfred.

These kings thought in 1265 that their resources could bring the best returns if they continued to conquer additional Muslim lands. They did that while the popes plotted with the French. With one crusade against the Christian Albigensians and another against the Catholic Germans, the papacy and the French considered another, this one against Catholic Aragon.

Putting all such threats aside, Jaime King of Aragon, the most powerful country in Europe, together with King Manfred of Sicily and Naples solemnized the marriage of the *Infante* Prince Pedro, and the *Infanta* Princess Constanza in one of the most elaborate and luxurious weddings of the age. Nobility acknowledged the bride as one of the most discreet, beautiful, and honorable maidens of all Europe.

Constanza proved worthy of her position. Like her mother-in-law before her, Constanza followed the Aragonese army into battle and gave birth a number of times in the thick of battle. The battles that took place involved her husband Pedro serving his father in continued penetration of Muslim lands.

Jaime and Pedro subdued the entire province of Valencia, bringing it into the Aragonese fold after a long war. At one point, Pedro sent a thousand head of great cattle, 20,000 Moorish slaves, and other treasures back to Barcelona. The pope, his cardinals, the German king, and the French king all received presents of slaves and other booty. These actions made Aragon the center of social and political relevance.

Constanza, with her father-in-law King Jaime, by then a widower, hosted the grand occasions of state, including the extraordinary visit of the entire Castilian court at Aragon, where royalty danced and celebrated for a two-month period. Dancing, tourneys, performances, mimes, mummers, marionettes, and acrobats all shared center stage[8]

Jaime tried in many ways to make peace with the French and the pope, including marrying of one of his daughters to the future king of France. None of Jaime's attempts to win peaceful coexistence succeeded. Like all tolerant governments, Jaime's tried peaceful overtures. Like all totalitarian regimes, the French and the pope accepted the gifts while plotting further mischief. The peace movement of Jaime amounted only to appeasement.

1266 CE

Jaime's son-in-law, Alfonso X "The Learned" of Castile also conquered land from the Muslims in southern Spain. Alfonso had married Jaime's daughter Isabella. Alfonso and Isabella were honored guests at the extravagant visit to Aragon in 1263.

After Alfonso annexed the Moorish province of Murcia in southern Spain, the subdued population rebelled when the noble given control of their territory abused their treaty of surrender. Jaime decided to act, as he relates.

"I went to lay siege to Murcia. In going thither I arrived among the first, that I might at once set my camp properly. In battle, kings should be in the rear guard, whilst in quartering their army they should be foremost, in order to place their men better. My guide conducted us to a spot and suggested, 'My lord, you may fix your tent here.' I asked how far to Murcia, and he showed me a city within a crossbow shot of the spot of my tent.

"I said, 'Sir, you have given me right perilous quarters. Since the tent is set, we shall remain or lose credibility.'

"The Saracens sallied out and my people exclaimed, 'My lord, they shoot hard at us with arrows and with stones, and have already hurt several men and beasts.'

"I told them, 'I know well the way of these Saracens. If we bear it for a day or two they will not repeat their attack. Wait a day or two. They will not repeat the attack, and then I shall give you crossbowmen to return fire.'

"I accordingly gave them thirty crossbowmen and stationed well-armed horsemen at the camp gates. The Muslims went into the city at sunset and did not come back for a month.

"I sent the knight Domingo Lopez and my Jewish interpreter and secretary Don Astruch into the city to negotiate with the Alguazir (mayor)...

"They returned with two negotiators. I bid everyone leave the tent except for Don Astruch...

"I explained to them of many Muslim vassals in my dominions. All had their laws respected if they put themselves at my mercy and submitted to me. Otherwise, I took their land by force and peopled it with Catholics...

"Then again came the Alguazir with a knight. Both were very influential men in their town. The Alguazir brought full power to negotiate. Again, I made everyone leave the tent except

Don Astruch and the Muslims...
"I said I would give them the entire town above the royal
palace on the camp side. This pleased them. I fixed a day by
which they should evacuate the other part..." [9]

Jaime I understood the ingredients for a successful government. He desired independence during his rule. He saw the ineffectual monarchs who succumbed to the rivalries of their nobility or to the dictates of the Church. His neighbor France, in particular, suffered from this tendency. In order to accomplish his goal, he needed the support of a diverse network. That network had to include the Muslims he conquered, knights and nobles not beholden to the Church, and an economy based on production rather than patronage.

To retain Muslims, religious tolerance had to occur. To gather a military whose first loyalty rested with the monarch, he looked to the societies of knights such as the Templars and the Hospitallers. To attract and retain a competitive economy, he passed hundreds of laws favorable to Jews and minorities.

The activity resulted in a government that instituted some of the most far-reaching reforms ever to grace a European government. The road to religious freedom traveled a path laden with practical measures against a thousand attempts of nobles, administrators, and Church authorities to disrupt the peace. Many European governments today, almost a thousand years after Jaime I, still have not equaled his perceptions.

In the area of medicine, economy, and administration, he wanted the advantages that Jews gave Charlemagne and Chilperic (sixth century Frank king). Jaime issued a strong call for Jews of the world to immigrate to Catalonia. He did this because they possessed the most independent and competent skills for forming an administration, and so Jaime made use of them. Jaime knew this from the experience of Charlemagne's family. Ever since France had chosen a system of prejudice, the country had suffered.

Jaime penned a letter to the community of Montpellier, in France.
"To the Jews of Montpellier,
You suffer a life of servitude in the realms of an unresponsive
Christian King. I am opposed to your humiliation, oppression,
and persecution. No lands under my rule will allow poor treat-
ment of Jews." [10]

They came and settled. Jaime wanted them also in his new Valencian and Majorcan territories. Jaime protected their rights to preserve Jewish identity, live according to ancient customs, maintain an independent judicial system, and operate their own administrative hierarchy. That community also took the responsibility of raising taxes for the crown, which placed the kingdom in a unique position of liquidity in a European environment of cash poor regimes. Royal charters specifically guaranteed freedom of worship and the right to consume kosher food.

Royal appointees tended to abuse their powers. When a custom of Jewish communities for giving a gift to new officials turned into an opportunity for those officials to extort large sums, a royal charter put an end to the practice.

The use of mobs by royal officials and priests, harkening back to the days when controlled rabble looted the University of Alexandria, caused problems. An official might enter a home to carry out an investigation accompanied by a large group of "volunteers" who beat and robbed in a spree of confiscation and abuse. A royal grant limited officials to groups of five when entering the Jewish quarter on official business.

Mob action tended to emanate from the efforts of the Church to propagate hatred and usurp property. Sermons suggested, especially on Good Friday, that mobs should throw stones at Jews. The king took detailed interest in halting that practice, including a letter of protection, closure of the towers and high ground overlooking Jewish quarters, and the stationing of guards.

Jaime showed great concern over the efforts of the Church to interfere with Jewish communal life and engage in coercive missionary practices. [11] One coercive technique involved forced lectures and forced debates. In an effort to set the record straight with comparatively honest debate rules, The king offered to host a debate. Nahmonides, physician to the royal family, a great scholar, and the king's advisor obeyed the king's wishes to enter such a debate.

The king hosted the debate in a great hall with a theatrical atmosphere: nobles of all faiths had gathered and the agenda was calculated to favor Catholics, but the king had limited the advantage. Nahmanides decidedly won the debate, known as the Barcelona Disputation.

After the disputation, Jaime further extended his protections for religious minorities. This ultimately resulted in letters of protection from the king to Jews in cities like Barcelona, assuring them that they need not obey orders to attend sermons outside their quarter or inside synagogues.

Many Catholic judges discriminated against Jews and Muslims. In order to insure a degree of fairness, a Catholic charge against a Jew went before a Jewish court and vice versa. A defendant received a copy of all charges, and the plaintiff bore the punishment and compensation if the accusation proved groundless. Some modern societies do not have this protection against malicious suits. The defendant could consult a lawyer, and the accuser could not remain anonymous. The accuser could, however, suffer the penalty for invalid cases. A Christian swearing in used a cross, while a Jew held the laws of Moses. [12]

In Spain, the position of the broker, or *sirsur*, from the Hebrew, grew into a well-recognized trade of providing a market for goods. Often the broker would manage to find an outlet half the world away, and thus earn his fee.[13]

Just when Jaime reached a pinnacle of power and prestige; when he thought his efforts to display peace towards France had brought results; and when he and Pedro were heavily involved in helping Alfonso defeat his Moorish rebels in the Spanish province of Murcia, Pope Clement IV and King Louis IX of France decided to throw off the niceties of appeasement and expose the sword of power.

In that same year of 1266, as the faithful Catholic kings of Aragon and Castile sewed up the latest campaign against Muslims of southern Spain, France and the papacy moved to kill King Manfred, father of Aragon's Princess Constanza. They planned to place Charles of Anjou, brother to the French king, on the throne of Sicily and Naples.

Pope Clement invited Charles to Rome. Charles slipped past a Sicilian fleet and entered Rome on May 23, 1265, and immediately began to raise an army. In January, he felt confident. Clement declared Charles of Anjou, brother to Louis IX King of France, the King of Sicily and Naples. Four cardinals especially accredited by Clement crowned him and his wife king and queen of Sicily and Apulia in the Church of Saint Peter. Clement, furthermore, placed the papal army at the behest of Charles and declared another crusade against a Catholic king.

The two new allies then took care of a little paperwork. They recognized the contract signed by Charles with Pope Clement's predecessor, Urban. Charles agreed to pay an annual sum of 8,000 ounces of gold to the papacy, to exempt clergy from taxes, and to otherwise ally himself with papal military ambitions.

Manfred assembled his army, with a special contingent of loyal Muslims who formed the backbone of his defense.

Anjou issued his challenge, with reference to the Muslims in Manfred's command, "to the sultan of Nocera, that G-d and the sword are umpire between us. Either he shall send me to paradise or I will send him to the pit of hell." [14]

The decisive battle commenced at Benevento. Outside that old papal city, Charles demolished the army of Manfred. Manfred met death in an intense skirmish and Charles claimed victory. The French forces of Anjou pillaged the moderate Catholic City of Benevento.

"The pope's champion sacked the old papal city, where women and children were mowed down with their men in the harvest of the sword. The town ran blood and wine, and Charles' threadbare Frenchmen filled their wallets and saddlebags with gold. The got fine silk and cloth of gold to their backs. For three days they sought Manfred's body among the festering slain. On the third day a peasant found it, and tied it upon an ass. He hawked it through the French camp, offering to sell it for money. Charles commanded it be buried in a ditch beside the bridge." [15]

Pope Clement wrote that "our dear son Charles is in peaceful possession of all the Kingdom of Sicily, having in his power the putrid corpse of that pestilential man, his wife, his children and his treasure." [16]

The pope spoke with some truth. Queen Helena of Sicily, her six-year-old daughter Beatrice, and her three young sons Enrico, Federigo and Anselmo hid in the royal castle of Trani on the Adriatic coast. In addition to their royalty, they had inherited extraordinary beauty from their dead father King Manfred, fair and handsome as his queen Helena was gorgeous. The children had looked extremely royal.

Agents of the pope and Charles of Anjou had searched for them as potential heirs of Manfred and to the Hohenstaufen line of Frederick II. The little group had looked for a ship to take them to the Greek home of Helena. Their hiding place, in retrospect, did not really seem so clever. Charles of Anjou knew of the castle and quickly rounded them up .

Clement wrote to the now King Charles Anjou regarding the boys, "They may live, but live as if they had never come into the world, live in order to die in jail." [17] Anjou placed the three princes in the dungeon of a castle at Apulia that their grandfather Frederick II had loved, and kept them, often chained like animals, for some twenty years until their death. Their mother and sister, separated from the condemned princes, entered prison in another castle.

Queen Helena could not survive the dungeon life or the separation and tension brought about from the capture of her three infant sons. She died in 1271 at age 29 deprived of any correspondence from the outside world.

Catholic - Jewish Renaissance

Charles of Anjou then added to his lands the bonus of Jerusalem and called himself the king of Sicily, Naples, Albania, and Jerusalem. Anjou ended the progressive culture of Sicily and Naples by instituting the most repressive of French feudal systems. Wholesale massacres of common people and executions of leaders prevailed as confiscated land found new French owners, taxes increased, and French military patrolled the streets to accept bribes and ravish the local women[18]

Constanza and her husband suffered greatly from the death of Constanza's father and stepmother and the internment of the rest of her family. Her father-in-law King Jaime, advancing in years, declined a response. He died in 1276. Pedro ascended to the throne of Aragon and Catalonia in the grandest of ceremonies.

At the time of the coronations of the new king and queen of Aragon and Catalonia, their country stood for freedom more than any other in the world. They were forced to defend that freedom against many incursions. Constanza and Pedro ascended to the throne, and followed in the footsteps of Jaime in rejecting the propositions of Imperial Rome. They choose freedom of religion, comparatively secular government, the rights of business and trade to conduct affairs without undue interference, a preference for Judeo-Christian law over the Roman Theodosian Code, the opportunity to enter a trade regardless of a father's position, and access to Greek or Jewish rational medicine rather than limitation to prayers to saints or dust from their tombs.

A civil vision of personal status arose. In the Roman model, military leaders forcefully acquired estates and slaves, which entitled them to nobility, clerical duties and political power. Even though this option remained, the practicing of trades, medicine, business, science, art, small farming, and teaching gained status. In Barcelona, free men rather than slaves engaged in metalwork and operated vineyards. They could form guilds and sell where they found a market. Knights like the Templars lent money at interest and owned shopping areas.

In areas of Roman control, diversity of thought, philosophy, and religion diminished. The great schools of Greek philosophy all met the Roman torch and no longer existed. The many strains of Christianity and their various interpretations of Christ and his divinity also lost their existence to the Roman monolith.

Despite the strenuous waves of battles and rivalries for power that swept Europe before 1400, Portugal, Aragon, Catalonia, and Castile maintained orderly governments. In an age where feudal lords warred constantly, groups of largely Jewish civil servants held together the economic life of the countries.

After 1100, records show clearly the names of these civil servants. For Instance,

"In Portugal, King Diniz (1279-1325) named Judah, the chief rabbi of the country, as minister of finance. King Ferdinand (1367-1387) appointed another Judah as his chief treasurer. The extraordinary Isaac Abravanel started his career as finance minister to Alfonso V (1483-1481).

The Spanish state of Aragon had even more significant figures. The 'Rothschild of Aragon,' Judah de la Cavalleria, served as controller-general of revenues and chancellor for James I. His son Pedro III employed Joseph Ravaya as treasurer of all Aragon-

Catalonia. Even up to 1490, Luis de Santagnel and Gebriel Sanchez held the highest treasury posts of Aragon.

Jews of Castile ran almost without interruption the finances of that state from its rise to the creation of a single Spanish nation. Starting in the twelfth[h] century and continuing through the fifteenth, every significant Castilian king employed Jewish treasurers.

These men did more than rule the treasury, farm the taxes, and run the mints – in these kingdoms, where feudal grandees warred with each other and their kings oer the heads of a groaning peasantry, they actually held together the economic life of the countries."[19]

With the precedent of so many Catholic monarchs before them, Queen Constanza and Pedro could distinguish between the Catholic faith and the machinations of imperial Rome embedded in the papacy. Hence, this royal couple proceeded to expose the oppression of France and Rome. They planned nothing less than the military defeat of the papal monarchy. In so doing, they guaranteed their excommunication, a Catholic Crusade against their Catholic royal persons, and war against the Vatican. During their reign, however, they never wavered from their Catholic faith.

Constanza and Pedro prepared to liberate Sicily from the tyranny of France and the Roman pope. If successful, this action would do much more than liberate Sicily. Constanza and Pedro could, once and for all, end the possibility of a papal monarchy in Europe and the Mediterranean, thus freeing the Church from the ambitions of its imperial Roman bonds. Then the Catholic Church could concentrate on the mission of religion rather than politics.

1279 CE

Some considered Charles Anjou the most powerful man in Europe and the Mediterranean. He called himself King of Sicily, Jerusalem, Albania and Naples; Count of Provence, Forcalquier, Anjou and Maine; Regent of Achaea; Overlord of Tunis and Senator of Rome. His proxy, Pope Martin IV did the king's bidding at the papal court.

Charles planned to capture northern Italy by subduing the remnants of the rebellious Ghibellines and the city of Genoa. In addition, with Pope Martin anxious to please, Charles expected to capture the great City of Constantinople to add to his glory.

Anjou enjoyed his power, but ignored his problems. In addition to the continuing resistance of the Ghibellines and Genoese in Italy, his Sicilian subjects did not take kindly to his imperial Roman style domination. And then, worst of all, he ignored Constanza, daughter of the killed Manfred, sister of the three boy princes and Princess Beatrice (who were still in dungeons), and heiress to the same throne of Sicily claimed by Charles Anjou. Constanza bid her time.

Ever since the death of her father, the Royal Aragon court at Barcelona had considered Constanza Queen of Sicily. After the deaths of her father King Manfred , and her uncle King Conrad, expatriates and disgruntled allies made their way to Barcelona and received a most gracious welcome.

Roger de Lauria, the most capable naval officer in the world at the time, made his way to Spain and soon found himself admiral of the Aragon fleet.

Catholic - Jewish Renaissance

Doctor John Procida, physician to Emperor Frederick II, physician to the beheaded King Conrad, and international diplomat, joined de Lauria. Constanza and Pedro made him Chancellor of Aragon in charge of foreign policy. Others followed.[20]

John Procida rapidly narrowed down potential allies to only the most motivated and trustworthy: Michael, Emperor of Constantinople, who possessed plenty of money but not much of a military; Genoa and the Ghibellines, with an excellent fleet and lots of gold.

John's office served as the center for the coordination for the invasion of Sicily. He or his sons traveled first to Constantinople. One of them disguised himself as a Franciscan in order to land in Sicily secretly and speak with leaders of an underground opposition. During the talks, he suggested that an appeal to Aragon, home of their lawful queen, would serve to build support and justification. He arrived back in Barcelona with a written request for help.

In 1281 the kings of Sicily and Aragon undertook assemblages of great fleets. They both claimed the desire to use the ships for differing crusades. The activity took on frenetic proportions.

All of the many peoples oppressed by Anjou and the papacy gathered around Aragon's effort, including Muslims thrown out of their homeland, persecuted Catholics, Greeks repulsed by the campaign against Constantinople, and nobles taxed and subjected to confiscation. Jews also harbored grievances, as Charles had evicted their community which had been built up under the protections of Frederick and Manfred.

Pedro III continued the policies of his father with regard to government administration. His formalization of a civil service that relied mainly on Jews came close to ending dependence on Roman clergy. His actions helped to end a feudal relationship in servitude to the pope.[21] The Aragon government funneled money and arms to the discontented Sicilians and Italians. On Easter Day, March 29, 1282 the residents of Sicily prepared for the holy occasion while the troops of Anjou commandeered stores of grain, cattle and horses from the country in preparation for their conquest of Constantinople. Their great armada sat in the harbor of Messina on the eastern side of the island.

On Easter Monday, the Church of the Holy Spirit near the city wall of Palermo opened its doors to celebrate its annual festival and vespers service. People brought baskets of food and drink to picnic during the hours prior to the service, and so a happy atmosphere prevailed. As a crowd accumulated in the square, waiting for a signal to enter the church, a group of drunken and carefree French officers sauntered into the scene. French sergeant Drouet playfully dragged a young married woman from the crowd and pestered her with groping attentions. Her husband could not stand by. He drew a knife and stabbed Drouet to death.

As the other French officers surrounded the husband to avenge their fallen comrade, a host of furious Sicilians armed with knives and swords went to work. Most of the soldiers died on their knees begging for mercy. A pile of French uniforms lay in the square clothing dead bodies. All of the church-bells in Palermo began to ring their call to vespers.

As the bells rang out so did the shouts of the woman's friends and relatives, along with the cries of a thousand heralds who scattered throughout the city, "Moranu li Franchiski," "Death to the French."

Riot and mayhem poured into the streets, and every Frenchman encountered fell to the mob. Sicilians attacked inns favored by the French and houses they called home. French friars suffered the same fate.

"Already news of the uprising spread throughout the island. Runners hurried out during the fierce Monday night from Palermo to tell all the towns and villages to strike at once, before the oppressor could strike back. On Tuesday the men of Palermo themselves marched out to destroy the castle of Vicari, where the Justiciar and his friends were taking refuge. The garrison was too small to resist for long, and the Justiciar offered to surrender if he were allowed to go down to the coast and embark for his native France. As the negotiations were beginning one of the besiegers fired an arrow at him and shot him dead. It was the signal for a general massacre of everyone inside the castle."[22]

Across the island, rebels repeated the actions of Palermo, with the exception of Messina, across the straits from Italy, where the large fleet of Charles Anjou awaited orders to depart and conquer Constantinople. Charles had spent time in Rome, instructing Pope Martin IV on his duties. Therefore, when the Sicilian rebels sent an emissary to the pope asking for support, the request received a rapid and distinctive rejection.

After a short time, the city of Messina submitted to its rebels from without and within. Torchbearers rushed through the harbor, and the entire French fleet quickly burned and sank. Thus Charles's ideas of expansion went up in smoke, and the contribution of gold by Emperor Michael of Constantinople to rebel arms proved an excellent investment.

A small group of Genoese vessels hastened to protect Sicily from the coming French invasion.

King Charles Anjou prepared to retake the island of Sicily in the most brutal of possible procedures. In preparation, pope Martin excommunicated all rebels and anyone giving them aid, such as the Ghibellines, King Pedro of Aragon and Emperor Michael of Constantinople. He lent papal money to Anjou. King Philip of France, nephew to King Charles and successor to Louis IX, lent a sympathetic ear, and France sent warnings to King Pedro of Aragon, threatening war with France should Aragon interfere.

But Pedro had already departed Catalan waters in order to accompany the fleet, leaving word that he planned a crusade. He docked in Africa close to Sicily. The spontaneous revolt there caught him by surprise, even though he had fomented and financed it. The revolt came a little prematurely.

As Pedro and his emissaries made contact with the rebels and began to accelerate plans, Anjou sent a hastily convened fleet against the city closest to his base in Italy, the city of Messina. The Sicilians repulsed the initial thrusts of Anjou, and more French and Italian allies of Charles rushed to punish Sicily.

At the same time, Pedro promised the rebels that, with his wife Constanza as queen of Sicily upon the throne of her ancestors, their liberties and rights would return. With that understanding reached, Pedro broke camp in Africa and ordered Admiral Roger de Lauria to set sail. A journey of two days at sea delivered a huge army of Aragonese upon the shores of Sicily at Trapani. The Sicilian Vespers revolt became a great European war with France and the papacy against Aragon. French knights massed in order to cross through Italy and challenge the Sicilian rebellion, but also to cross the Pyrenees and conduct an invasion of Aragon with the intent to ravage Barcelona.

Pedro moved his army, swelling it with Sicilian supporters on the way to Palermo, where he accepted a grant of kingship and then set a course eastward to the harbor city of Messina. His fleet paralleled troop movements with its progress around the island. Pedro sent a warning to Charles Anjou to withdraw from the island.

Because the troops of the French Anjou in Sicily did not possess adequate arms to fight the huge aragon army, Charles ordered a quick retreat across the Strait of Messina to the boot of Italy. The advance brigades of Aragonese arrived outside of Messina as the last of the French attempted to board their ships. The Spanish knights mowed down their adversaries in immense carnage and captured large stores of material. Aragonese Admiral de Lauria made quick work of the French ships that dared to approach the island, capturing twenty-one galleys filled with arms in several pitched naval battles. The successes of Pedro and de Lauria encouraged the Ghibellines in north Italy, who rallied to capture several towns and burn the hated Pope Martin in effigy.

But Pope Martin IV raised the stakes. He began preaching another crusade of Catholic versus Catholic, the papacy against Aragon, making the number of crusades against Christians about as numerous as those against Muslims. Any participant in the war against Aragon received privileges granted to those who fought Muslims in the Holy Land. Martin declared Pedro deprived of his dominions; he ordered the King Edward of England to cancel the proposed marriage of his daughter to Pedro's eldest son. The pope, claiming power over kings, offered the throne of Aragon to King Philip's son, the Count of Valois. King Philip of France accepted. Papal legates flooded Italy with money and encouragement for the allies of Anjou, including the Guelphs.

Pedro and Constanza hosted a week of revelry in Barcelona to celebrate the queen's acceptance by the population of Sicily. The monarchs and their parliament, called the Cortes, decided to send Constanza and two of her sons for an extended visit to Sicily, showing the support of the realm.

The queen, escorted by the King of Majorca, fifty gentlemen of Aragon and Catalonia, and various other dignitaries, made way to the ship *La Bonne Adventure*. She stopped first at the cathedral and offered prayers. Constanza and Pedro had shown, once again, as Kings Chilperic, Charlemagne and his family, Frederic II, and others had before, that faithful Catholics could rule in perfect harmony with secular governments, granting religious liberty and general toleration. Constanza proved that, in so doing, they could still stand up to a Roman papacy, demand justice, win the admiration of the population and secure the needed military victories. The royal couple showed that crusades made in the name of oppression deserved to fail.

Constanza sailed with a small flotilla to the capital of Sicily, Palermo. There, the party was

> "*received with every outward expression of delirious joy by the inhabitants. To Constanza, the moment was one of intense emotion. Confronted as she was by the acclaiming welcome of a populace who regarded her as a guardian angel, the harbinger of a new era of hope and peace for their distracted island, she could not but remember that the homecoming was empty of the presence and embraces of all from whom she parted some twenty-five years before... The veil of death or of captivity had fallen over those other faces of father, mother, uncle, nephew, sister, for*

which she looked in vain among the surging crowds that hurried to quayside to bid her welcome...

"The queen, on landing, made the sign of the cross, raised her eyes to heaven, kissed the ground, weeping, and entered the Church of St. George, where she prayed, together with the Infante, her sons. On emerging into the streets, more than five hundred mounts awaited her and her retinue. A handsome white horse, on which were placed her own trappings, emblazoned with the arms of Aragon and Sicily was the gift of Palermo to the Queen. The city provided two other white steeds for her sons.... Dinner was served. From the royal table, food was sent to the ships and galleys in such abundance that the supply lasted for a week. During the whole seven days, not only Palermo, but the whole of Sicily gave itself up to rejoicing.

"The queen and her sons continued the journey through Sicily attended by universal popular demonstrations of joy. Their escort consisted of five hundred crossbowmen, the same number of friendly Almogarves, and all the knights of the household...

"The fleet of Charles Anjou continued to threaten the coasts and the pope continued his adverse attitude. Suddenly aspects brightened as the great seaman, Roger de Lauria gained a notable victory over the galleys of the enemy, which had rashly ventured out of the port of Naples. De Lauria destroyed or captured thirty-seven sails. A frantic welcome awaited the victorious navy at Messina, Sicily..."[23]

De Lauria produced other naval victories, constantly out-maneuvering the French. The three brothers of Queen Constanza, however, were killed after their long imprisonment as chained dungeon dwellers.

1285 CE

In May, 1285, the crusading army of France set out to conquer Aragon. King Charles Anjou raised another army and fleet in his Provence domains.

The brilliance of Admiral de Lauria once again saved his native kingdom of Sicily and Naples. His mastery of the Mediterranean enabled him to defeat French shipping and to land raiding parties along the Italian coast at will. The attackers struck their targets quickly. By the time the troops of Charles pursued them, they had already boarded a vessel and moved on to the next attack.

De Lauria blockaded the entire Bay of Naples, sinking any ship that attempted to exit. This induced a rebellion within the City of Naples. The son of King Charles Anjou attempted to break the embargo and insurrection by loading galleons with knights and challenging an isolated group of Aragon ships. De Lauria had set a trap.

The son of Anjou ended up a prisoner to de Lauria, along with his compatriots and those ships not sunk. News of this naval battle reached Naples, where the rebels immediately massacred all French found in the streets and houses. Neighboring cities followed suit.

The admiral rescued the sister of Queen Constanza, Beatrice, who had been kept a prisoner almost twenty years. Constanza sent a message to the French that the son of Anjou might meet a sudden death if her sister were not set free. De Lauria himself sailed to pick up the princess. Beatrice married Manfred, Marquis of Saluzzo from the area east of Rome, and thereafter led a contented life. Queen Constanza, however, kept the son of Anjou in prison for some years.

Anjou reached Naples in time to suppress the rebellion in that city and hang 150 rebel leaders. After a further injection of money from Pope Martin, Charles marched with a massive army through Italy towards Sicily, with his new fleet keeping pace in the sea. Charles then commanded a larger fleet than Roger de Lauria. This enabled the French to blockade de Lauria in Messina harbor.

The better sailor prevailed. De Lauria waited for a storm that obliged the French to disperse their ships and then he slipped out of the harbor to join additional Aragonese warships in a relentless ravaging of the Italian coast. Desertion depleted the French army as Charles waited to invade Sicily. He wanted his invasion to coincide with the invasion of Aragon by King Philip of France. Illness overtook the grand King Charles Anjou and he died in the middle of his great crusade.

Pedro hastened home to Aragon in order to meet a French crusader force of 100 ships, 16,000 knights, 17,000 crossbows and 100,000 infantry. Pedro's Castilian allies abandoned him in the face of what seemed impossible odds.

The French moved rapidly through the Pyrenees mountain passes as had Charlemagne before. They first descended on the Catalan city of Elna.

"Now the French soldiers advanced in such force and the assaults they made were so many that they took the city by storm and entered. They then let themselves loose upon men, women ,and children and spared none. They broke into the churches of the city and pillaged them and dashed in pieces the crucifixes and the images of the saints that were therein. They seized little children and flung them against the walls and outraged widowed women and maidens and others, showing no reverence for church nor altar, and violated women even in the sanctuaries, and when they had satisfied their lust, they maimed them cruelly and afterwards put them to death. Cries for mercy brought no pity, for at no time whatsoever was there such torture nor such fierce savagery wrought by men of any faith.

After the city of Elna was subdued and the French had put to the sword all the men and women who were therein, they tore down all the houses of the city both large and small, so that there remained scarcely one stone upon another. They unroofed the churches and set them on fire, and all the city was in flames."[24]

A siege against Spanish Gerona followed, and the French captured that city in August 1285. In a spirited defense that delayed capitulation, the inhabitants gave Pedro a chance to organize his strategy. In the meanwhile, Pedro showed his military skills with guerrilla harassment of the French to such a degree that the crusaders could not disperse and began to suffer illnesses that spread through their ranks.

Many nobles of Aragon shirked their duty to King Pedro III, who then called upon his special knights, including the Templars, to fight his Catholic enemies. His strategy of remaining independent from Rome came into use. He issued a summons and a request for a loan, referring to the specific clause in the law of the land, the Usatges.[25]

Section 64. Indeed if the prince should be besieged, holds his enemies under siege, or hears that a certain king or prince is coming against him to wage war, he must warn his land by both letters and messengers or by the usual customs. Then all men, knights and footmen alike must come to his aid.

The Templars had to choose between obeying the law of their country, Aragon and Catalonia, or their own rules, which included.

~ The most serious crimes for a Templar are simony, heresy, revealing secrets of the order, and killing a Christian.

~Killing of infidels is not only sanctified, but can lead to martyrdom in the name of Christ.[26]

Pope Innocent II had made it official.

"You Templars are not at all afraid to lay down your lives for your brothers and to defend them from the pagans' invasions. You are known by name to be the Knights of the Temple. The Lord has established you as defenders of the Church and assailants of the enemies of Christ. Although with endeavor and praiseworthy devotion you are toiling with all your hearts and all your minds in so sacred an undertaking, nevertheless we exhort all the members of your Order in the Lord. We enjoin both you and those serving you for the remission of sins, by the authority of G-d and Blessed Peter the Prince, to protect the Catholic Church. Also, by fighting the enemies of the cross, to rid that part of the Church which is under the tyranny of the pagans from their filth."[27]

The Templars nevertheless honored their allegiance to the King of Aragon and came to his aid against the French, and later, the forces of Castile. Pedro and his father Jaime before him would call on their knights to divert efforts from the *Reconquista* against Muslims and fight Catholics a number of times against both France and Castile.

Roger de Lauria maneuvered his Catalan fleet into the Bay of Rosas and destroyed the French armada. He landed marines on the ground to block supplies destined for the main French army. Pedro closed in on the dispirited force, whereupon the French panicked and ran. French King Philip, for his troubles, contracted a fever and died during the retreat. The French, just as in the time of Charlemagne, lost their entire baggage. The Catalans picked through an immense treasure.[28]

"It is not possible to give any idea of the gold and silver which fell into the hands of our knights and foot soldiers. Precious stones, collars embroidered with gold, and silken gowns relieved the poverty of all Catalonia."[29]

Pedro punished Castile for its help to the French by annexing some of its land. He also invited members of its royal family who laid claim to the throne of Castile to seek protection in Aragon. He used the Templars in these actions.

Upon the death of Pope Martin IV, his successor excommunicated the entire population of Sicily.

Merchants of Catalonia rapidly extended their bases forward to Sicily, enabling them to better serve their interests in North Africa and the East.

Pedro acted as a good Catholic, faithful to universal morals, as a person of any religion should. His grandfather died opposing the French crusade against the Albigensian Christians; his father was excommunicated, and

Pedro himself fought for freedoms and secular government despite a Crusade against him and his Queen Constanza accompanied by excommunication. Combating totalitarianism cannot succeed with halfway measures. Pedro's victories ended forever the papal ambitions to religious monarchy and empire, but did not end the latent imperial Roman desire for control. Even after hundreds of years, that desire festered. All imperial Rome needed was one susceptible king, one person to do its bidding, just like the weakling Visigoth Recared, who jettisoned the ancient Arian religion and substituted a constitution with dictatorship, in order to cancel centuries of advances.

For the moment, in 1286, Catalans dominated the Mediterranean, and:

"by the fourteenth century, Catalonia was the largest mercantile country in the Mediterranean.... Barcelona became the market place and point of supply for commodities of an extensive hinterland reaching far beyond the principality, and, like her rivals, Genoa and Venice, was one of the great banking places of medieval Europe."[30]

Northern Spain enjoyed an increase in trade, but nowhere did that increase take place so dramatically as in Catalonia, anchored by Aragon and Barcelona.

"Aragonese wheat, wood, fruits, and vegetables flowed to the chronically hungry Barcelona and beyond to Majorca and Valencia. The products of the sea came back, to be sure, and also such things as the oranges and the rice of Valencia. The conquest of the valley of Guadalquivir in the thirteenth century meant the yet more unrestricted passage of the olive and olive oil, wines, and the fruits of that region" and brought flocks of sheep to the ports. Industry increased including steel products such as armor, Jewish glass and carpets.

"The business of fairs was tied into a financial network that covered all of western and central Europe. Archbishop Sancho of Toledo borrowed 4,000 solidi from a French (probably Jewish) merchant in 1256, the agreement stipulating that it was to be repaid at the fair of Alcala de Henares after Easter or the fair at Pamplona after the feast of the Ascension....

"Bolstered by the control of Provence and much of the Midi by the dynasty of Barcelona, and successively reinforced by the conquest of the Balearics and Valencia in the 1230's and the annexation of Sicily in 1282, the seagoing merchants of Catalonia bid fair to dominate the trade of western Mediterranean. In this case though, the flag followed the trade. For a century before the acquisition of Sicily the Catalans had become very active players in a maritime trade which, as in antiquity, was based essentially upon the traffic in manufactured goods, spices, wheat, slaves, and piracy. Vessels coasted from Montpellier to Genoa to Palermo to Tunisia and Almeria in search of occasional cargo, such as the silk of Valencia and the paper of Jativa, which might be saleable in their climes, but the great staples were those three.

"At home both Barcelona and Valencia now possessed an organized and fertile hinterland in Aragon from which and to which they could organize exports. Jaime and then Pedro negotiated favorable conditions for the merchants with the various portions

of the decayed North African Empire of the Muslims and even in Alexandria. To accommodate the results Pedro III began the issuance of a heavier silver coinage, after the precedent of the Italian towns, better adapted for use in the European market. "[31]

During this time a continuous state of war existed between the Spanish Catholic states of Europe and the Muslim states of Spain and the Mediterranean. Hence trade with cities such as Muslim Alexandria could be made only by noncombatants or neutral parties. The Jewish community served as such a neutral party. Because Aragon contained such a vibrant Jewish trading center, its commerce sailed throughout the entire Mediterranean.

Unlike the dictatorships of France and Rome, Aragon increasingly practiced separation of power and consent of the governed. Public opinion mattered:

"Royal revenue that was obtained only with the gravest difficulty in the thirteenth century (northern Spain). Public opinion was conservative in the extreme, demanding that the ruling dynasty live 'of its own' just as any other family.' The dynasties never had, of course, but their shortfalls were larger and more frequent because the success of the Reconquista had brought an end to the parias (protection taxes) that could be exacted from the south...

"Already in the twelfth century one can detect, in a rough way, the increasing tendency of the crown to secure more widespread support for the most important policies or initiatives by summoning more and more magnates and prelates to court. The resulting larger meetings were sometimes called a 'general curia' or a 'general council' by the chroniclers. The practice continued but when townsmen as well were summoned to attend them people called them cortes, or corts. It appears that the first such assembly in Iberia took place in Leon in 1188 on the troubled accession of Alfonso IX. While the record is not entirely clear, by the first quarter of the thirteenth century such meetings were being held in all of the Iberian kingdoms. They treated questions of war and peace, of the royal succession and of dynastic marriage but above all they met to consider the crown's request for a special grant-in-aid. Most frequently, to obtain his funds, the king had to promise that he would not debase the currency for a stipulated period, often seven years.

"This new institution can claim to represent the realm in a particular way. It came to have its own organization; usually the three houses of clergy, nobles, and burghers, each with it's own speaker. They developed their own procedures, meeting jointly to hear the requests of the crown from the royal chancellor and to deliver their own petitions for redress of grievance, deliberating separately on the crowns agenda, and reassembling with the other houses to respond to the latter. These assemblies came to validate the credentials of their own members and to keep records of their own proceedings. They, at various times, attempted to control the selection of royal ministers, the disbursement of royal revenues, the implementation of royal policies, and even the business of their own regular convocation, without obtaining final success in any one of these. Nevertheless, by 1300 the courts became not only a central institution but also a symbol of the realm in a degree second only to that of the king himself."[32]

In 1383 the Catalan Franciscan theologian Francesc de Eiximenis wrote about the virtues of the merchant in his *Regiment de la Cosa Publica:*

"The land where the market flourishes unimpeded is full, and

fertile, and in the best of shape. And so ... merchants should be favored above all other lay people in the world ... they are the life of the people, the treasure of public interest. They are the food of the poor, the arm of all good commerce, and the fulfillment of all business matters. Without merchants societies fall apart, princes become tyrants, the young are lost and the poor weep. For knights and citizens who live as renters do not take care of large charities. Only merchants are big givers and great fathers and brothers of the common good." [33]

Contrast this to the France of Phillip Augustus or the Spain of Ferdinand and Isabelle. When Phillip Augustus needed money, he raided the Knights Templar, the Jews, and any business he could lay his hands on. France therefore did not enjoy prosperity, but it did suffer central power and state religion.

1300 CE

Philip the, Fair king of France needed money, as he always did. The France of that day did not include Normandy or Aquitaine and engaged in plans to annex those lands from England. The annexation of Provence during the Cathar Crusade had almost doubled the size of France, but Philip put a quick end to the prosperity of Provence.

France desired to live from the proceeds of booty. The king turned to plundering its own citizens, starting with the Cathars, Lombards and Jews. Campaigns for external plunder from Aragon ended only in debts, as Aragon proved superior both in military and financial matters. This came about because Aragon gave freedom and security to its economy.

France employed extreme measures of tax collection. In the southern village of Laurac, for instance, a royal knight and clerk executed a tax hunt. A band of collectors including 26 sergeants came to levy the money the monarch claimed.

"At once they went briskly into action, taking securities from houses, even including clothes and bedding, and in some cases turning out the inhabitants, locking their houses and confiscating the keys ... They then summoned fifty or sixty notables to the local hotel and explained what payments they required. One man who refused to go was punched in the back.

"The agents transported the consuls and notables to Toulouse and were not allowed to leave until they agreed to payments of 25,000 sous toulousains over five years.

"Back in the village, royal sergeants rounded up about 200 heads of households in order to force the village to ratify the agreement. The village refused, whereupon the village men faced indefinite confinement. In the end, each man filed past the royal representative, Bible in hand, to swear adherence to the agreement.

"Later, when the village missed a payment, the collectors returned and imprisoned villagers until the leaders agreed to borrow money at usury rates in order to meet the terms of the agreement. Also a procedure of confiscating grain, movables, and animals left the villagers destitute.

"The king also descended upon Church grounds with carpenters and woodcutters to harvest trees. As the Bishop of Angers and his clerk dismounted their horses on return from a trip, tax collectors grabbed the steeds and made off with them. The tax collectors carried off sacred vessels and movable goods from other monasteries." [34]

Philip of France decided to turn to the Templars who resided in France for his next campaign of acquisition. Crusaders like the Templars lost prestige in this era because the Islamic leader Saladin repossessed Jerusalem. But, the loss of that city did not hinder other activites, as their wealth increased. The Templars also earned the enmity of William Archbishop of Tyre, the very same man who had inspired the Third Crusade. The patriarch of Jerusalem complained about the abuse of privileges by the Templars, who in response shot arrows at his door.

The loss of Jerusalem also weakened the power of the papacy in favor of the European monarchs. The pope could no longer raise large armies, as he could not deliver booty and land. Knights looked for gold, slaves, and property at the end of the battle, not death and ignomiy. Kings of England and France used knights to fight each other and followed the policy of Charlemagne's family in taxing the clergy for their efforts.

The Templar knights did have gold and property, but now their income came from commercial transactions, shipping, and banking. Their power brought them into competition with their old friends, the pope and the king of France. Those powerful figures did not believe in competition, and withdrew support from the Templars.

Support from the royalty of Spain, however remained strong.

King Philip of France, with the pope as a virtual prisoner, issued a secret arrest order, purporting to act on accord of the papal duties of heresy.

"A bitter thing, a lamentable thing, a thing horrible to think of and terrible to hear, a detestable crime, an execrable evil deed, an abominable work, a detestable disgrace, a thing wholly inhuman, foreign to all humanity, has reached our ears. The Order of the Knights of Templars is a wolf in sheep's clothing guilty of astonishing bestiality, supremely abominable crimes, and acting like beasts.

"We have decreed that all the members of the said order within our realm will be arrested, without any exception, imprisoned, and reserved for the judgement of the Church, and that all their moveable and unmovable property will be seized, placed in our hands, and faithfully preserved.

Arresting officers shall put the arrested Templars in isolation under a good and secure guard, make a preliminary inquiry about them, and then call the inquisitor's assistants and examine the truth with care, using torture if necessary." [35]

The King's order had to do with the seizure of wealth. But without their mandate to fight a holy war against the Muslims, the Templars remained as just another wealthy victim for the king of England, the pope, and, especially, the king of France. Once exempt from papal taxes, the order sent money to finance Pope Gregory IX's battles against the emperor of Germany. Bishops complained of Templar independence in the administration of Templar churches, the unjust acquisition of churches, and other special Templar privileges. [36]

An unusual concentration of Templar leaders in Paris at the time of the arrests brought the very highest-ranking members into the hands of the Inquisition. Methods of torture perfected against the Christian Cathars were readied for the Catholic knights.

The rack, the pulley, the ordeal of water, and the ordeal of fire did their job. Confessions abounded, in about eight categories:

Denial of Christ, G-d, the Virgin, and the saints.

Sacrilegious acts on the cross or Christ's image

Obscene kisses

Sodom.

Failure to consecrate the Host

Non-belief in the sacraments

Idolatry

Absolution of sins by Templar leaders[37]

The king of Aragon defended the Templars, who continued their strong relations with the monarchy and the Jewish community. The Jewish Cavalleria family, long administrators for the Templars also produced Judah, bailiff for King Jaime in Zaragossa and Valencia. Judah raised large sums of money for the king's activities, including the outfitting of fleets to continue the *Reconquista*.[38] Templars undoubtedly contributed to these loans.

Several bishops in Aragon, however, circumvented royal officials by capturing several Templars and began to torture some of them. Aragon laws prohibited torture and the king immediately put a stop to the practice. When the pope weighed in with the opinion that the Templars needed dismantling, the king protested, but acquiesced.[39]

As Templars came out of the torture chambers into the light of the court proceedings, they started to recant their confessions and insist on their innocence. Philip of France marched fifty-four of them to a field outside of Paris on May 12 and burned them all. The victims maintained their denials and complained that the death sentences without cause or justification.

The grand master of the Templars and his assistant retracted their confessions. Jacques de Molay and Geoffroi de Charney were then burned to death declaring their orthodoxy on a small island in the River Seine on March 18, 1314.

Those writers of medieval chronology in the Church then discarded the Templars into the heap of hidden history. Pope Clement wanted the Templars tried in Church court and their property turned over the Church, as Templars served as members of a monastic order. The king's minister replied that Jews and Muslims were of more value than Templars, and that laws obliged Catholics to put Templars to death. Pope Clement only agreed that Catholics should hate Templars and avoid their company. He insisted that only the Church could give the death penalty and that the Church should get the property.

The king kept the property.

The era closed with French and Roman imperial power firmly in control of northern Europe and a more open society with constitutional freedoms operating successfully in Spanish Catalonia, Aragon, Castile, and Portugal. The Muslim regime in the south of Spain, formerly enlightened, wealthy, and powerful, sank into a mess of intolerance, dictatorship, and incompetence.

It would take the Rennaissance and the Enlightenment to return Europe to the laws and culture of Moses.

APPENDIX A: THE SPANISH FLAG

The Lion of Judah begins it's life in *Genesis* and *Numbers* as the symbol of the Tribe of Judah. That Lion travelled with Jews to Spain where it proudly posed on the seals of Jewish families and cities with large Medieval Jewish populations such as the Shatiel family and its adopted City of Zaragossa; the Jewish City of Lucena; Cordova, the Abravanel family, the Andias, the Calvos the Barreiras, and others.

The venerable Tribe of Simeon accompanied this Lion with its symbol of the Fortress, as exemplified on the seals of the Abinion family, the Ablanedos, the Jewish City of Carcao, the Aristizabal family, the Ladneres family, and many others.

The early Kingdom of Leon, home to many Jews, used the Lion of Judah as a flag and the Kingdom of Castile, in the same situation with Toledo as its capital, used a castle, that of the Tribe of Simeon with three parapets. At the time for forming the joined Kingdom of Castile-Leon, Jews commonly used these symbols on synagogues such as that of Halevi and even in their grammer books such as that of Kimchi. Relationships were strong between three religions as Ferdinand III emblazoned his tomb with Hebrew, Arabic, and Latin. The Almighty was referred to as He who only could absolve those of the three religions. The flag of Castile-Leon features the Lion and the Fortress.

The People of the Book paid strict attention to their traditions. They would instinctively, in 800, 900, 1000, 1100, or 1200 recognize themselves also as the People of the Exodus, celebrated as Pesach or Passover. The mystical number of four accompanies this holiday due to ritual involving four glasses of wine, four sons, four questions, and four promises of the Almighty. So it is not surprising to find four strips represented in places such as the Barcelona Haggadah (narrative of the Exodus) and others. The towns of Cerdagne and Urgell, original home of early Jewish Counts of Barcelona, use the four stripe motif, as does Barcelona and Catalunya. Other towns and families show these stripes.

And so, out of respect for history, from the intimate friendly relationship of many Catholics and Jews, or as a result of conversions, these symbols entered the world of medieval nobility and nationhood.

In the formation of Spain, comprised of the leading Kingdoms of Castile, Leon, Bacelona-Aragon-Catalunya, and Navarre the same symbols emerge. The flag of Spain takes from these Kindgoms the Fortress, Lion, and four stripes. That flag also features the gold chains of Navarre. The symbols spread throughout the Medieval world, on the shields of armies, the crests of families, and the flags of nations. These are some of the many clues to the intense friendship of Christians and Jews and the basis of modern civilization: Torah and Talmud.

APPENDIX B

COUNTS OF BARCELONA

Starting with Rule of Charlemagne, 802

802-820	Bera	Largely Jewish Force ousted Muslims
820-827	Rampo	
827-844	Bernard	Grandson of Aimeri, son of William
844-846	Sunifred	
846-848	Aleran	First Christian (Catholic)
848-850	William	Great grandson of Aimeri
850-852	Aleran	Defeated w/ Babylonian help
852-863	Independent country	W/ Babylonian help to Hebrews
864-869	Solomon	Jewish ally of Charles the Bald
869-877	Bernard	Son of Solomon
878-897	Gulfre I	The Hairy, secured Catholic presence
898-910	Bulfre II Borell	
911-947	Sunyer	
947-966	Miro	
966-991	Borell II	
992-1018	Ramon Borell III Berenguer	
1018-1034	Ramon Berenguer I	The Crooked
1035-1076	Ramon Berenguer I	The Elder
1076-1082	Ramon Berenguer II	The Fratricide
1082-1097	Ramon Berenguer II	
1097-1131	Ramon Berenguer III	The Great
1131-1162	Ramon Berenguer IV	The Saint
1162-1196	Alfonso I	The Chaste, King of Aragon
1196-1213	Pere I	King of Aragon
1213-1276	Jamie	King of Aragon
1276-1285	Pedro	King of Aragon

APPENDIX C

ROYAL LIBRARY OF ALEXANDRIA

Alexander the Great expanded a little-known town on the coast of Egypt into one of the greatest cities in the world and named it after himself (in 332 BCE). Its strategic trading location, its natural harbor, and its superb defensive geography enabled it to quickly grow. His successor Ptolemy II Soter founded the Museum or Royal Library of Alexandria. The establishment housed over a half million documents from around the world and over a hundred scholars.

The library, along with the famous lighthouse (280 BCE) and Serapeum, home of the Egyptian-Greek god Serapis, formed the cored of an ardently metropolitan environment where Christians, Jews, Greek thinkers, pagans, and even Buddists created an intellectual heaven. Here the Jewish Philo presided over the translation of the Bible into Greek.

Other scholars of note include Euclid, the Greek mathematician, Archimedes as a student before his tenure in Syracuse, the surgeons Herophilus and Erasistratus, the inventor of keyboard instruments Ctesibius, Eratosthenes the mathematician and astronomer, Arius the theologian, Hypatia the philosopher, and many others.

Its most famous occupant was Cleopatra. Events surrounding Roman conquest and specifically the interactions between Caesar, Antony, and Augustus brought the city under Roman rule.

It all came to an end with the Imperial Roman regime created by Constantine that deplored intellectual curiosity and brutally enforced conformity of thought. Under that bias, the Archbishop Theophilous transformed intellectual debates into intimidation by mob action. His mobs set the Serapeum on fire, destroyed the Royal Museum and Library, and ended the era of open-ended thinking. The library burned in 391 CE. In the process, his mob cornered the mathematician Hypatia, dragged her through the streets, and killed her.

APPENDIX D: JUDEO-CHRISTIAN
BASIS OF MODERN CIVIL SOCIETY
A BRIEF SAMPLING

1. **No murder, lying, stealing,** *Ten Commandments:* Amazingly enough, some societies permit this, and end up disfunctional.
2. **Government must get consent of the governed (elections or such)**, and the governed must be a free people. Hebrews, once free, agree voluntarily to follow the new laws of their Maker, and do so often. Also do politicians and sermons in the House of Commons, US, Calvin, *Exod.* 19.8, 24.7; D 5.3, 29.10-13; *Josh* 25.16-28; *2Kings* 23:2-3, *Neh.* 8.3-18 & 9.38 with many other references in Exodus and Revolution by Michael Walzer.
3. **Obtain a constitutional republic** where neither majority or leader can void particular rights and responsibilities, outlined in the many Israelite covenants.
4. **Separation of government powers**, in the case of *Deut.* etc., king, prophets, priests, judiciary. Judges should be impartial.
5. **Science and religion are compatable**, science venerated in many texts, i.e. "Geometry and astronomy are appetizers of wisdom." *Pirket Avot*, 3:23.
6. **Base leadership on merit, not heredity.** "appoint a king" (anyone among you) *Deut.* 17.14-15.
7. **Honor contracts freely entered.** Everything from the Hebrew covenants to the entire *Talmud Seder Nezikin.*
8. **Charity** Exhortations to help the needy from Moses to Maimonides to today.
9. **Provide education.** *Deut.* 6.6-7
    a. **Study Hebrew.** It is the source, relied on by leaders over the course of thousands of years from Moses to Jerome to Aquinas to Kepler to Dante to Bacon to Grotius.
    b. **Universal education.** *Deut.*
10. **Pay your workers.** *Deut.* 25:14 - 18
11. **Insure property rights** *Isaiah* 65.21-23 Because when they were slaves, Hebrews could not benefit from their own production. That should not happen again.
12. **Rights to minorities, maids, indentures, freedom for slaves** Exod. 21:12, 20
13. **Create a civil society** "Do unto others..." *Leviticus*
14. **Community health.** From *Deut.* 23.12-13 to *Talmud.*
15. **Religion and morals.**
16. **Work for these attributes:** to the extent a society lacks them, it is more oppressive and requires more opposition and replacement. That is a lesson of Exodus, American Revolution, Jewish German Revolution, Muslim capture of Spain, and the ascendency of Castile, Leon, and Aragon in 1100 Catholic Spain.

The references here are by no means complete, but only quick examples.

APPENDIX E:
JUDEO-CHRISTIAN COLLABORATION

A SAMPLING OF RENAISSANCE FIGURES WHO LEARNED HEBREW OR WORKED WITH HEBREW PARTNERS AND ASSISTANTS

Bede
Alcuin of York
Paul the Deacon,
Peter of Pisa
Rabanus Maurus, Bishop of Fulda
Pope Gregory I
Walafrid Strabo
Haimon of Halberstadt
Paschasius Radbertus
Saint Augustine
Claudius of Turin
Engelmann of Luxueil
Remi of Auxerre
Notker Balbulus
Bruno of Wuerzburg
Hartmorte of St. Gall
Christian Druthmar
Alduin of Limoges
Siegebert of Gemblours
Abelard
Heloise
Stephen Harding
Raymond Lully
Nicholas of Lyra
Nicholas Manjacoria
Thomas Aquinas
John Huss
Radulphus Niger
William Breton
William Tyndale
Kepler
Roger BaconTheobald
Hugo of Saint Caro
Gerard de Hoyo
William de Mara
Galileo
Dante

Thomas Matthews
Anselm,
Bernard
John of Salisbury
Abelard
William of Auvergne
Alexander of Hales
John Duns Scotus
Albertus Magnus
Pico di Mirandola
Vincent of Beauvais
Michael Servetus
Leibnitz
Immanuel Kant
Arthus Schopenhauer
Friedrich Nietzsche
Theocracy of Milan
Kepler
Passagii
Zwingli
Jacob Ceporinus
Felix Manz
Johann Eck
Martin Luther
Johann Reuchlin
Montesquieu
John Locke
Thomas Hobbes
John Stuart Mill

ENDNOTES

CH 3 GERMANS AND JEWS: THE EARLY YEARS

[1] Pirenne, Henri, *Mohammed and Charlemagne,* pp. 28-30, 49, 76, 122.

[2] Slouschz, *Travels in North Africa,* p. 274.

[4] Anderson, W.B., ed., *Sidonius, v. I,* pp. xx-xxi.

[3] Wolfram, Herwig, *The Roman Empire and Its Germanic Peoples,* pp. 159-182.

[4] Isadore of Seville, *History of the Kings,* G. Donini, tr., p. 30-36.

[5] St. Augustine, EP, 71, 3-5.

[6] St. Augustine, *City of God, IV,* Intro.

[7] Reilly, Bernard F. *The Medieval Spains,* pp. 30-33.

[8] St. Augustine, *City of God,* V. 12, 18, 25.

[9] St. Augustine, letter to Paulinus of Nola and *The Correction of the Donatists,* as in James Carroll, *Constantine's Sword,* NY: Houghton Mifflin, 2001, p. 211.

[10] Sidonius, Epithalamium V 1 231-233.
Anderson, W.B. ed., *Sidonius,* V.II, *p. 83, 277*

[11] Ibid., pp. xxvii-xxx.

[12] The Roman Theodosian Code forbade Christian sects other than Catholic, but permitted, with many restrictions, Jewish existence, which was not always honored by bishops.

[14] Anderson, W.B., ed., *Sidonius* V. II, *p. 37*

[15] Not to be confused with Theodoric, king of the Ostrogoths in Italy.

[16] Sidonius, *Letters and Poems Epist.,* I, II: vol. I pp. 335-345.

[17] Under King Euric, a vigorous Arian Christian and anti-Catholic, who attracted Roman nobles.

[18] Ibid., Sidonius, *Epist. VII, VII.*

[19] Gregory, *History of the Franks,* IV, p. 31.

[20] Sidonius, *Epist. VIII, IX*

[21] Gibbon, Edward, *The Decline & Fall of the Roman Empire,* pp. 1192-1193. King Euric first arranged the codification of Gothic law, a group of four Frank kings ordered the Salic law, and Emperor Theodosius II issued the *Codex Theodosianus,* all in the fifth century.

[21] Gibbon, Edward, *The Decline & Fall of the Roman Empire,* pp. 1194-1196.

[22] Sidonius, *Letters and Poems,* V.1, p. 334, note *

[23] Scott, S.P., tr., *The Visigothic Code,* pp. 337-340.

[24] The Theodosian Code, Clyde Pharr, tr.

[25] King, P.D., *Law and Society in the Visigothic Kingdom,* pp. 1-5.

[26] See Rashi's comments on Deuteronomy, and the writings of Athanasius in his *Select Works, pp. 337-415.* Scott, S.P., *The Visigothic Code.* This version reflects a late edition, when Catholic Goths inserted anti-Semitic clauses and pro Roman clauses. Projections back to the time of Euric have been made.

[28] Gregory, *The Four Books on the Miracles of St. Martin,* in Van Dam, *Saints,* p. 255.

[29] Gregory, *History,* V.6.

[30] *Ibid., III.50*

[31] Gregory, *History,* V, *43.*

[32] *Leviticus,* 20:18.

[33] Scherman, Katharine, *The Birth of France* (New York: Randon House, 1987), p. 192.

[34] Katz, Solomon, *The Jews in the Kingdoms of Spain and Gaul,* pp. 122-123.

[35] Chilperic, *Hymn for the Feast of St. Medard,* in *Monumenta Germaniae Historica Poetarum Latinorum MedII AeVI Tom I IV Fasciculus I, p*p. 455-458. Luciano Nar-

End Notes

done, tr. The poem continues:
> You dispelled many fevers and sicknesses. You revived many feeble limbs. Endowed with great virtues, you crucified your body and despised the world. You lived in this world as an angelic being, constantly dwelling with your mind in heaven.
> A sweet celestial voice always resounded in your soul; well done, O good and faithful servant. Enter into the joy of the Lord.
> You have been faithful over a few things. I will make you ruler over many things.
> You have been poor in spirit. Yours is the kingdom of heaven. Your have been meek; you shall inherit the earth.
> O you who now in heaven enjoy the voices of the angels, intercede for us, your faithful servants.
> Don't forsake us who sing hymns in your honor, O you that now experience celestial delights.
> Remember us and pray for us to the Lord, who always listens to the prayer of his saints.
> Glory be to the Father, to the Son and to the Holy Spirit, Holy God, who bestows crowns on his Saints forever and ever.

[36] Paul, Catholic deacon of Merida, in *Medieval Iberia*, Olivia Constable, ed., pp. 5-11, and E.A. Thompson, *The Goths in Spain*, 78-81.

[37] Thompson, E.A., *The Goths In Spain*, pp. 92-94.

[38] Heather, Peter, *The Goths*, pp. 288-290

[39] Bachrach, Bernard, *Armies and Politics in the Early Medieval West*, pp. 13-14

[40]. Coppee, Henry, *History of the Conquest of Spain*, V.1 , pp. 204-205.

[41] *Gregory, Epp. ix. 204.*

[42] *Gregory, Epp. i. 45.*

[43] Moreno, Garcia in *Prosopografria*, p. 37. N. 28 as in Wolfram, Herwig, *History of the Goths*, p. 516, n. 400.

[44]. Wolfram, Herwig, *The Roman Empire and Its Germanic Peoples*, pp. 272-273.

[45] E.A. Thompson, *The Goths in Spain*, pp. 219-229.

[46] Kurinsky, Samuel, *The Eighth Day*, p. 271.

CHAPTER 4
ISLAMIC LIBERATORS

[1] Slouschz, *Travels in North Africa*, pp. 306-316

[2] Al-Makkiri, *The History of the Mohammedan Dynasties in Spain*, V.1., pp. 12-93.

[3] Rosenthal & Mozeson, *Wars of the Jews*, p. 196, and Ibn El Athir, *Annales du Maghreb & du Espagne*, E. Fagan, tr., p. 32.

[4] Slouschz, *Travels in North Africa*, p. 365.

[5] Ashtor, Eliyahu, *The Jews of Muslim Spain*.

[6] Eliyahu Ashtor, *The Jews of Muslim Spain*, pp. 1-8.

[7] Al- Makkiri, v.1., p. 268. Roderic was the Gothic king.

[8] Eliyahu Ashtor, *The Jews of Muslim Spain*, pp. 1-20; Ibn El-Athir, *Annales du Maghreb & de L'Espagne*, pp. 32-71; Samuel Kurinsky, T*he Berbers and the Jews*, pp. 1-12. Al-Makkiri V.1., pp. 273-299, And others.

[9] *Treaty Between Arab Leader Musa and Theodemir*, in *Medieval Iberia*, Olivia Constable, ed., pp. 37-38.

[10] Scherman, Katharine, *The Birth of France*, p. 250.

[11] Perry, *The Franks*, quoting Archbishop Hincmar or Rheims.

[12] Lewis, Bernard, *The Muslim Discovery of Europe*, pp. 19-20, 185-186, 221.

[13] Ashtor, Eliyahu, *The Jews of Muslim Spain*, p. 34.

[14] Bachrach, Bernard, *Armies and Politics in the Early Medieval West,* p. 67.
[15] *Royal Frankish Annals,* 749.
[16] Katz, Solomon, *The Jews in the Kingdoms of Spain and Gaul,* pp. 127-136.
[17] Efron, John, *Medicine and the German Jews,* p. 34.
[18] Pirenne, Henri, *Mohammed and Charlemagne,* pp. 168-185.
[19] Port, Celestin, *Histoire du Commerce Maritime de Narbonne* (Paris, 1854), pp. 168-9.
[20] Devic & Vaissete, *Histoire Generale de Languedoc,* V2, p. 806, written by clerics who did not disclose much of Jewish history, including the religion of Amoroz.
[21] The presence of these persons is generally attested, from the sources referred to in footnotes above and below. The Jewish heritage is attested to by their names, which many use as a yardstick for Goths, Romans, etc.; by their actions, which favor Jewish causes; by their Jewish associations; and by scarce documents, many of the key ones having suspiciously disappeared.

CH 5 FIRST CATHOLIC - MUSLIM - JEWISH ALLIANCE

[1] See Henri Pirenne's *Mohammed and Charlemagne* and his conclusions on 284.
[2] Dupont, A., *Les Cites,* p. 211-213, 287-294; Zukerman, A., *A Jewish Princedom,* pp. 48-49.
[3] Zukerman, Arthur, *A Jewish Princedom,* pp. 379-381, which is a reprint of F. Schneegans, ed., *Gesta Karoli Magni ad Carcassonam et Narbonam,* Romanische Bibliothek, ed. Wendelin Foerster, XV, pp. 176-180, 186-190.
[4] Schneegans, F., ed., *Gesta Karoli Magni ad Carcassonam et Narbonam,* Romanische Bibliothek. Hrsg. Von Dr. Wendelin Foerster. XV. Halle a.d.s. 1898, pp. 176-180; 186-190. This manuscript, written by a 13th century monk, does not avoid the status of Jews in France, unlike many other Church works. Zuckerman, Arthur J., *A Jewish Princedom in Feudal France,* pp 52-73. Zuckerman, with much research, lays out the facts regarding Jews in Narbonne.
[5] Katz, *The Jews in the Kingdoms of Spain and Gaul,* pp. 135-136.
[6] Einhard, *The Life of Charlemagne,,* translated by Evelyn Scherabon Firchow and Edwin H. Zeydel, p. 43.
[7] Buckler, F.W., *Harunu'll Rashid and Charles the Great,* pp. 8-36.
[8] Slouschz, Nahum, *Travels in North Africa,* p. 276.
[9] Explained in *The Jewish Princedom,* pp.77-97, with additional references to J. Schor, ed., *Sefer ha'Ittim,* Yhudah Barzilai Al-Barceloni, pp. xi-xii, B.M. Lewin, *Otsar ha-Geonim. Thesaurus of the Gaonic Responsa and Commentaries…*Haifa-Jerusalem: 1928-43, I. p. 20; Abraham ibn Daud, *Sefer ha-Kabbalah* in Neubauer, I, p. 82. Fredric Cheyette refers to another source by Abraham ben David of Toledo in his 1160 *Book of Traditions or Sefer Hakabala,* quoted by many including Fredric Cheyett in his *Ermengard,* p. 16, and Aryeh Grabois, "'Roi juif' de Narbonne" and "Dynastie des 'rois juifs' de Narbonne."
[10] *Gesta Caroli Magni ad Carcassonam et Narbonam* and letter of Pope Stephen III in Solomon Katz, *The Jews in the Kingdoms of Spain and Gaul,* pp. 95-95
[11] Zukerman's *A Jewish Princedom in Feudal Fran* does an excellent diagnosis of the available literature. Katz, Solomon, *The Jews in the Visigothic and Frankish Kingdoms of Spain and Gaul,* (Cambridge, Mass.: 1937), pp. 94-96; Rabbi Benjamin B. Jonah, *The Travels of Rabbi Benjamin of Tudela in Early Travels in Palestine,* New York (Ktav Publishing House, Inc.: 1968), p. 64, Abraham ibn Daud, (*Sefer Seder haKabbalah,* in Neubauer, Adolph, ed., *Midieval Jewish Chronicles and Chronological Notes* (Oxford: Documents and Extracts from Manuscripts in the Bodleian and Other Oxford Libraries. Semitic Series), vol. I, p. 82; Dumege, A., in an 1829 report recited in *A Jewish Prince,* p. 63; Peter the Venerable, abbot of Cluny, in an 1143 letter to King Louis VII, see I. Loeb, "Polemistes chretiens et juifs en

End Notes

France et en Espagne," in "Revue des Etudes Juives," XVIII, 1889, p. 45: an 1144 claim of the Cambridge monk Theobald, see Thomas of Monmouth, *The Life and Miracles of St. William of Norwich*, ed. and transl. Augustus Jessopp and Montague R. James, Cambridge, 1896, 135,306, The *Annals of Aniane in Veterum Scriptorum et Monumentorum Historicorum...* Collectio,, V, cols. 884-916 from the Latin 5941 of the Bibliotheque Nationale in Paris; see *Jewish Princedom*, p. 39-45; Brody, Robert, *The Geonim of Babylonia*, p. 77. *The Histoire of Languedoc* refers to the Jewish grants as the privileges of the Jews, v. 2, p. 1014.

[12] See note 16.

[13] Pepin III, *Capitulary of Aquitaine* in *The Jewish Princedom*, p. 85; ibid, pp. 83-85.

[14] Bachrach, Bernard S., *Early Carolingian Warfare*, p. 65.

[15] Ibid.

[16] Abraham ben David, *Sefer HaKabbalah*, in Neubauer, Adolf, *Medieval Jewish Chronicals*, pp. 82-84.

[17] Stow, Kenneth, *Alienated Minority*, pp. 70-71, 123.

[18] Zuckerman, Arthur, *A Jewish Princedom*, pp. 62-170. Zuckerman makes many references to different Jews by the name Todros and their association with writing. The significance here is that the author of the *Song of Roland* signed his name as a variant of Todros. More on this later.

[19] *Talmud Ketubbot 105b* as in Katz & Schwartz, *Swimming in the Sea of Talmud*, p. 195.

[20] Einhard, *The Life of Charlemagne*, pp. 50 - 54.

[21] *A Cyclopeidia of Education* Vol. 3, p. 548 and also Jewish Encyclopedia.com

[22] Solomon Grayzel, *A History of the Jews*.

[23] Devic & Vaissett, *Histoire Generale de Languedoc*, p. 842.

[24] Oelsner, Ludwig, *Jahrbucher des Frankischen Reiches unter Konig Pippin*, Leipsic: Jahrbucher der Deutschen Geschichte, IV, 1871, pp. 412-415, as presented in Zuckerman's *A Jewish Princedom*..

[25] *The Histoire Generale de Languedoc v. 2* pp. 842-876. The ethnicity of names often serves as sufficient evidence of heritage or religion. In these cases, other criteria pertain as per note 11 above. Jewish names appear in religious material such as the Bible, that that alone is not sufficient. The case of Bera exudes Jewish heritage as the root is used for prayers, the first word of the Torah, the Hebrew town, and reference to scholarly commentary known as *beraisha*. Finally, Jews use Jewish names, as appearing in Jewish name lists or references. Names take different spellings over years and countries. Ansell may appear as Amsel, Ancel, Enzel, Inzel, Enzel, Inzel, Insel, Anselle, etc., Curson or Chorson as Khorson, Gherson, Garson, Korzen, Kuson, Courshon, Carson, Korczeny, Gruzin, Gerson, etc.

[26] Zuckerman, Arthur, *A Jewish Princedom*, p. 128.

[27] *Royal Frankish Annals*, 777-778, and B. Scholz, *Carolingian Chronicles*, p. 184-185. *The Histoire Generale de Languedoc* pp. 851-853 says that Solomon and Joseph were only ambassadors and that Ibin Alarabi was governor of Zaragossa. Franks killed Waifre, rebel Duke of Aquitaine, and Lupus, his son staged the ambush. Einhard only refers to Gascon treachery, but who other that the leadership had the wherewithall to commit "treachery." When Romans used secret service to stage this type of attack, "treachery" became bold fighting for a good cause.

[28]Einhard, *The Life of Charlemagne*, 778.

[29] Pidal, R. Menendez, *Flor Nueva de Romances Viejos*, # 1-7, pp. 85-98.

[30] *Royal Frankish Annals*, 777-778, and B. Scholz, *Carolingian Chronicles*, pp. 184-185.

[31] *The Song of Roland*, selected portions, with careful interpretations in areas such as Roland's shofar, which is not the prevailing translation. Countless studies on this important ballad have not yielded the underlying proto-Roland, which has been sub-

jected to intense rewriting by various Catholic clerics with points to make. George Jones studied the ethos of *Roland* and proclaimed it the work of an Old Testament, not New Testament, people. Joan Ferrante, Glanville Price, and Arthur Zuckerman, among others, point out that in other chansons, relatives of the heroes in Roland speak Hebrew. Of the actuality of the Roncesvals battle, ample sources in Spanish, French, Latin, Hebrew, and Arabic confirm the event. Ex: Annals of St. Bertin, Einhard's *Charlemagne,* and the *Nota Emilianense.* Also see Scholz, *Carolingian Chronicles,* p. 185.

[32] Einhard, *Life of Charlemagne, yr. 778* and numerous other sources. Collins in *The Basques* emphasizes attempts by Catholics to color the battle as Muslim vs. Frank rather than Basque vs. Frank, p.121. *The Annals of the Kingdom of the Franks* casually mentions the disaster in its year 778.

[33] Katz, Solomon, *The Jews in the Visigothic and Frankish Kingdoms,* p. 109; Agobard, *Ep. 4, 7, 9.*

[34] Charlemagne, *Capitulary of Herstal, 3/779,* in P. King, *Charlemagne: Translated Sources,* pp. 203-205.

[35] *Capitularies of Charlemagne, 806, 807,* in P. King, *Charlemagne: Translated Sources,* pp.260-261.

[36] Bachrach, Bernard S. *Early Carolingian Warfare,* pp. 53-56 & 148-149.

[37] Hughes, Robert, *Barcelona* (New York: Alfred A. Knopf, 1992), pp. 56-67. Also see Katz, Solomon, *The Jews in the Visigothic and Frankish Kingdoms,* p. 54.

[38] *Frank Annals,* pp. 801-2.

[39] *Annals of the Kingdom of the Franks,* p. 801.

[40] Pifford, Guerard, tr., *The Cycle of William of Orange, v. I,* p. 389 Some attempts by early monks to claim that William founded a monastery and became a monk are demolished by, among others, Francis Nachtmann's *History of Studies of the Old French William Cycle.*

[41] *La Chancon de Williame,* vv. 1039-41, 1331, 1421, 3358-79, and the *Continuation w* 2170-71 as analyzed by Zukerman in *A Jewish Princedom,* pp. 116-117; *Song of William,* tr. Glanville Price, Lynette Muir, and David Hoggan, p. 174; *The Cycle of Willame of Orange,* by Guerard Piffard tr, v. I, pp. 467,481.

[42] Bachrach, Bernard, *Armies and Politics in the Early Medieval West XIII,* p. 26. See chapter 9.

[43] Astronomer, *Life of Louis,* in P.D. King, *Charlemagne Translated Sources,* p. 174.

[44] Astronomer, *Life of Emperor Louis,* ch. 8-10

[45] Bachrach, Bernard, *Armies and Politics in the Early Medieval West,XIII,* p. 27.

[46] Astronomer, *Life of Louis,* in P.D. King, *Charlemagne Translated Sources,p. 176.*

[47] See also *Milhemet Mitsvah* by Meir Simeon in Neubauer, "Documents sur Nabonne," *Revue des Etudes Juives,* X, 1885 reprinted in Zuckerman, *A Jewish Princedom,* pp. 387-388; the William cycle of Franch Chancons; the Zuckerman book.

[48] Devic & Vaissett, *Histoire Generale de Languedoc* v. 2, p. 912-926. Who was William? What a question and controversy! Between the French chansons and extant records some ten or twenty candidates line up. Much attention focuses on a William who could be William of Toulouse; Saint William of Gellone; William who speaks his vernacular, Hebrew; Count William who with Counts Bera and Borell populates empty cities of Catalonia with Jews; William, son of Theodore; or William, son of Aimeri. The written record confuses because documents of ecclesiastics and monarchs reek with forgery, propaganda, and gross rewriting. Detective work in the form of reading between the lines must take place. So, if certain clerics wrote complaints that they saw Jews every day at the royal court and Christians prefer the lectures of rabbis, we can conclude a prominent Jewish presence. When records indicate Jews in majorities or large quantities residing within certain cities

End Notes

and archaeology uncovers major portions of old towns containing Jewish sections, obvious conclusions follow. Combine this with practices of the day. For instance, exploits of Charlemagne's father and son are often credited to Charlemagne. And then, of course, add the actions, life and heritage of the man. Hence our conclusion: a Jewish Count William existed. The history of this William, for various natural or nefarious reasons, fused with the history of other Williams. Also see Bachrach, Bernard, *Armies and Politics in the Early Medieval West*, pp. 15-19.

[49] Collins, R.J.H., "Wifred the Hairy," in Gibson, Margaret, and Nelson, Janet, *Charles the Bald*, PP. 185-188. Collins suggests that the Hispani were refugees from non-Frank Spain, some with Arabic names. Also Kagay, *The Usatges of Barcelona*, pp. 5-7.

[50] Zuckerman, Arthur, *A Jewish Princedom*, pp. 135-136, 318-319, who quotes various sources.

[51] Devic & Vaissett, *Histoire Generale de Languedoc*, v. 2, p. 889.

[52] Devic & Vaissett, *Histoire Generale de Languedoc*, v.5, preuves, col. 117.

[53] Collins, *The Basques*, p. 141. The Banu Qasi joined Basques.

54 Collins, *The Basques*, pp. 157-159.

[55] Charlemagne, *811 memorandum*, in P.D.King, *Charlemagne: Translated Sources*, pp. *264-265*.

[56] Charlemagne, *811 Capitulary* in P.D. King, *Charlemagne: Translated Sources*, p. 262.

[57] Einhart, *Life of Charlemagne*, p. 810.

[58] Einhard, *Life of Charlemagne*, p. *801*.

[59] Charlemagne, *Captiularies*, in P.D. King, *Charlemagne: Translated Sources*, pp. 208-220, 256.

[60] Charlemagne, *Capitularies*, in P.D. King, *Charlemagne: Translated Sources*, p. 257.

[61] Bishop Wolfran of Sens, as quoted in Sergeant, *The Franks*, Scherman, Katharine, (*The Birth of France*, New York: Randon House, 1987), p. 259.

[62] Scherman, Katharine, *The Birth of France*, (New York: Random House, 1987), p. 260, 261.

[63] Fichtenau, Heinrich, *The Carolingian Empire*, pp. 40-45.

[64] Bachrach, Bernard, *Jews in Barbarian Europe*, p. 42.

[65] Efron, John, *Medicine and the German Jews*, p. 18, who also quotes an unpublished work by Edwin Mendelssohn, *The Popes' Jewish Doctors*.

[66] Agobard, *Ep. MGH, ep. V*, ed E. Dummler, in Bachrach, Bernard, *Jews in Barbarian Europe*, p. 63-64.

[67] Airlie, Stuart, "Bonds of Power..." in *Charlemagne's Heir*, Godman and Collins ed., pp. 191-196.

[68] Allen Cabaniss, *Judith Augusta*, p. 13, although Cabaniss does not identify the name as Hebrew.

[69] Duckett, Eleanor Shipley, *Carolingian Portraits*, pp. 34-37.

[70] Duckett, Eleanor Shipley, *Carolingian Portraits*, pp. 43-45.

[71] Katz, Solomon, *The Jews in the Visigothic and Frankish Kingdoms*, p. 69.

[72] Charlemagne, *Capitulary in June 794*, in King's *Charlemagne: Translated Sources*, p. 224.

[73] Cabaniss, Allen, *Judith Augusta*, pp. 65-103., and Devic & Vaissett, *Histoire Generale de Languedoc*, v. 2. pp. 904-907.

[74] Reilly, Bernard, *The Medieval Spains*, pp. 80-81.

[75] Zuckerman, Arthur, *A Jewish Princedom*, pp. 289-371.

[76] Nelson, Janet, "The Reign of Charles the Bald," in Gibson, Margaret, and Nelson, Janet, ed., *Charles the Bald*, pp. 1-22. Nelson gives an organized overview of a chaotic period.

[77] Lewis, Archibald, *Southern French and Catalan Society*, pp. 136-154.

[78] pp. 179-190.

CH 6 MUSLIM RENAISSANCE

[1] Exodus, 30, 22-25.

[2] Kurinsky, Samuel, The Glassmakers, p.1.

[3] Isaiah, 49, 11-12 The interpretation of China has its advocates and disagreements. S.M. Perlmann and Pan Guangdan agree.

[4] Kurinsky, Samuel, The Glassmakers, pp. 250-310.

[5] Ibn Khordadhbeh, Book of Ways and Kingdoms, in Elkan Adler, ed., Jewish Travelers in the Middle Ages (NY: Dover, 1987).

[6] Pirenne, Henri, Economic and Social History of Medieval Europe, pp. 11-12.

[7] Goitein, S.D., Jews and Arabs, p. 99.

[8] Goitein, S.D., Jews and Arabs, p. 110.

[9] Adler, Elkan Nathan, Jewish Travelers in the Middle Ages, pp. 39-49.

[10]Lewis, Bernard, Music of a Distant Drum, p. 118.

[11] Yellin, David, and Abrahams, Israel, Maimonides, pp. 2-6.

12 Wikipedia.org,, also Mann, Vivian, Convivencia: Jews, Muslims, and Christians in Medieval Spain, p. 84, fromVernet and Catala, "Las obras matemataticas de Maslama d Madrid," Al-Andalus 30 (1965):19

13 Messahalah, De scientia motus orbis (1504): Widiedia.org, also David Pingree: "The Byzantine Translations of Māshā'allāh on Interrogational Astrology", in The Occult Sciences in Byzantium. Ed. Paul Magdalino, Maria V. Mavroudi. Geneva 2006. 231-243.

[14]Paul Alvarus, Catholic writer, quoted in Maria Rosa Menocal, The Ornament of the World, p. 66.

[15] Menocal, The Ornament of the World, pp. 32-34.

[16] Miron, E., The Queens of Aragon, pp. 24-25.

[17] Reinhart Dozy, Spanish Islam pp. 431-443. Queen Theuda ruled Navarre for herself and then as regent for her son Garcia. Dozy quotes the German envoy from Vita Johannis Abbatis Borziensis by Perez in Mon. Germ. Hist (Scriptores), tom iv., p. 371. Also in Al Makkiri, The History of the Mohammedan Dynasties in Spain p. 55-60, among others.

[18] Graetz, History of the Jews, iii. 232.

[19] Rabbi Chasdai and King Joseph, in The Jew in the Medieval World, Jacob Marcus, ed. pp. 227-232.

[20] Dozy, Reinhart, Spanish Islam, pp. 444-554.

[21] Dozy, Reinhart, Spanish Islam, pp 607-610.

[22] Slouschz, Travels in Africa, pp. 104-5.

[23] Pidal, R. Menendez, The Cid and His Spain, 26-27.

CH 7 CATHOLICS JEWS AS ALLIES

[1] Kagay, Donald J., The Usatges of Barcelona, p. 8. In 1059. It is our assumption, not Kagay's, that Geribert is Jewish. This name would also be Herbert, Grubert, Garfried, or Graubart.

[2] Lewis, Catalan Society pp. 336- 381.

[3] Lewis, Archibald R. The Development of Southern French and Catalan Society. pp. 379-381.

[4] Collins, R.J.H., "Charles the Bald and Wilfred the Hairy," in Gibson, Margaret, and Nelson, Janet, Charles the Bald, pp. 183-186. Collins gives an excellent summary of the era, but confuses the Jewish code, new and vigorous, with the Visigoth, gone for over a century. The Jewish population, as many do even today, utilize both a Jewish and a local name. In Carolingian times, one could also have a Frank and Latin name, etc.

[5] Baer, Yitzhak A History of the Jews in Christian Spain, p. 50.

End Notes

[6] Information about El Cid is summarized from Butler Clarke, *The Cid Campeador;* Ramon Pidal, *The Cid and His Spain;* the anonymous *Historia Roderici;* and the anonymous *Epic of the Cid.*

[7] Clarke, Butler, *The Cid Campeador,* pp. 110-112.

[8] Clarke, Butler, *The Cid Campeador,* pp. 164-171.

[9] Barnes, *Western Civilization I,* p. 798.

[10] Pope Urban II at Clermont, 1095, announcing the first Crusade as reported by Robert the Monk and printed at www.wwnorton.com, 2001.

[11] Kagay, Donald, *The Usatges of Barcelona,* pp. 64-102.

[12] Hughes, Robert, *Barcelona,* p. 119.

[13] Castro, Americo, *The Spaniards,* Willard King and Selma Margaretten tr., p. 61.

[14] Forey, A.J., *The Templars in the Corona de Aragon,* pp. 2-9.

[15] Reilly, Bernard, *The Medieval Spains,* pp. 104-120.

[16] Forey, A.J., *The Templars in the Corona de Aragon,* pp. 23-40. 159, 286.

[17] Baer, Yitzak, *History of the Jews in Christian Spain,* p. 57.

[18] *Encyclopedia Judaica.*

[19] Forey, A.J., *The Templars in the Corona de Aragon,* pp. 346-349.

[20] Baer, Yitzhak, *History of the Jews in Christian Spain,* p. 61.

[21] Baer, Yitzhak, *History of the Jews in Christian Spain,* pp. 59-77.

[22] Neuman, Abraham, *The Jews in Spain,* Philadelphia: Jewish Publication Society, 1942.

[23] Baer, Yitzhak, *History of the Jews in Christian Spain,* pp. 40-50.

[24] Castro, Americo, *The Spaniards,* Willard King and Selma Margaretten tr., p. 89.

[25] Reilly, Bernard, *The Medieval Spains,* pp. 125-126.

[26] Baer, Yitzhak, *History of the Jews in Christian Spain,* p. 55.

[27] *Chronica Adephonsi Imperatoris,* as in Castro, Americo, *The Spaniards,* Willard King and Selma Margaretten tr., p. 66.

[28] Goitein, S.D., *Jews and Arabs,* p. 114.

[29] Zeitlin, Solomon, *Maimonides,* pp. 14-17.

[30] Zeitlin, Solomon, *Maimonides,* p. 24-142..

[31] Maimonides, *Guide to the Perplexed, Introduction,* David Hartman, tr. in *Maimonides,* p. 127.

[32] Zeitlin, Solomon, *Maimonides,* p. 169.

[33] Ahimaaz, *Chronicle of Ahimaaz,* pp. 88-92.

[34] Oldenbourg, Zoe, *Massacre at Montsegur,* p.8.

[35] O'Shea, Stephen, *The Perfect Heresy,* pp. 7-56.

[36] Pegg, Mark Gregory, *The Corruption of Angels,* p. 4.

[37] Paul Wiegler, *The Infidel Emperor,* pp. 18-19; Catholic.org; catholic forum.com; goacon.com/overseas-digest.

[38] O'Shea, Stephen, *The Perfect Heresy,* pp. 57-73.

[39] O'Shea, Stephen, *The Perfect Heresy,* pp. 5-6.

[40] Pedro II

[41] Oldenbourg, Zoe, *Massacre at Montsegur,* pp. 160-170.

[42] Ballad of the period in Oldenbourg, Zoe, *Massacre at Montsegur,* p. 201.

[43] Pegg, Mark Gregory, *The Corruption of Angels,* pp. 5-14.

[44] *Capitula of Council of Toulouse 1229, & Proclamation of Council of Narbonne, 1243,* in Oldenbourg, Zoe, *Massacre at Montsegur,* pp. 377-381.

[45] O'Shea, Stephen, *The Perfect Heresy,* pp. 191-195.

[46] Pegg, Mark Gregory, *The Corruption of Angels,* pp. 45-46.

[47] O'Shea, Stephen, *The Perfect Heresy,* pp. 2-5, 211-246.

[48] Jacobs, Joseph, *Jewish Contributions of Civilization,* p. 212.

CH 8 CATHOLIC JEWISH RENNAISSANCE

[1] Assis, Yom Tov, *The Golden Age of Aragonese Jewry,* pp. 2-3.

[2] King Jaime of Aragon, *Chronicles,* pp. 24-26.

[3] King Jaime of Aragon, *Chronicles,* pp. 112, 167-172.

[4] King Jaime of Aragon, *Chronicles,* pp. 151, 212.

[5] Joseph ben Juday Ibn Aqnin, *Tibb al-Nufus,* tr. Jacob R. Marcus, *The Jew in the Medieval World,* pp. 374-77, abbreviated.

[6] A number of commentators have pointed out the parallels between Romeo and Juliet and the Italian Guelphs and Ghibellines. See Isaac Asimov, *Asimov's Guide to Shakespeare,* pp. 475-477.

[7] Miron, E., *The Queens of Aragon,* p. 111.

[8] Miron, E., *The Queens of Aragon,* pp. *112-116.*

[9] King Jaime of Aragon, *Chronicles,* pp. 557-572

[10] Assis, Yom Tov, *The Golden Age of Aragonese Jewry,* p. 20, from S. Kahn, "Documents Inedits sur les Juifs de Montpellier" in *Revue de Etudes Jeives,* Paris, xix 1889 259-81 and xxii 1896 265-279.

[11] Assis, Yom Tov, *The Golden Age of Aragonese Jewry,* pp. 20-28.

[12] Assis, Yom Tov, *The Golden Age of Aragonese Jewry, p*p.28-38.

[13] Neuman, Abraham, *The Jews in Spain v. I,* p. 179.

[14] Gibbons, *The Decline and Fall of the Roman Empire,* p. 2183, and Steven Runciman, *The Sicilian Vespers,* pp. 69-84.

[15] Francis Marion Crawford, *The Rulers of the South,* v. 2, p. 308.

[16] Runciman, Steven, *The Sicilian Vespers,* p. 96.

[17] Wiegler, Paul, *The Infidel Emperor,* p. 299.

[18] Crawford, Francis Marion, *Rulers of the South,* pp. 315-316, Steven Runciman, *The Sicilian Vespers,* pp. 117-13.,

[19] Friedenberg, Daniel, *Jewish Minters & Medalists,* pp. 31-32.

[20] The account that follows of the War of the Sicilian Vespers utilizes the excellent work of Steven Runciman, *The Sicilian Vespers;* Francis Marion Crawford, *The Rulers of the South;* Paul Wiekler, *The Infidel Emperor;* G.G. Coulton, *From St. Francis to Dante* (abstracting the Chronicle of Salimbene).

[21] Assis, Yom Tov, *The Golden Age of Aragonese Jewry,* p. 3

[22] Runciman, Steven, *The Sicilian Vespers,* p. 216.

[23] E.L.Miron, *The Queens of Aragon,* pp. 119-124

[24] Desclot, Bernat, *Chronicle of the Reign of King Pedro III,* V. 2 F.L. Critchlow tr., p. 246.

[25] Forey, A.J., *The Templars in the Corona de Aragon,* p. 135-136.

[26] Burman, Edward, *The Templars,* p. 38.

[27] Riley-Smith, *The Crusades: Idea and Reality,* pp. 92-93

[28] Read, Jan, *The Catalans,* pp. 71-75.

[29] *Gesta Comitum,* in Jan Read, *The Catalans,* p. 74.

[30] Read, Jan, *The Catalans (*London: Faber and Faber, 1978), p. 20.

[31] Reilly, Bernard, *The Medieval Spains,* pp. 140-142.

[32] Reilly, Bernard, *The Medieval Spains,* pp. 151-153.

[33] Hughes, Robert, *Barcelona (*New York: Alfred A. Knopf, 1992), pp. 113-114.

[34] Barber, Malcolm, *The Trial of the Templars,* pp. 30-37.

[35] Burman, Edward, *The Templars,* pp. 158-163.

[36] Forey, A.J., *The Templars in the Corona de Aragon,* pp. 167-181.

[37] Burman, Edward, *The Templars,* pp. 166-167.

[38] Forey, A.J., *The Templars in the Corona de Aragon,* pp. 356-363.

[39] Barber, Malcolm, *The Trial of the Templars,* pp. 96-97. Guillame de Plaisans was the king's minister.

BIBLIOGRAPHY

Abadal, Ramon. *Catalunya Carolingia Volume III Pt 2*. Barcelona: Institut D'Estudis Catalans, 1955.

Abulafia, David. *Frederick II*. NY: Penguin, 1988.

Abadal, Ramon. *Catalunya Carolingia Volume II Pt 1 & 2*. Barcelona: Institut 'Estudis Catalans, 1952.

Adler, Elkan Nathan. *Jewish Travelers in the Middle Ages*. NY: Dover, 1987.

Aeschylos. *Tragedies*. Philadelphia: David McKay.

Ahimaaz. *The Chronicle of Ahimaaz*. Marcus Salzman New York: AMS Press, 1966.

Alic, Margaret. *Hypatia's Heritage*. Boston: Beacon Press, 1968.

Al-Makkari, Ahmed Ibn-Mohammed. *The History of the Mohammedan Dynasties in Spain*. Pasqual De Gayangos tr., London: Oriental Translation Fund, 1840.

Annals of St. Bertin. Janet Nelson, tr. NY: Manchester U. Press, 1991.

Annals of the Kingdom of the Franks. In *Charlemagne: Translated Sources*, P.D. King tr. Lancaster, G.B.: U of Lancaster, 1987.

Aristotle. *The Basic Works of Aristotle*. R. McKeon, ed. NY: Random House, 1941.

Ashtor, Eliyahu. *The Jews of Moslem Spain*. Aaron & Jenny Klein, tr. Philadelphia: Jewish Publication Society, 1992.

Armstrong, A.H. & Markus, R.A. *Christian Faith and Greek Philosophy*. NY: Sheed and Ward, 1960.

Assis, Yom Tov. *The Golden Age of Aragonese Jewry*. London: Littman Library, 1997.

Assis, Yom Tov. *The Jews of Spain*. Jerusalem, 1988.

Astronomer. *Life of the Emperor Louis*, in *Charlemagne: Translated Sources*. P.D. King tr., Lancaster, G.B.: U of Lancaster, 1987

Athanasius and Schaff, Philip. *Select Works and Letters*. Grand Rapids, Eerdmans, 1891.

Atlas of the World. NY: Times Books and Random House, 1985.

Athanassiadi, Polymnia, and Michael Frede, ed., *Pagan Monotheism in Late Antiquity*. Oxford: Clarendon Press, 1999.

Audisio, Gabriel. *The Waldensian Dissent*. Cambridge: Cambridge Univ., 1999.

Augustine. St. *City of G-d*. V. 12,18,25. Marcus Dods, tr., NY: Modern Library,1950.

Avicenna. *The Canon of Medicine*. Cameron Gruner, tr. London: Luzac, 1930.

Avicenna. *Avicenna Commemoration Volume*. Calcutta: Iran Society, 1956.,

Asimov, Isaac. *Asimov's Guide to Shakespeare*. NY: Avenel Books, 1978.

Bacon, Lord Roger. *Compendium of the Study of Theology*. Thomas Maloney tr., Leiden: E.J.Brill, 1988.

Bacon. Lord Roger, *Novum Organum*. NY: Collier & Son, 1902.

Baer, Yitzhak. *A History of the Jews in Christian Spain*. Louis Schoffman tr., Philadelphia: Jewish Publication Society, 1992.

Bachrach, Bernard S. *Armies and Politics in the Early Medieval West*. Brookfield, VA, Variorum, 1993.

Bachrach, Bernard S. *Early Carolingian Warfare*. Philadelphia: Univ. of Penna., 2001.

Bachrach, Bernard S. *Jews in Barbarian Europe*. Lawrence, Kansas: Coronado: 1977.

Bachrach, Bernard, S. *The Anatomy of a Little War*, Boulder. CO: Westview Press, 1994.

Baigent, Michael, Leigh, Richard, & Lincoln, Henry. *Holy Blood, Holy Grail*. NY: Dell, 1982.

Balaguer. Victor, *Historia de Calaluna* 12 vol. Madrid: Manuel Tello, 1885.

Barder, Malcolm. *The trial of the Templars*. Cambridge: Cambridge Univ., 1978.

Barnes, Henry. *History of Western Civilization*. NY: Harcourt Brace, 1935.

Barton, Simon, and Fletcher, Richard. *The World of El Cid*. Manchester: Manchester U., 1988.

Ben-Sasson, H.H., ed. *A History of the Jewish People*. Cambridge, MA: Harvard U., 1976.

Benbassa, Esther. *The Jews of France*. Princeton: Princeton University Press: 1999

Bendiner, Elmer. *The Rise and Fall of Paradise*. NY: Barnes & Noble, 1983.

Benjamin of Tudela. *The Travels of Rabbi Benjamin of Tudela*. In Thomas Wright, Ed. *Early Travels in Palestine*. New York: Ktav Publishing, 1968.

Ben-Sasson, H.H., ed. *A History of the Jewish People*. Cambridge: Harvard U Press,

1976
Bentwich, Norman. *Philo-Judaeus of Alexandria*. Philadelphia: Jewish Publication Society, 1910.
Berber, Malcolm. *The Trial of the Templars*. Cambridge:Cambridge University, 1978.
Berman, Joshua A. *Created Equal*. Oxford: Oxford Press, 2008
Bible. Catholic Family Edition. New York: Crawley, 1953.
Bickell, Prof. *The Lord's Supper and the Passover Ritual*. Skene, William F., tr. Edinburgh: Clard, 1891.
Bloomberg, Jon. *The Jewish World in the Middle Ages*. NY: Ktav Publishing, 2000.
Boccaccio, Giovanni. *The Decameron*. London: Henry Bumpus, 1906. tr: J.M.Rigg. Illus: Charon.
Book of Deeds of James I of Aragon. Damian Smith and Helena Buffery tr.: Burlington, VT: Ashgate, 2003.
Brody, Robert. *The Geonim of Babylonia*. New Haven, CT: Yale, 1998.
Brooks, E. W. *Select Letters of Severus*. London: Williams & Norgate, 1903.
Bryar, William, and Stengren, George. *The Rebirth of Learning*. NY: Putnam, 1968.
*Buckler, F.W. *Harunu'll Rashid and Charles the Great*. Cambridge, Mass.: 1931.
Burman, Edward. *The Templars, Knights of God*, Rochester. VT: Destiny Books, 1986.
Burns, Robert I., ed., *The Worlds of Alfonso the Learned and James the Conqueror*, Princeton: Princeton U. Press, 1985.
Cabaniss, Allen. *Charlemagne*. NY: Twayne, 1972.
Cabaniss, Allen. *Judith Augusta*. NY: Vantage, 1974.
Cadiou, Rene. *Origen*. London: Herder Book, 1944.
Cahill, Thomas. *The Gifts of the Jews*. NY: Doubleday, 1998
Cantor, Norman F. *In the Wake of the Plague: The Black Death and the World it Made*. New York: Free Press, 2001.
Cantor, Norman F. *The Civilization of the Middle Ages*. NY: Harper Perennial, 1994
Cantor, Norman F. *Encyclopedia of the Middle Ages*. New York: Viking, 1999.
Cantor, Norman F. *The Civilization of the Middle Ages*. NY: Harper Perennial, 1993
Cantor, Norman F. *Inventing the Middle Ages*. New York: William Morrow, 1991.
Cantor, Norman F. *Medieval History*. NY: MacMillan, 1969.
Carr, Raymond, Ed. *Spain: A Histor,*. New York: Oxford, 2000.
Castro, Americo. *The Spaniards*. Berleley: Univ. CA Press, 1971.
Castro, Don Adolfo. *The Jews in Spain*. tr: Kirwan, E. Cadiz, 1847
Carroll, James. *Constantine's Sword*. New York: Houghton Mifflin, 2001.
Chaliand, Gerard. Penguin *Atlas of the Diasporas*. New York: Penquin, 1997.
Chansons de Geste.
Chazan, Robert. *Barcelona and Beyond*. Berkeley, U. of California, 1992.
Chazan, Robert. *European Jewry and the First Crusade*. Berkeley & Los Angeles: Univ. of California Press, 1987.
Chazan, Robert. *In the Year 1096*. Philadelphia: The Jewish Publication Society, 1996.
Chazan, Robert, ed. *Medieval Jewish Life*. NY: Ktav Publishing House, Inc., 1976.
The Cid, J Markley tr.. NY: Bobbs-Merrill. 1961.
Clarke, Butler, *The Cid Campeador*, NY: Putnam's Sons, 1897.
Cheyette, Fredric L. *Ermengard*. Ithaca, NY: Cornell Univ., 2001.
Cohen, Mark R. *Under Crescent & Cross*. Princeton, NJ: Princeton U., 1994.
Constable, Olivia. *Medieval Iberia: Readings from Christian, Muslim & Jewish Sources*. Philadelphia: Univ. PA Press, 1997.
Coogan, Michael, ed. *Oxford History of the Biblical World*. Oxford, Oxford U, 1998.
Cooper, David. *G-d is a Verb*. NY: Riverhead Books, 1997.
Coppee, Henry. *History of the Conquest of Spain*. Boston: Little, Brown, 1881.
Coulton, G.G. *From St. Francis to Dante*. London: David Nutt, 1906.
Crawford, F. Marion. *The rulers of the South*. NY: McMillan, 1900.
Crubellier, M., and Juillard, Charles. *Histoire de la Champagne*. Paris: Presses Universitaires de France, 1952.
Dan, Joseph. *Jewish Mysticism*,.Northvale, NJ: Jason Aronson, 1998.
Davies, J.G. *The Early Christian Church*. NY: Barnes & Noble, 1965.
Desclot, Bernat. *Chronicle of the Reign of King Pedro III of Aragon*. F. Critchlow, tr., Princeton: Princeton Univ. Press, 1928-34.
De Faye, Eugene. *Origen and his Work*. New York. Columbia U., 1929.
Deshpande, V.W. *The Impact of Ancient Indian Thought on Christianity*. New Delhi: APH Publishing, 1996.
De Sismundi, Simonde. *The French Under the Merovingian and Carolingian*. London: Piper, Paternester, Row, 1950.

Bibliography

Devic & Vaissett. *Histoire Generale de Languedoc.* Toulouse: Edouard Privat, 1875.
Dougherty, David M. and Barnes, E.B. ed. *La Geste de Monglane.* Eugene, OR: U. of Oregon, 1966.
Dozy, Reinhart. *Spanish Islam.* London: Chatto & Windus, 1913.
Duckett, Eleanor Shipley. *Carolingian Portraits.* Ann Arbor: University of Michigan Press, 1969.
Dudden, F. Homes. *Gregory the Great.* London: Longs, Green, 1905.
Dudden, F., Homes. *Saint Ambrose.* 2 vol. Oxford: Clarendon Press, 1935.
Duggan, F. Joseph. *The Song of Roland.* Berkeley: UCB, 1973
Durant, Will. *The Story of Civilization.* NY: Simon and Schuster, 1935-1975.
Dvornik, Francis. *Origins of Intelligence Services.* New Brunswick, NJ: Rutgers U., 1974.
Dzielska, Maria. *Hypatia of Alexandria.* F. Lyra, tr., Cambridge, MA: Harvard U., 1995.
Eban, Abba. *My People.* New York: Random House, 1968.
Edbury, Peter, ed. *The Conquest of Jerusalem, the Third Crusade.* Brookfield, VT: Scolar, 1996.
Ed-Din, Beha. *The Life of Saladin.* London: Committee of Palestine Exploration, 1897.
Efron, John. *Medicine and the German Jews.* New Haven, CT: Yale, 2001.
Efron, John. *Judaism and Science.* CA: Greenwood, 2007
Einhard. *Life of Charlemagne.* Coral Gables: University of Miami Press.
El-Athir, Ibn. *Annales du Machreb & de L'Espagne.* tr.Fagnan, Alger: Adolphe Jourdan, 1898.
Engelman, Uriah Zevi. *The Rise of the Jew in the Western World.* New York: Arno Press, 1973.
Ermoldi, Carmen Nigelli. *Exulis in Laudem Gloriosissimi Pippini Regis,* in *Monumenta Germaniae Historica.* Stuttgart: Anton Hiersemann Kraus, 1963.
Esler, Philip. *The Early Christian World.* NY: Routledge, 2000.
Eusebius. *The Ecclesiastical History.* J. Lawlor & J Leonard Oulton, tr., London: Society for Promoting Christian Knowledge, 1927.
Eusebius. *Life of Constantine the Great.* Philip Schaff & Henry Wace ed. NY: Christian Literature.,1890.
Eusebius, *Oration.* Philip Schaff & Henry Wace ed. NY:Christian Literature.,1890
Ferrante, Joan M. *Guillaume d'Orange.* NY: Columbia University Press, 1974.
Ferrante, Joan, M., tr. *Guillaume d'Orange.* NY: Columbia University Press, 1974.
Fichtenau, Heinrich. Trans. By Peter Munz. *The Carolingian Empire,* New York: Harper & Row, 1964.
Fletcher, Richard. *The Quest for El Cid.* NY: Knopf, 1989.
Fletcher, Richard. *Moorish Spain.* U. of CA, 1992.
Forey, A. J. *The Templars in the Corona de Aragon.* London: Oxford U. Press, 1973.
Fouracre, Paul. *The Age of Charles Martel,.*Essex: Pearson Education, 2000.
Fortunatus, Venantius, George, Judith W. trans. *Venantius Fortunatus: Personal and Political Poems.* Liverpool: Liverpool University Press, 1995.
Friendenberg, Daniel M. *Jewish Minters & Medalists.* Philadelphia: The Jewish Publication Society, 1976.
Friedlander, Gerald, *The Jewish Sources of the Sermon of the Mount,* London: Routledge, 1911.
Garcia Lopez, Jose. *Historia de la Literatura Espanola.* Barcelona: Vicens Vives, 1999.
Gavilanes, Jose Luis and Apolinario, Antonio eds. *Historia de la literatura Portuguesa.* Madrid: Catedra, 2000.
Geffre, Claude, and Dhavamony. *Mariasusai, Buddhism and Christianity.* NY: Seabury Press, 1979.
George, Judith W. *Venantius Fortunatus.* Oxford: Clarendon Press, 1992.
Gerberding, Richard A. *The Rise of the Carolingians.* Oxford: Clarendon Press, 1987.
Gersh, Harry. *The Sacred Books of the Jews.* NY: Stein and Day, 1968.
Gibbon, Edward. *The Decline and Fall of the Roman Empire.* NY: Heritage Press, 1946.
Gibson, Margaret, and Nelson, Janet, ed. *Charles the Bald.* Hampshire, Gt.Britain:Variorum, 1990.
Godman, Peter, and Collins, Roger. *Charlemagne's Heir.* Oxford: Clarendon Press, 1990.
Golb, Norman. *The Jews in Medieval Normandy.* New York: Cambridge University Press, 1998.
Goitein, S.D. *Jews and Arabs.* NY: Schocken Books, 1955.

Jewish German Revolution of 400

Goldin, Hyman. *Hebrew Criminal Law and Procedur.,* NY: Twayne, 1952.
Gooch, G.P. *English Democratic Ideas.* NY: Harper, 1959.
Gordis, Robert. *Koheleth.* NY: Schocken, 1968.
Grayzel, Solomon. *A History of the Jews.* Philadelphia: Jewish Publication Society, 1948.
Green, J.R. *Conquest of England.* London 1884
Gregory the Great. *Selected Epistles.* Grand Rapids, MI: Eerdmans Pub., 1983.
Gregory of Tours. *History of the Franks.* tr. Brehaut, New York 1916
Gregory of Tours. *History of the Franks.* tr. Thorpe, Lewis, New York Penguin, 1985.
Guizot, Francois. *History of France.* Robert Black, tr., Boston: Estes & Lauriat.
Hadas, Moses. *Rome.* Philadelphia: Jewish Publication Society, 1940.
Halkin, Abraham, and Hartman, David, ed. *Epistles of Maimonides.* Philadelphia, Jewish Publication Society, 1985.
Hamilton, Edith. *The Greek Way.* New York: W.W. Norton, 1930.
Harris, Michael H. *A History of Libraries in the Western World.* NY: Scarecrow Press, 1984.
Hartman, David. *Maimonides.* Philadelphia: Jewish Publication Society, 1986.
Hatch, Edwin. *The Influence of Greek Ideas on Christianity.* NY: Harper, 1957.
Hatch, Edwin. *the Organization of the Early Christian Churches.* London: Longmans, Green, 1901.
Heather, Peter. *The Goths.* Cambridge, Mass: Balckwell, 1996.
Heinzelmann, Martin. *Gregory of Tours.* C. Carroll, tr. Cambridge: Cambridge U. Press, 2001.
Hornblower, Simon, and Spawforth, Antony, ed. *The Oxford Companion to Classical Civilization.* Oxford: Oxford U., 1998.
Hughes, Robert. *Barcelona.* New York: Alfred A. Knopf, 1992
Husik, Isaac. *A History of Mediaeval Jewish Philosophy.* Philadelphia: Jewish Pub. Society, 1948.
Isidore of Seville. *History of the Kings.* Leiden, E.J. Grill, 1966.
Jacobs, Joseph. *Jewish Contributions to Civilization.* Philadelphia: Jewish Publication Society, 1919.
James I, King of Arogon. *Chronicles.* John Forster, tr. London: Chapman & Hall, 1883.
James, Edward. *The Franks.* New York: Basil Blackwell Ltd.: 1988
Johnson, Elmer. *A History of Libraries in the Western World.* NY: Scarecrow Press, 1965.
Jones, George Fenwick. *The Ethos of the Song of Roland.* Baltimore: Johns Hopkins, 1963.
Jones, Joseph Ramon and Keller, John Estern. *The Scholar's Guide.* Toronto: Pontifical Inst. 1969.
Jordon, William Chester. *The French Monarchy and the Jews.* Philadelphia: University of Penna. Press, 1989.
Kagag, Donald J.tr. *The Usatges of Barcelona.* Philadelphia: U of Penn, 1994.
Katz, Michael, and Schwartz, Gershon. *Swimming in the Sea of Talmud.* Phila.: Jewish Pub. 1998.
Katz, Solomon. *The Jews in the Visigothic and Frankish Kingdoms of Spain and Gaul.* Cambridge, Mass., 1937
Keller, Hans-Erich, ed. *La Geste de Garin de Monglane.* Aix: Cuer Ma, 1994.
King, P.D. *Charlemagne Translated Sources.* Great Britain: University of Lancaster, 1987.
Kingsley, Charles. *Hypatia.* Boston: Joseph Knight, 1897.
Koss, Ronald G. *Family, Kinship and Lineage in the Cycle De Buillaume d'Orange.* Lewiston, NY: The Edwin Mellen Press, 1990.
Kurinsky, Samuel. *The Glassmaker.,* New York: Hippocrene Books, 1991.
Kurinsky, Samuel. *The Eighth Day.* Northvale, NJ: Jason Aronson, Inc., 1994.
Kurinsky, Samuel. *The Berbers and the Jews.* Hebrewhistory.org.
Lacroix, Paul. *Military and Religious Life In the Middle Ages.* London: Bickers & Son
La Geste De Garin De Monglane en Prose. ed. Hans-Erich Keller, Center Universitaire d'Etudes et de Recherches Medievales d'Aix, 1994. O'Callaghan, tr. , Arizona, Arizona Center for Medieval & Renaissance Studies, 2002
Latourette, Kenneth Scott. *The Expansion of Christianity.* NY: Harper, 1937.
LeGentil, Perrre. *The Chanson de Roland.* tr. Frances F. Beer, Cambridge: Harvard, 1969
Le Goff, Jacques. *Medieval Civilization.* London: Balckwell, 1990.

Bibliography

Lee, A.C. *The Decameron*. NY: Haskell House, 1972.
Leroy, Beatrice. *The Jews of Navarre*. Israel: Magnes Press Hebrew U., 1985.
Lewis, Archibald R. *The Development of Southern French and Catalan Society*. 718-1050, Austin, TX: Univ. of Texas, 1965.
Lewis, Bernard. *The Muslim Discovery of Europe*. New York: Norton, 2001.
Lewis, Bernard. *The Jews of Islam*. Princeton, NJ: Princeton U.:1984.
Lewis, Bernard. *Music of a Distant Drum*. NY: Simon and Schuster, 2001.
Lindo, E. H. *The Jews of Spain and Portugal*. London: Longman, Brown, Green & Longman, 1848.
Lopez, Robert S. and Raymond, Irving W. *Medieval Trade in the Mediterranean World*. NY: Columbia University, 1955.
Lorenz. *Arius Judaizans*? Gottingen, Vandenhoeck & Ruprecht, 1979.
Lowenthal, Marvin. *The Jews of Germany*. New York: Longmans, Green & Co., 1936.
Mackay, Angus. *Atlas of Medieval Europe*. New York: Routlege, 1997.
Macmullen, Ransay. *Christianity & Paganism*. New Haven: Yale, 1997.
Maimonides, Moses. *The Guide for the Perplexed*. M Friedlander tr. NY: Dover, 1956.
Maimonides, Moses. *Medical Aphorisms*. F. Rosner & S. Muntner, tr., NY: Yeshiva U., 1970.
Maimonides, Moses. *Epistles*. Abraham Halkin, tr. Phila.: Jewish Publication, 1985.
Manm, Milton, ed. *Selections from Early Greek Philosophy*. NY: Crofts & Co., 1947.
Mann, Vivian; Glick, Thomas; Dodds, Jerrilynn. *Convivencia: Jews, Muslims, and Christians in Medieval Spain*. George Braziller & The Jewish Museum, NY, 1992.
Markoe, Glenn. *Phoenicians*. Berkeley: Univ. CA Press, 2000.
Marcus, Jacob. *The Jew in the Medieval World*. Cincinnati, Union of American Hebrew Congregations, 1938
Mashallah. *De Scientia Motus Orbis*. as found in *The Irish Astronomical Tract*, originally in Hebrew and Arabic, written about 780, translated into many languages
Menn, Hermann. *Die Chanson Garin De Monglene*. Greofswald: Univ. of Greifswald, 1913.
Merriam Webster's Biographical Dictionary. Springfield, Mass.: Merriam-Webster, 1995.
Milton, John. *Of Education*. Mishnah, Neusner, Jacob, tr. New Haven, Conn.: Yale Univ., 1988.
Monumenta Germaniae Historica. Berlin: 1887-1899.
Moore, R.I. *The Formation of a Persecuting Society*. Oxford: Blackwell, 1987.
Muller, Max. *Die Chanson Garin De Monglene*. Greifswald: Univ. of Greifswald, 1913.
Nachtmann, Francis Weldon. *A History of Studies of the Old French William Cycle*. Urbana, Ill: Univ. of Ill., 1958.
Nelson, Eric. *The Hebrew Republic*. Cambridge: Harvard, 2010.
Nelson, Janet. *Politics and Ritual in Early Medieval Europe*. Harlow: Longman Group, 1994.
Newark, Tim. *The Barbarians*. Poole: Blandford Press, 1985.
Neubauer, Adolph, Ed. *Midieval Jewish Chronicles and Chronological Notes*. Oxford: Oxford U., 1887-1895.
Neuman, Abraham, A. *The Jews in Spai.*, Philadelphia: Jewish Publication Society, 1942.
Newman, Louis Israel. *Jewish Influence on Christian Reform Movements*. NY: Columbia U.,1925.
Nicolle, David. *Attila and the Norman Hordes*. Oxford: Osprey Publishing, 1990.
Nithard. *Histories, in Carolingian Chronicles*. B. Scholz tr.:Ann Arbor: U. Michigan, 1970.
Odegaard, Charles E. *Vassi and Fideles in the Carolingian Empire*. Cambridge, Mass.: Harvard Historical Monographs, XIX, 1945.
O'Donovan, Oliver and Joan Lockwood, ed. *Fron Irenaeus to Grotius*. Grand Rapids, MI: Eerdmans Pub., 1999.
Oldenbourg, Zoe. *Massacre at Montsegur*. Peter Green, tr., NY: Pantheon, 1961.
Orosius, Paulus, *Seven Books of History Against the Pagans*. NY: Columbia U., 1936.
O'Callaghan, Joseph F. *The Learned King*. Philadelphia, U Penn, 1993.
O'Shea, Stephen. *The Pefect Heresy*. NY: Walker, 2000
Parkes, Henry Bamford. *The Divine Order*. New York: Alfred A. Knopf, 1969.

Pegg, Mark Gregory. *The Corruption of Angels.* Princeton: Princeton U.:2001.
Pentateuch, w Targum Onkelos, Haphtaroth, Rashi. tr. M. Rosenbaum and A.
        Silbermann, NY. Hebrew Pub. Co., 1934.
Perlmann, S.M. *Jews in Old China.* NY: Paragon, 1971.
Philostorgius. *The Ecclesiastical History.* tr. E. Walford, London: Hengy Bohn,
        1855.
Pidal, R. Menendez. *The Cid and His Spain.* Harold Sunderland, tr. London:J.
        Murray, 1934.
Pidal, R. Menendez. *Flor Nueva de Romances Viejos.* 1928.
Pidal, R. Menendez. *Spaniards in their History.* New York: 1951.
Piffard. *Guerard, William of Orange.* Vol. I – III, San Diego: San Diego State
        University Press, 1977.
Pinski, David. *Temptations.* tr. Goldberg, Isaac, NY: Brentano's, 1919.
Pipin III. *Capitulary of Aquitaine.* 768 in The Jewish Princedom, p. 84.
Piffard, Guerard, Trans. *Willame of Orange.* Ann Arbor: San Diego State University
        Press, 1977.
Pingree, David: "The Byzantine Translations of Māshā'allāh on Interrogational
        Astrology", in *The Occult Sciences in Byzantium.* Ed. Paul Magdalino,
        Maria V. Mavroudi. Geneva 2006. 231-243.
Pirenne, Henri. *Economic and Social History of Medieval Europe.* NY: Harcourt
        Brace Jovanovich, 1936.
Pirenne, Henri. *Mohamed and Charlemagne.* Mineola, NY: Dover, 2001.
Plato. *The Republic.* Allan Bloom, tr. NY: Basic Books, 1968.
Plutarch. *Plutarch's Lives,* NY: A.L. Burt,
Porphyry. *Letter to His Wife Marcella.* tr. A. Zimmern, Grand Rapids, MI: Phanes
        Press, 1986.
Porphyry. *Against the Christians.* Joseph Hoffmann, tr. Amherst, NY: Prometheus,
        1994.
* Port, Celestin. *Histoire du Commerce Maritime, de Narbonne.* Paris: 1854
Powers, James F. *A Society Organized for War.* Berkeley: U. of CA, 1988.
Price, Glanville, ed.. *William, Count of Orange.* Totowa, NJ: Rowman and
        Littlefield, 1975.
Rebinowitz, Isaac. *Jewish Merchant Adventurers.* London: Edward Goldston, 1948
Radin, Max. *The Jews Among the Greeks and Romans.* Philadelphia: Jewish
        Publication Society, 1915.
Radbertus, Paschasius. *The Life of Saint Adalard – The Life of Wala.* in
        Charlemagne's Cousins, Allen Cabaniss tr., Syracuse, NY: Syracuse U.,
        1967.
Radhakrishnan, S. *Eastern Religions and Western Thought.* London: Oxford U.,
        1939.
Rand, Edward Kennard. *Founders of the Middle Ages.* NY: Dover Publications,
        1957.
Randers-Pehrson, Justine Davis. *Barbarians and Romans.* Norman: Univ. of
        Oklahoma, 1983.
Raphael, Chaim. *Minyan.* Malibu. *CA,* Joseph Simon, 1992.
Read, Jan. *The Catalans.* London: Faber and Faber, 1978
Regan, Geoffrey. *Lionhearts.* London: Constable, 1998.
Regan, Geoffrey. *Saladin and the Fall of Jerusalem.* NY: Croom Helm, 1987.
Regne, Jean. *Etude sur la condition des Juifs de Narbonne du Ve au XIVe siecle.*
        Narbonne: Caillard, 1912.
Reilly, Bernard F. *The Medieval Spains.* Cambridge: Cambridge University, 1993.
Rice, Wallcae, ed. *Pagan Pictures.* NY: Boni & Liveright, 1927.
Riley-Smith, Jonathan & Louise. *The Crusades: Idea and Reality 1095-1274.*
        London: Edward Arnold, 1981.
Royal Frankish Annals in Carolingian Chronicles. B. Scholz tr. Ann Arbor: U.
        Michigan, 1970.
Rosenthal, Monroe, & Mozeson, Isaac. *Wars of the Jew.,* NY: Hippocrene Books,
        1990.
Roth, Norman. *Daily Life of the Jews in the Middle Ages.* Westport: Greenwood
        Press, 2005.
Rothwell, Fred. *Origen and His Work.* NY: Columbia U., 1929.
Rouche, Michel. *L'Aquitaine.* Paris: Bibliotheque Benerale, 1979.
Runciman, Steven. *The Sicilian Vespers.* Cambridge: Cambridge U., 1958.
Schenck, David P. *The Myth of Guillaume.* Birmingham, AL: Summa Pub., 1988.
Scherman, Katharine. *The Birth of France.* New York: Random House, 1987.
Scholasticus, Socrates. *The Ecclesiastical History.* ed, O. Schaff & H. Wace. NY:
        Christian Literature, 1890.

Bibliography

Schuppe, Erich. *Die Chanson Garin De Monglene.* Greifswald: Univ. of Greifswald, 1914.

Scholz, Bernhard, tr. *Carolingian Chronicals,* Ann Arbor: U. Michigan, 1970.

Schwarz, Leo, ed. *Great Ages and Ideas of the Jewish People.* NY: Modern Library, 1956.

Scott, S.P. *The Visigothic Code.* Boston: The Boston Book Co., 1910.

Severus. *Select Letters of Severus.* E. W. Grooks, ed & tr., London: Williams & Norgate, 1903.

Severus. *Letter on the Conversion of the Jews.* Scott Bradbury, ed., Oxford: Clarendon, 1996.

Sharf, Andrew. *Byzantine Jewry.* NY: Schocken Books, 1971.

Shakespeare, William. *The Tragedy of Macbeth.* NY: Washington Square Press, 1932, 1992.

Shapiro, Sidney, ed. *Jews in Old China.* New York: Hippocrene, 2001.

Sidonius. w/Anderson, W.B. ed. *Sidonius Poems and Letters* vol. I & II, Cambridge, MA: Harvard, 1963.

Sismondi, Simonde de. *The French under the Merovingians and the Carlovingians.* London, Piper, Paternoster Row, 1850.

Slouschz, Nahun. *Hebraeo-Pheniciens et Judeo-Berberes.* Paris: Ernest Leroux, 1908.

Slouschz, Nahum. *Travels in North Africa.* Philadelphia: Jewish Publication Society, 1927.

Smith, John Holland. *Constantine the Great.* New York: Scribner, 1971.

Sombart, Werner. *The Jews and Modern Capitalism.* M. Epstein tr., NY: Collier, 1962.

Sozomen. *The Ecclesiastical Histor.,* tr. E. Walford, London: Hengry Bohn, 1855.

Sozomen. *The Ecclesiastical History.* ed. O. Schaff & H. Wace. NY: Christian Literature, 1890.

Starr, Joshua. *The Jews in the Byzantine Empire.* NY: Burt Franklin, 1939.

Steinsaltz, Adin. *The Essential Talmud.* Chaya Galai, tr. USA: basic Books, 1976.

Stegemann, Ekkehard & Wolfgang. *The Jesus Movement.* tr. O. Dean, Minneapolis: Fortress Press, 1999.

Stevens, C. E. *Sidonius Apollinaris and His Age.* Oxford: Clarendon Press: 1933.

Stone, Edward Noble, Translator. *The Song of William.* Seattle: University of Washington Press, 1951.

Stow, Kenneth C. *Alienated Minority.* Cambridge, MA: Harvard, 1992.

Strabo. *The Geography of Strab.,* H. Jones, tr., NY: Loeb Library, 1923.

Strayer, Joseph R. *The Albigensian Crusades.* NY: Dial Press, 1971.

Streeter, Burnett Hillman. *The Buddha and the Christ.* NY: Macmillan, 1933.

Schwarz, Leo W. *The Jewish Caravan.* NY: Farrar & Rinehart, 1935.

Schwarz, Leo W. *Great Ages and Ideas of the Jewish People.* NY: Modern Library, 1956.

Synesius. *Essays and Hymns.* 2 vol. A. Fitzgerald, Tr. London: Oxford U. Press, 1930.

Synesius. *Letters.* 2 vol. A. Fitzgerald, Tr. London: Oxford U. Press, 1926.

Talmud

Tambyah, T. Isaac. *Hinduism, Budhism and Christianity.* Delhi: Indian Book Ballery, 1925.

Tanach, The Holy Scriptures. Vol. I & II,. Philadelphia, Jewish Pub., 1955.

Taylor, Nathaniel. "Saint William, King David, Makhir," The American Genealogist, v.72 # 3-4.

Theodosian Code. Phar, Clyde, tr. Princeton: Princeton Univ., 1952.

Toaff, Ariel, and Schwarzfuchs, Simon,ed. *The Mediterranean and the Jews,* Israel: Bar-Ilan University, 1989.

Thomas, Hugh. *A History of the World.* NY: Harper & Row, 1979.

Thompson, E.A. *The Goths in Spain.* Oxford: Clarendon, 1969.

Todros. *The Song of Roland.* tr. Patricia Terry. Indianapolis: Bobbs-Merrill, 1965.

Taitz, Emily. *The Jews of Medieval France.* Westport, CN: Greenwood Press, 1994.

Terry, Patricia, tr. *The song of Roland.* Indianapolis: Bobbs-Merrill Ed. Publishing, 1965.

Tolan, John. *Petrus Alfonsi.* Florida: University Press of Florida, 1993.

Van Dam, Raymond. *Saints.* Princeton, NJ: Princeton U., 1993.

Von Soden, Wolfram. *Sumerian and Babylonian Science.* tr. Donald Schley. Grand Rapids: Eerdmans Pub., 1985.

Walzer, Michael. *Exodus and Revolution.* US: Basic Books, 1984.

Waithe, Mary Ellen. *A History of Women Philosophers.* Vol. 1-4, Boston: Martinus

Nijhoss, 1987.
Wein, Berel. *Herald of Destiny.* Brooklyn: Shaar Press, 1993.
Weston, Jessie, L. *The Romance Cycle of Charlemagne and his Peers.* NY: AMS, 1905.
Wiegler, Paul. *The infidel Emperor.* NY: E.P. Dutton, 1930.
Wolfram, Herwig. *History of the Goths.* Berkely: U. of Cal.: 1988.
Wolfram, Herwig, tr. By Thomas Dunlap. *The Roman Empire and its Germanic Peoples.* Berkeley, CA, Univ. of California, 1997.
Wood, Ian. *The Merovingian Kingdoms.* London, Longman, 1994.
Yellin, David, and Abrahams, Israel. *Maimonides.* Philadelphia: Jewish Publication Soc., 1936.
Yu, Chai-Shin. *Early Buddhism and Christianity.* Delhi: Motilal Banarsidass, 1981.
Zeitlin, Solomon. *Maimonides.* NY: Ganis and Harris, 1955.
Zink, Michael. *The Enchantment of the Middle Ages.* Baltimore, MD: Johns Hopkins, 1998.
Zuckerman, Arthur J. *A Jewish Princedom in Feudal France 768-900,* New York: Columbia University Press, 1972.

PICTURES

9. Constantine statue in Milan, Renaissance sketch of Arius, Arian Visigoth churches in Banos de Cerrate and Lara, miniature of Pedro III and Usatges. 10. Abraham by Jan Provost , Joseph sold into Egypt by James J. Tissot , Commandments by Aron de Chavez in 1674 , 11. Solomon by Edward Paynter, ship unknown, 12. Gregory I by Meister Theoderich von Prag -- Deborah by Narcisse-Virgile Diaz de la Pena – lions of ancient Israel, 13-16. author and public domain, 17. Ancient Alexandria by Adolf Gnauth in "Egypt" by Georg Ebers, 1878 – 19th century woodcut of lighthouse and engraving of library – Hypatia, part of larger painting by Raphael -- Beruriah by Luba in play by Pinski, 18. Constantine by Rubens lions under glass Israel - Canadian Museum of Civilization, 19. Theodosius by Ambrose Peirre Subleyras, Death of hypatia by William Mortensen, 5th century scroll showing Bishop Theophilus atop a destroyed Serapeum, 20. Roman Slave by Gerome, Titus Arch in Rome, Church of The Visitation in Jerusalem, Romans during the Decadence by Couture. 21. Akiba by Rembrant, Moses by Rembrant, Christ by Bloch, 22. 16C Rashi woodcut, St. Athanasius in the Mar Musa Chapel, Arian church ruins in Spain, St. Nicholus punching Arius on wall of Soumela Monastery of Turkey, Exiling of Arius in Megalo Meteoron Monastery, Visigoth jewelry, 23. *Cruce Liber Tres by* Justus Lipsius, Constantine edict to burn Arius' books, Greek tile in Cologne in 300, Constitine edict to recognize Jewish political position in Cologne, Arian alter, 24. Gregory of Tours by Boulanger, Sidonius letters and poems, Euric statue in Madrid, 26. Recared by Antonio Degrain, Moor Chief by Eduard Charlemont -- statue of Abd al Rahman -- Hasdai Ibn Shaprut in the court of Abderramán by Dionis Baixeras, 27. Scientia Orbis by Mashalla, Marshalla on Climate, Anatomica de Motv Cordis et Sanguinis in Animali by Harvey, Aid to Health , 28 . Gabirol statue in Israel, Roger Bacon statue at Cambridge U. Museum – Summa Universai Theologiae -- Guide for the Perplexed 1347 Royal Library in Copenhagen -- engraving of Moses Maimonides approx. 1190 in Granger collection, NY -- Duns Scotus by Joos van Gent, 29. Bust of Charlemagne in Aachen (Aix-la-Chapelle) Cathedral –, print of Charlemagne and Pipin, von Steuben medieval battle, 30. Early Hebrew grammer book fr. Cairo Geniza -- Illustration by Todros Geller from The Great March by Rose Lourie -- Rome jewish ghetto by Ettore Roesler Granz 1880 -- Radinnate routes fr. Louis Rabirowitz, Jewish Merchant Adventures, London: Edward Goldston, 32. Halevi Synagogue in Toledo, grammar book by David Kimchi, 33. Sister, Sarajevo, and Barcelona Haggadot, 35. Alfonso VI. 12th century painting at the Cathedral of Santiago de Compostela -- tomb of Ferdinand III , Libro Des Jueg with Alfonso X, 36. Zacuto and da Gama mural by Amshewitz in U or Witwatersrand, Johannesburg, Jacob's staff fr. John Sellers' Practical Navigation (1672), Statue of Moses de Leon in Guadalajara, Spain, book on Kabbalah from 1250, Templars burned at state anonymous chronicle "From the Creation of the World until 1384," 37. Albegesians from Les Chroniques de Saint-Denis, 14th century, Sicilian Vespers by Grancesco Hayez, French carpet w jousting theme, Medieval depiction of trades 38. Pico Mirandola by Cristofano del Altissimo , 1600 Galileo inquisition paint by Cristiano Bant, Fibonacci statue in Pisa, More engraving by D. Loggan 1679 -- Divine Comedy depiction by William Blake, Roger Bacon statue at Cambridge, Aquinas from old calendar 39. Ten Commandments by Aron de Chavez in 1674.

Index

THAT'S RIGHT !!

MANY OF OUR AUTHORS ARE AVAILABLE FOR SPEAKING ENGAGEMENTS. CHECK IT OUT ON OUR WEBSITE OR EMAIL

www.pavilionpress.com
webmaster@pavilionpress.com